A
DICTIONARY
OF WIT,
WISDOM, & SATIRE

A
DICTIONARY
OF WIT,
WISDOM,

SATIRE

by

HERBERT V. PROCHNOW

HERBERT V. PROCHNOW, JR.

CASTLE BOOKS

This edition published in 2005 by
CASTLE BOOKS ®
A division of Book Sales, Inc.
114 Northfield Avenue
Edison, NJ 08837

This edition published by arrangement with
HarperCollins Publishers, Inc.
10 East 53rd Street
New York, NY 10022

ISBN-13: 978-0-7858-2024-6
ISBN-10: 0-7858-2024-8

Printed in the United States of America

Preface

This book with approximately five thousand definitions is a new type of dictionary. These definitions come from hundreds of authors, statesmen, businessmen, historians, philosophers, teachers, scientists, and military leaders. Over the centuries men and women with unusual insight and understanding, and from many walks of life, have given new and colorful meanings to words.

In these definitions one finds the sharp wit of brilliant minds and the profound wisdom of great thinkers. Here also inspiration, sarcasm, irony, and satire are used to define terms covering a wide range of subjects and interests.

It is hoped that this book will be a valuable reference source on countless occasions for many different groups of persons, including all who make speeches, preside at meetings, and deliver sermons, as well as attorneys, businessmen, teachers, presidents of associations, and writers of scripts for radio and television.

The book is also meant for general readers who enjoy wit tersely expressed and sentences that define a word ingeniously, often with humor, and frequently with wisdom and inspiration.

The authors have given credit for every definition of whose origin they were aware. The sources of many of the definitions for which no credit could be given have been lost over the years. The definitions which the editors of this book themselves created are also unsigned. If in any instance credit has been withheld, or given in error, the reader should understand that it is sometimes impossible to trace to their original source epigrams and witticisms that have become a part of the world's literature and conversation.

The arrangement of a dictionary is obviously alphabetical and makes an index superfluous.

If some persons find this dictionary useful and practical as a reference work, and if others find it a pleasant and enjoyable book in which to browse, it will have earned the place it was hoped it might fill.

HERBERT V. PROCHNOW

HERBERT V. PROCHNOW, JR.

A
DICTIONARY
OF WIT,
WISDOM, & SATIRE

• A •

A. B.

A degree that means the holder has mastered the first two letters of the alphabet.

ABSENCE

That common cure of love. *Miguel de Cervantes*

Absence diminishes little passions and increases great ones, just as the wind blows out a candle and fans a fire. *La Rochefoucauld*

Absence is death, or worse, to them that love. *Philip Sidney*

Absence and death are the same—only that in death there is no suffering. *Walter Savage Landor*

Absence is the enemy of love. *Italian Proverb*

ABSTAINER

A weak person who yields to the temptation of denying himself a pleasure. *Ambrose Bierce*

ABSTINENCE

The surety of temperance. *Plato*

ABSURDITY

A statement or belief manifestly inconsistent with one's own opinion. *Ambrose Bierce*

ACCELERATOR

A device in an automobile which enables a person to die with his boots on.

ACCENT

The soul of talk; it gives it feeling and verity. *Jean-Jacques Rousseau*

ACCURACY

The twin brother of honesty; inaccuracy, of dishonesty. *Charles Simmons*

ACQUAINTANCE

A degree of friendship called slight when its object is poor or obscure, and intimate when he is rich or famous. *Ambrose Bierce*

A person whom we know well enough to borrow from, but not well enough to lend to. *Ambrose Bierce*

ACROBAT

The only person who can do what everyone else would like to do—pat himself on the back.

ACTING

The lowest of art; if it is an art at all. *George Moore*

ACTOR

The only honest hypocrite. *William Hazlitt*

A sculptor who carves in snow. *Lawrence Barrett*

ACTOR (HAM)

The drama critic's meat.

ACTOR (TV WESTERN)
Someone who is quick on the drawl.

ADHERENT
A follower who has not yet obtained all that he expects to get. *Ambrose Bierce*

ADMIRATION
Our polite recognition of another man's resemblance to ourselves. *Ambrose Bierce*
A youthful fancy which scarcely ever survives to mature years. *Josh Billings*
The daughter of ignorance. *Benjamin Franklin*
A very short-lived passion, that immediately decays upon growing familiar with its object. *Joseph Addison*

ADOLESCENCE
That period when children feel their parents should be told the facts of life.
That period of life when a boy refuses to believe that someday he will be as dumb as his father.

ADULT
One who has stopped growing except in the middle.

ADULT (EDUCATION)
The education parents receive from their children.

ADVENTURER
An outlaw. Adventure must start with running away from home. *William Bolitho*

ADVENTURES
An indication of inefficiency. Good explorers don't have them. *Herbert Spencer Dickey*

ADVERSITY
The state in which a man most easily becomes acquainted with himself, being especially free from admirers then. *Samuel Johnson*
The first path to truth. *Lord Byron*
A medicine which people are rather fond of recommending indiscriminately as a panacea for their neighbors. Like other medicines, it only agrees with certain constitutions. There are nerves which it braces, and nerves which it utterly shatters. *Justin McCarthy*
An experience that introduces a man to himself.
An experience that makes a man wise, not rich. *English Proverb*
Adversity makes men; prosperity, monsters. *French Proverb*
A medicine people recommend as good for the neighbors.

ADVERTISEMENTS

The only truths to be relied on in a newspaper. *Thomas Jefferson*

ADVERTISING

Publicity has been developed into a fine art, being able, for instance, to make you think you've longed all your life for something you never even heard of before. *Ohio State Journal*

The science of arresting the human intelligence long enough to get money from it. *Stephen Leacock*

The principal reason why the businessman has come to inherit the earth. *James R. Adams*

A racket, like the movies and the brokerage business. You cannot be honest without admitting that its constructive contribution to humanity is exactly minus zero. *F. Scott Fitzgerald*

The mouthpiece of business. *James R. Adams*

Advertising nourishes the consuming power of man . . . sets up the goal of a better home, better clothing, better food for himself and his family. It spurs individual exertion and greater production. It brings together in fertile union those things which otherwise would not have met. *Winston Churchill*

ADVERTISING (AGENCY)

Eighty-five per cent confusion and fifteen per cent commission. *Fred Allen*

ADVICE

What people who live in glass houses shouldn't give. *Judge*

A word of advice: Don't give it. *Life*

What you take for a cold.

The suggestions you give someone else which you believe will work to your benefit.

Like castor oil, easy enough to give but dreadful uneasy to take. *Josh Billings*

Something sold by your lawyer, given away free by your mother-in-law, but impossible to dispose of yourself.

A drug in the market; the supply always exceeds the demand. *Josh Billings*

What we ask when we seek approbation. *Adapted from Charles Caleb Colton*

ADVICE (FREE)

The kind that costs you nothing unless you act upon it.

ADVICE (GOOD)

One of those injuries which a good man ought, if possible,

to forgive but at all events to forget at once. *Horace Smith*

AFFECTATION

The product of falsehood. *Thomas Carlyle*

Affectation is an awkward and forced imitation of what should be genuine and easy, wanting the beauty that accompanies what is natural. *John Locke*

AFTER-THOUGHT

A tardy sense of prudence that prompts one to try to shut his mouth about the time he has put his foot in it. *Gideon Wurdz*

AGE

To know how to grow old is the master-work of wisdom, and one of the most difficult chapters in the great art of living. *Henri-Frédéric Amiel*

What a woman is often shy in telling—in more ways than one.

Thirty is a nice age for a woman, especially if she happens to be forty.

Some people age gracefully; others attempt the new dances.

A man is old when he can pass an apple orchard and not remember a stomach-ache. *Lowell Sun*

What a woman is shy in giving.

The most terrible misfortune that can happen to any man; other evils will mend, this is every day getting worse. *George Payne Rainsford James*

Only a number, a cipher for the records. A man can't retire his experience. He must use it. Experience achieves more with less energy and time. *Bernard Baruch*

That period of life in which we compound the vices that we still cherish by reliving those that we no longer have the enterprise to commit. *Ambrose Bierce*

AGE (MIDDLE)

The time when the average man is going to begin saving next month.

When you begin to exchange your emotions for symptoms. *Irvin S. Cobb*

The period in life when man has baldness, bridgework, bifocals, bay windows, and bunions.

The period when a man believes the thinning of his hair is only a temporary matter.

That period in a man's life when he'd rather not have a good time than have to get over it. *Oscar Wilde*

Ten years older than you happen to be at the time. *Oscar Wilde*

The time when a man is always thinking that in a week or two he will feel as good as ever. *Don Marquis*

When you know how to take care of yourself and expect to one of these days.

When you are too young to take up golf and too old to rush up to the net. *Franklin P. Adams*

When your narrow waist and broad mind begin to change places.

> Youth without its levity
> And age without decay.
> *Daniel Defoe*

Our judgment ripens; our imagination decays. *Thomas B. Macaulay*

AGE (OLD)

A period in life when you bend over once to pick up two things.

The time a man prepares for by saving and a woman prepares for by dieting and beauty treatments.

Always fifteen years older than I am. *Bernard M. Baruch*

The only thing that comes to us without effort.

Intelligence, and reflection, and judgment, reside in old men, and if there had been none of them, no states could exist at all. *Cicero*

A dreary solitude. *Plato*

The sanctuary of ills: they all take refuge in it. *Antiphanes*

An incurable disease. *Seneca*

AGENT (PRESS)

Supposed to be a genial guy with a one-track mind that makes him look over the papers and wonder why such trifles as wars and politics are cluttering up the front page. *George Washburn*

AGNOSTICISM

The philosophical, ethical, and religious dry rot of the modern world. *F. E. Abbot*

AGREEABLE

To agree with me.

AGRICULTURE

Something like farming only farming is doing it.

The first and most precious of all the arts. *Thomas Jefferson*

AGRICULTURIST

A farmer who owns a station wagon.

AID (FEDERAL)

Simply a system of taking money from the people and making it look like a gift when you hand it back.

ALARM CLOCK

A mechanical device that annoys you when good sense tells you that you should continue sleeping. Most of us do not like that sort of ting.

The symbol of civilization, that is, of voluntary submission, of free-will obedience. *Joyce Kilmer*

ALASKA

Miles and miles of miles and miles.

ALIENIST

A person who "finds you cracked, and leaves you broke." *Keith Preston*

ALIMONY

Alimony is a system by which, when two people make a mistake, one of them continues to pay for it. *American Lumberman*

Marry in haste and repent insolvent. *Life*

Matrimonial insurance for women paid by men for having poor judgment. *Cincinnati Cynic*

The wages of sin. *Carolyn Wells*

The billing without the cooing.

The cash surrender value of a husband.

ALL-EXPENSE TOUR

The perfect example of truth in advertising.

ALLIANCE

In international politics, the union of two thieves who have their hands so deeply inserted in each other's pocket that they cannot separately plunder a third. *Ambrose Bierce*

ALTRUISM

A noble sentiment but no lasting social order has ever been built upon it alone. *James T. Shotwell*

The art of doing unselfish things for selfish reasons.

AMATEUR GARDENER

A person who overworks the soil.

AMATEUR HUNTER

One who mistakes a guide for a deer and invariably hits him.

AMBASSADOR

An honest man sent to lie abroad for the good of his country. *Henry Wotton*

A spy.

Ambassadors are the eyes and ears of states. *Francesco Guicciardini*

A politician who is given a job abroad in order to get him out of the country.

AMBITION

The main thing that keeps people moving, but the "No Parking" sign is doing its part.

The last refuge of the failure. *Oscar Wilde*

Avarice on stilts and masked. *Walter Savage Landor*

Aggravated itching of the wishbone.

An insatiable desire for honor, command, power, and glory. *Cicero*

AMERICA

A place where the people have the right to complain about the lack of freedom. *Louis Hirsch*

The melting pot of the world. *Israel Zangwill*

A country where an hour is forty minutes. *Adapted from a German Proverb*

A great nation in which a cigarette testimonial by a famous football player who has never smoked in his life is regarded as persuasive publicity.

The last abode of romance and other medieval phenomena. *Eric Linklater*

A nation that conceives many odd inventions for getting somewhere but can think of nothing to do when it gets there. *Will Rogers*

A country where "the young are always ready to give to those who are older than themselves the full benefits of their inexperience." *Oscar Wilde*

A nation that has more highways than any other country, but they're so crowded you can't use them.

A country where they lock up the jury and let the criminal out.

An overwhelming country to a stranger. It is the country where humanity, for the first time in modern history, was let loose. *Hans Bendix*

A country where "there is more space where nobody is than where anybody is. This is what makes America what she is." *Gertrude Stein*

Not a mere body of traders; it is a body of free men. Our greatness is built upon our freedom—is moral, not material. We have a great ardor for gain; but we have a deep passion for the rights of man. *Woodrow Wilson*

America is God's Crucible, the great Melting Pot—where
all the races of Europe are melting and re-forming! God
is making the American. *Israel Zangwill*

America means opportunity, freedom, power. *Ralph Waldo
Emerson*

The country where you buy a lifetime supply of aspirin for
one dollar, and use it up in two weeks. *John Barrymore*

Lo! body and soul!—this land!
Mighty Manhattan, with spires, and
The sparkling and hurrying tides, and the ships;
The varied and ample land—the South
And the North in the light—Ohio's shores,
    and flashing Missouri,
And ever the far-spreading prairies,
    covered with grass and corn.
Walt Whitman

AMERICAN

A person who complains about the government spending
too much and then asks for more government spending
for his community.

One who is an incurable optimist. He admits the necessity
for saving for his old age, but puts it off with the expectation that a miracle will come along and do it for him.

One who loves justice and believes in the dignity of man.
Harold L. Ickes

One who will fight for his freedom and that of his neighbor. *Harold L. Ickes*

One who will sacrifice property, ease, and security in order
that he and his children may retain the rights of free
men. *Harold L. Ickes*

The great idealist among mankind. *Leon Samson*

That singular people who know a little, and but a little, of
everything. *John Neal*

Two great classes: those who think they are as good as anybody, and those who think they are better.

Persons who cheer for the bull at a bullfight.

People who trust in God. You can tell by the way they
drive. *Sharon (Pennsylvania) Herald*

AMERICAN GOVERNMENT

A rule of the people, by the people, for the boss. *Austin
O'Malley*

AMERICAN LIBERTY

A religion. It is a thing of the spirit. It is an aspiration on the part of the people for not only a free life but a better life. *Wendell L. Willkie*

AMERICAN (LOYAL)
One who gets mad when an alien cusses the institutions he cusses. *Huntington Herald*

AMERICAN MOTION PICTURES
Entertainment "written by the half-educated for the half-witted." *St. John Ervine*

AMERICANISM
An endless quest after something new—a hero, a car, or a President.

AMNESTY
The state's magnanimity to those offenders whom it would be too expensive to punish. *Ambrose Bierce*
The most beautiful word in all human speech. *Victor Hugo*

AMPLIFIER
A device that enlarges the speaker's voice but not his ideas.

AMUSEMENT
The happiness of those who cannot think. *Alexander Pope*

ANANIAS
The honorary president of a club of press agents. *Adapted from John Kendrick Bangs*

ANARCHISM
The doctrine that all the affairs of men should be managed by individuals or voluntary associations, and that the State should be abolished. *Benjamin R. Tucker*

ANCIENTS
Those who "were really new in everything." *Blaise Pascal*

ANGER
An emotion that "makes dull men witty—but it keeps them poor." *Attributed to Queen Elizabeth I*
To women it is a balm, a nepenthe, a release, a relief, a divine comfort to their nerves, and a consummation of all their suppressed feelings. *J. C. Powys*
A condition where the tongue works faster than the mind.
Momentary madness, so control your passion or it will control you. *Horace*
A brief lunacy. *Horace*
A vulgar passion directed to vulgar ends, and it always sinks to the level of its object. *Ernest von Feuchtersleben*
Anger begins with folly, and ends with repentance. *H. G. Bohn*

ANGLING
An innocent cruelty. *George Parker*

ANIMALS

A great many animals laugh, says a scientist. And, of course, a great many people give them good cause to. *San Diego Union*

Creatures that do not keep on grabbing for more when they have enough.

Agreeable friends—they ask no questions, they pass no criticisms. *George Eliot*

Beasts that "glory in being cynics. Having no education, they are devoid of prejudices." *J. O. de La Mettrie*

ANT

An insect that "finds kingdoms in a foot of ground." *Stephen Vincent Benét*

ANTI-VIVISECTIONIST

One who gags at a guinea pig and swallows a baby. *H. L. Mencken*

ANTHOLOGY

A complete dispensary of medicine for the more common mental disorders, and may be used as much for prevention as cure. *Robert Graves*

ANTIQUE

A piece of furniture on which you have finally paid the last installment.

An object that has been to the attic and has come back.

An old virtue.

ANXIETY

Fear of one's self. *Dr. Wilhelm Stekel*

APATHY

Political repletion. *Nikolai Lenin*

APHORISMS

Portable wisdom, the quintessential extracts of thought and feeling. *W. P. Alger*

APIARY

A house you keep apes in.

APOLOGIZE

To lay the foundation for a future offense. *Ambrose Bierce*

A desperate habit—one that is rarely cured. Apology is only egotism wrong side out. *Oliver Wendell Holmes*

APPENDIX

An organ that is useless to man but of value to the doctors.

APPETITE

The best sauce. *French Proverb*

APPLAUSE

The echo of a platitude. *Ambrose Bierce*

A demonstration by an audience. At the beginning of a speech, it expresses faith. In the middle of a speech, it expresses hope. At the end of a speech, it expresses charity.

A strange beating together of hands which has no meaning, "and to me it is very disturbing. I do not like it. It destroys the mood my colleagues and I have been trying to create with our music." *Leopold Stokowski*

The spur of noble minds, the end and aim of weak ones. *Charles Caleb Colton*

APPLE

A fruit you eat to keep the doctor away. The more you eat and the more doctors you keep away, the better.

A fruit that keeps the doctor away unless you get the seeds in your appendix.

The fruit that brought all evil into the world. *Adaptation of a Medieval Latin Proverb*

APRIL 1

The day upon which we are reminded of what we are on the other 364. *Mark Twain*

> The first of April, some do say,
> Is set apart for All-Fools' Day;
> But why the people call it so
> Nor I nor they themselves do know.
> > *Poor Robin's Almanac, 1760*

ARCHAEOLOGIST

The best husband any woman can have: the older she gets, the more interested he is in her. *Agatha Christie*

ARCHITECT

One who drafts a plan of your house, and plans a draft of your money. *Ambrose Bierce*

A man who could build a church, as one may say, by squinting at a sheet of paper. *Charles Dickens*

ARCHITECTURE

The flowering of geometry. *Ralph Waldo Emerson*

Frozen music. *J. W. van Goethe*

In architecture the pride of man, his triumph over gravitation, his will to power, assume a visible form. Architecture is a sort of oratory of power. *F. W. Nietzsche*

ARGUMENT

The worst sort of conversation. *Jonathan Swift*

When two people each try to get the last word in first.

Arguments are to be avoided; they are always vulgar and often convincing. *Oscar Wilde*

ARISTOCRACY

A combination of many powerful men for the purpose of maintaining and advancing their own particular interests. It is consequently a concentration of all the most effective parts of a community for a given end; hence its energy, efficiency, and success. *James Fenimore Cooper*

ARISTOCRAT

The aristocrat is the democrat ripe and gone to seed. *Ralph Waldo Emerson*

A demokrat with hiz pockets filled. *Josh Billings*

ARITHMETIC

One of the oldest branches, perhaps the very oldest branch, of human knowledge; and yet some of its most abstrusive secrets lie close to its tritest truths. *H. J. S. Smith*

ARIZONA

Where Summer spends the Winter. *Arizona Boosters' Slogan*

ARMOR

The kind of clothing worn by a man whose tailor was a blacksmith. *Ambrose Bierce*

ARMY

An organized group which travels on its stomach in contrast to some individuals who travel on their gall.

A body of humanitarians that seeks to impress on another body of men the beauty of non-resistance, by exterminating them. *Elbert Hubbard (The Roycroft Dictionary)*

The army has always been the basis of power, and it is so today. Power is always in the hands of those who command it. *Leo Tolstoy*

ARROGANCE

The obstruction of wisdom.

Arrogance and boldness belong to those that are accursed of God. *St. Clement*

ART

The expression of an emotional experience in some medium —stone, bronze, paint, words, or musical tone—in such a way that it may be transferred to other people. *F. E. Halliday*

All art, has this characteristic that it unites people. *Leo Tolstoy*

A human activity consisting of this, that one man, usually by means of external signs, hands on to others feelings he has lived through, and that other people are infected by these feelings, and also experience them. *Leo Tolstoy*

The expression of something one has seen which is bigger than oneself. *Oliver La Farge*

A collaboration between God and the artist, and the less the artist does the better. *André Gide*

Nothing more than the shadow of humanity. *Henry James*

Not an end in itself, but a means of addressing humanity. *M. P. Moussorgsky*

A delayed echo. *George Santayana*

The stored honey of the human soul, gathered on wings of misery and travail. *Theodore Dreiser*

A kind of illness. *Giacomo Puccini*

All art consists in bringing something into existence. *Aristotle*

The perfection of nature. *Sir Thomas Browne*

A work of art is a corner of creation seen through a temperament. *Emile Zola*

ART OF GOVERNMENT

Consists in taking as much money as possible from one class of citizens to give to the other. *Voltaire*

ARTIST

A dreamer consenting to dream of the actual world. *George Santayana*

A person who "should be fit for the best society and keep out of it." *John Ruskin*

A vessel of freedom. *H. M. Kallen*

The artist appeals to that part of our being which is not dependent on wisdom; to that in us which is a gift and not an acquisition—and, therefore, more permanently enduring. He speaks to our capacity for delight and wonder, to the sense of mystery surrounding our lives; to our sense of pity, and beauty, and pain. *Joseph Conrad*

Not the mouthpiece of a century, but the master of eternity. *Oscar Wilde*

ASCETIC

One who "makes a necessity of virtue." *F. W. Nietzsche*

ASH TRAY

Something to put cigarette ashes in when the room hasn't a fine table top or expensive rug.

ASPIRATION

To love the beautiful, to desire the good, to do the best. *Moses Mendelssohn*

ASSASSINATION
The extreme form of censorship. *George Bernard Shaw*

ASTRONOMER
One who "can predict with absolute accuracy just where every star in the heavens will be at half-past eleven tonight. He can make no such prediction about his young daughter." *James Truslow Adams*

Earthly godfathers of Heaven's lights
That give a name to every fixed star.
Shakespeare

ATTENTION
The stuff that memory is made of, and memory is accumulated genius. *James Russell Lowell*

AUCTIONEER
One who admires all schools of art. *Adapted from Oscar Wilde*
One who picks people's pockets. *Adapted from Samuel Johnson*
The man who proclaims with a hammer that he has picked a pocket with his tongue. *Ambrose Bierce*

AUDIENCE
Like hungry guests, a sitting audience looks. *George Farquhar*

AUDITOR
A person who manipulates the records of a business so they satisfy the stockholders, the income tax authorities, and the management.

AUTHOR
A fool who, not content with having bored those who have lived with him, insists on boring future generations. *C. L. de Montesquieu*
A person who is turned down by numerous publishers and then decides to write for posterity. *Adapted from George Ade*
A person who departs; he does not die. *Dinah Maria Mulock*
One who makes the sweets which others buy. *Adapted from Leigh Hunt*

AUTHORITY
A stubborn bear, yet he is oft led by the nose with gold. *Shakespeare*

AUTOBIOGRAPHY
An alibiography.
The books which I give away. *Charles Lamb*

An unrivaled vehicle for telling the truth about other people. *Philip Guedalla*

AUTOMOBILES

A machine that eliminated horses but made horse sense necessary.

A machine for transportation that has a 200-inch wheel base and is about the width of a prostrate pedestrian.

AUTUMN

The season which "repays the earth the leaves which summer lent it." *Georg C. Lichtenberg*

Season of mists and mellow fruitfulness,
Close-bosom-friend of the maturing sun;
Conspiring with him how to load and bless
With fruit the vines.
John Keats

When the frost is on the punkin and the fodder's in the shock. *James Whitcomb Riley*

The melancholy days are come, the saddest of the year,
Of wailing winds and naked woods,
    and meadows brown and sear.
William Cullen Bryant

AVARICE

The besetting vice of a propertied society, but that avarice is in fact a vice is nowhere questioned. *Max Radin*

The spur of industry. *David Hume*

Generally the last passion of those lives of which the first part has been squandered in pleasure, and the second devoted to ambition. *Samuel Johnson*

The ruin of every great state. *Livy*

The lust of gold, unfeeling and remorseless,
The last corruption of degenerate man.
Samuel Johnson

AVERAGE MAN

A married man who expects his wife to be a sweetheart, valet, audience, and nurse.

A person who seldom increases his average.

A person who thinks he isn't.

One who enjoys going places where a social error won't be recognized if he commits it.

We are such stuff as dreams are made on. *Shakespeare*

• B •

BABY

A form of minority rule in families.

A mother's anchor. She cannot swing far from her moorings. *Henry Ward Beecher*

A bald head and a pair of lungs. *Eugene Field*

BABY SITTER

A term formerly applied only to mothers.

Someone you pay to watch your television set while your children cry themselves to sleep.

One who gets paid hush money.

BACHELOR

One who "gets tangled up with a lot of women in order to avoid getting tied up to one." *Helen Rowland*

A person who "never quite gets over the idea that he is a thing of beauty and a boy forever." *Helen Rowland*

One who thinks one can live as cheap as two. *Eleanor S. J. Ridley*

A man who wouldn't take yes for an answer.

A man who shirks responsibilities and duties. *George Bernard Shaw*

A man who gives in when he is wrong; a married man gives in when he is right.

A man who gets all the credit when he accomplishes something great.

A man who knows the precise psychological moment when to say nothing.

A man who is footloose and fiancé free. *F. G. Kernan*

A man who has never told his wife a lie.

A man who never made the same mistake once.

The only good husbands stay bachelors; they're too considerate to get married. *F. P. Dunne*

One who enjoys the chase but does not eat the game.

A souvenir of some woman who found a better one at the last minute.

A permanent public temptation. *Adapted from Oscar Wilde*

BACHELOR OF ARTS

One who makes love to a lot of women, and yet has the art to remain a bachelor. *Helen Rowland*

BAD MANNERS

What it takes to "make a journalist." *Oscar Wilde*

BANK

An institution which will lend you money if you can prove that you do not need it.

BANKER

A fellow who lends you his umbrella when the sun is shining and wants it back the minute it begins to rain. *Mark Twain*

BARGAIN

Something you can't use at a price you can't resist. *Franklin P. Jones*

Pickpockets.

Anything a customer thinks a store is losing money on. *Kin Hubbard*

BARGAIN SALE

A sale at which a woman ruins a $50 street dress to get a house dress for $2.98.

BASHFULNESS

An ornament to youth, but a reproach to old age. *Aristotle*

BATHING SUIT

A device to keep people from bathing. It lets the water in, but it doesn't let the dirt out.

BATTLEFIELD

> They there may dig each other's graves,
> And call the sad work glory.
> > *Percy Bysshe Shelley*

BAYONET

A weapon with a worker at each end. *Slogan of English Pacifists, 1940*

BEARD

A thing you need to wear with gift neckties.

That ornamental excrement which groweth beneath the chin. *Thomas Fuller*

BEAUTY

The only thing that time cannot harm. Philosophies fall away like sand, and creeds follow one another like the withered leaves of Autumn, but what is beautiful is a joy for all seasons and a possession for all eternity. *Oscar Wilde*

Only skin.

Something wonderful and strange that the artist fashions out of the chaos of the world in the torment of his soul. *W. Somerset Maugham*

A form of genius—is higher, indeed, than genius, as it needs no explanation. *Oscar Wilde*

The mark God sets on virtue. *Ralph Waldo Emerson*

Like a rainbow—full of promise but short-lived. *Josh Billings*

The first present Nature gives to women, and the first it takes away. *George B. Mere*

What is beautiful is good, and who is good will soon be beautiful. *Sappho*

Beauty is silent eloquence. *French Proverb*

BEAUTY (RAVING)
A girl who finishes last in a beauty contest.

BED
A bundle of paradoxes; we go to it with reluctance, yet we quit it with regret; we make up our minds every night to leave it early, but we make up our bodies every morning to keep it late. *Charles Caleb Colton*

A place of luxury to me. I would not exchange it for all the thrones in the world. *Napoleon Bonaparte*

BEE
An insect "more honored than other animals, not because she labors, but because she labors for others." *St. John Chrysostom*

BEGINNER'S LUCK
A college freshman with an idea.

BEHAVIOR
The theory of manners practically applied. *Mme. Necker*

A mirror in which everyone shows his image. *J. W. von Goethe*

BEING NATURAL
Simply a pose. *Oscar Wilde*

BELL
Bells are music's laughter. *Thomas Hood*

BENEFACTOR
One who makes two smiles grow where one grew before. *Chauncey Depew*

BENEVOLENCE
A natural instinct of the human mind; when A sees B in distress, his conscience always urges him to entreat C to help him. *Sydney Smith*

One of the distinguishing characters of man. *Mencius*

BEST
The best is the enemy of the good. *English Proverb*

BEST REFORMERS
Those who commence on themselves. *George Bernard Shaw*

BEST SELLER
The gilded tomb of a mediocre talent. *Logan Pearsall Smith*

BETTING

Sometimes a means of getting something for nothing, but generally a method of getting nothing for something.

BIBLE

A book so great it survives all the translations that are made of it.

Born in the East and clothed in Oriental form and imagery, the Bible walks the ways of all the world with familiar feet and enters land after land to find its own everywhere. It has learned to speak in hundreds of languages to the heart of man. Children listen to its stories with wonder and delight, and wise men ponder them as parables of life. *Henry Van Dyke*

One mighty representative of the whole spiritual life of humanity. *Helen Keller*

A window in this prison-world, through which we may look into eternity. *Timothy Dwight*

A book which, if everything else in our language should perish, would alone suffice to show the whole extent of its beauty and power. *Thomas B. Macaulay*

This is a work too hard for the teeth of time, and cannot perish but in the general flames, when all things shall confess their ashes. *Thomas Browne*

BIBLE (TABLOID)

What this generation needs.

BIGAMIST

A man who doesn't know when he has got enough.

BIGAMY

Having one wife too many. Monogamy is the same. *Oscar Wilde*

BIGOT

A person who, under an atheist king, would be an atheist. *Jean de La Bruyère*

BIGOTRY

Has no head and cannot think, no heart and cannot feel. When she moves it is in wrath; when she pauses it is amid ruin. Her prayers are curses, her God is a demon, her communion is death, her vengeance is eternity, her decalogue written in the blood of her victims, and if she stops for a moment in her infernal flight it is upon a kindred rock to whet her vulture fang for a more sanguinary desolation. *Daniel O'Connell*

Chronic dogmatism. *Horace Greeley*

BIOGRAPHY

One of the new terrors of death. *John Arbuthnot*

A region bounded on the north by history, on the south by fiction, on the east by obituary, and on the west by tedium. *Philip Guedalla*

An interpretive, selective, and analytic, not a creative art. *Claude M. Fuess*

Biography, like big game hunting, is one of the recognized forms of sport, and it is as unfair as only sport can be. *Philip Guedalla*

The only true history. *Thomas Carlyle*

BIPED

Anything that goes on two feet, for instance a pair of socks.

A two-legged animal with or without feathers.

BIRD IN THE HAND

Bad table manners.

BIRTH

Our birth is but a sleep and a forgetting,
The soul that rises with us, our life's star,
Hath had elsewhere its setting,
And cometh from afar;
Not in entire forgetfulness,
And not in utter nakedness,
But trailing clouds of glory do we come
From God, who is our home.
                    William Wordsworth

BISHOP

A clergyman with political interests. *Adapted from St. John Hankin*

The bishop is in the nature of an ecclesiastical sheriff. *Chief Justice North*

A bishop . . . must be blameless, the husband of one wife, vigilant, sober, of good behavior, given to hospitality, apt to teach; not given to wine, no striker, not greedy of filthy lucre; but patient, not a brawler, not covetous; one that ruleth well his own house, having his children in subjection with all gravity. *I Tim. 3: 2-4*

BLIND ALLEY

Easy street.

BLOCK

The distance between some people's ears.

BLOTTER

A porous substance you spend your time looking for while the ink is drying.

BLUSH
> Blushing is virtue's color. *English Proverb*
> Modesty's first impulse and sophistication's afterthought.

BLUSTERING
> The characteristic manners of cowardice. *Edward Everett*

BOASTER
> First cousin to a liar. *From a German Proverb*

BOBBED HAIR
> One of those things that grow on you.

BODY
> A house of clay not built with hands. *Samuel Taylor Coleridge*
> The body of a man is not a home but an inn—and that only briefly. *Seneca*
> Your body is the temple of the Holy Ghost. *I Cor. 6: 19*

BOLDNESS
> Boldness is a mask for fear, however great. *Lucan*
> Boldness is a child of ignorance. *Francis Bacon*

BOMB
> A device for making "ruins in a flash where it takes nature centuries." *Adapted from Raymond Clapper*

BOOK
> A garden carried in the pocket. *Arabian Proverb*
> A garden, an orchard, a storehouse, a party, a company by the way, a counsellor, a multitude of counsellors. *Henry Ward Beecher*
> The only immortality. *Rufus Choate*

BOOK BORROWERS
> Mutilators of collections, spoilers of the symmetry of shelves, and creators of odd volumes. *Charles Lamb*

BOOK COLLECTOR
> The hermaphrodite of literature: neither a reader nor a writer. *Shane Leslie*

BOOK (COOK)
> A book whose only "object can conceivably be no other than to increase the happiness of mankind." *Joseph Conrad*

BOOKS
> Men of higher stature, and the only men that speak aloud for future times to hear. *Elizabeth Browning*
> Ships which pass through the vast seas of time. *Francis Bacon*
> The children of the brain.
> The true university. *Thomas Carlyle*

The ever-burning lamps of accumulated wisdom. *G. W. Curtis*

Books are the legacies that genius leaves to mankind, to be delivered down from generation to generation, as presents to those that are yet unborn. *Joseph Addison*

Books extend our narrow present back into a limitless past. They show us the mistakes of the men before us and share with us recipes for human success. There's nothing to be done which books will not help us do better. *T. V. Smith*

They are the voices of the distant and the dead, and make us heirs of the spiritual life of past ages. *William E. Channing*

Books are sepulchers of thought. *Henry Wadsworth Longfellow*

BOOM

The ineluctable antecedent of the depression. *Carl Snyder*

BORE

A man who spends so much time talking about himself that you can't talk about yourself. *Melville D. Landon*

A person who talks when you wish him to listen. *Ambrose Bierce*

A man who deprives you of solitude without providing you with company. *Gian Vincenzo Gravina*

A man who, when you ask him how he is, tells you.

A guy who wraps up a two-minute idea in a two-hour vocabulary. *Walter Winchell*

One who keeps you from being lonely and makes you wish you were.

A person who puts his feat in his mouth.

A person who is here today and here tomorrow.

BORROWER

The borrower is servant to the lender. *Prov. 22:7*

BOSTON

The home of the bean and the cod, where the Cabots speak only to Lowells, and the Lowells speak only to God. *Credited to Samuel C. Bushnell*

The town of the cries and the groans, where the Cabots can't see the Kabotschniks, and the Lowells won't speak to the Cohns. *Franklin P. Adams*

BOSTONIAN

An American, broadly speaking.

You may know a Boston man by two traits . . . he thinks he knows and he thinks he is right. *G. E. Woodberry*

A comfortable man with dividends. *Henry Wadsworth Longfellow*

BOTTOMS UP

A toast you never make to the crew in a boat race.

BOY

Of all wild beasts, the most difficult to manage. *Plato*

A boy is truth with dirt on its face, beauty with a cut on its finger. *Allan Beck*

A boy is a magical creature—you can lock him out of your workshop, but you can't lock him out of your heart. *Allan Beck*

BRAGGART

A person who enters a conversation feat first.

BRAIN

An organ that "starts working the moment you get up in the morning, and does not stop until you get into the office." *Robert Frost*

There are three kinds of brains: one understands of itself, another can be taught to understand, and the third can neither understand of itself or be taught to understand. *Niccolo Machiavelli*

The greatest natural resource. *Karl Brandt*

BRAVERY

A cheap and vulgar quality, of which the brightest instances are frequently found in the lowest savages. *Paul Chatfield*

It is an accident of circumstances. *Michael J. Dee*

BRAVERY (PHYSICAL)

An animal instinct; moral bravery is a much higher and truer courage. *Wendell Phillips*

BREAD

An army's greatest ally: the soldier marches no further than his stomach.

The staff of life. *Jonathan Swift*

Jesus said unto them, I am the bread of life: he that cometh to me shall never hunger; and he that believeth on me shall never thirst. *John 4:35*

BREAKFAST (NOOK)

A space so small the architect could find no practical use for it.

BREEDING (GOOD)

Consists in concealing how much we think of ourselves and how little we think of the other person. *Mark Twain*

An expedient to make fools and wise men equals. *Richard Steele*

BREVITY

Almost a condition of being inspired. *George Santayana*

The soul of wit. *Shakespeare*

Let thy speech be short, comprehending much in few words. *Ecc. 32:8*

BRIDE

A woman with a fine prospect of happiness behind her. *Ambrose Bierce*

BRIDEGROOM

Something they use at weddings.

A man who thought he would became a ruler because he had once been Prince Charming.

BRIDGE

Next to hockey the most dangerous shin-bruising game in America.

BRITISHER

One who "imagines God is an Englishman." *George Bernard Shaw*

BROAD-MINDEDNESS

The result of flattening high-mindedness out. *George Santayana*

The ability to smile when you learn that the ten dollars you lent your roommate is taking your girl to the theater.

BROADWAY

The longest street with the shortest memory. *Maurice Barrymore*

America's hardened artery. *Mark Kelly*

A place where people spend money they haven't earned to buy things they don't need to impress people they don't like. *Walter Winchell*

BROOKLYN

The borough of homes and churches, always has suffered from a community inferiority complex because of its proximity to the wicked and glamorous borough of Manhattan. *Charles Van Devander*

BROTHERHOOD

Brotherhood, according to the dictionary, is the relationship of two male persons having the same parents—or the members of a fraternity or organization. I don't think the dictionary goes far enough. To me brotherhood isn't just something you're born with or something you join. It's something deep inside you, like love or loyalty, that reaches out to all the world and everybody in it—men, women, children. Just the thought of brotherhood has a sobering effect on me, for it reminds me that I am only a transitory member of a very large family called Humanity. *Bellamy Partridge*

Brotherhood must have a religious basis if it is to have any real significance. Without faith in the Fatherhood of God, as Jesus and the prophets preached it, people have a pretty hard time being brotherly. They drift off into hate societies, or more often, into the society of the indifferent. *Edwin T. Dahlberg*

BRUTALITY

Pleasure in forcing one's will upon other people; courage is indifference to personal misfortunes. *Bertrand Russell*

BUDGET

A mathematical confirmation of your suspicions. *A. A. Latimer*

The family's attempt to live below its yearnings.

BUDGET (GOVERNMENTAL)

The balance wheel of the economy. *Douglas Abbott*

BUFFER STATE

One that's between two biffer states.

BUREAU (GOVERNMENT)

The nearest thing to immortality in this world. *Adapted from General Hugh S. Johnson*

BUREAUCRAT

The cancer-cell of the nation. *E. S. P. Haynes*

BUSINESS

Business underlies everything in our national life, including our spiritual life. Witness the fact that in the Lord's Prayer, the first petition is for daily bread. No one can worship God or love his neighbor on an empty stomach. *Woodrow Wilson*

A combination of war and sport. *André Maurois*

Often a battle of the wits, and some businessmen are unarmed.

The playthings of our elders. *St. Augustine*

The nature of business is swindling. *August Bebel*

BUSINESS ECONOMY

A reduction in some other employee's salary.

BUTLER

A solemn processional of one. *P. G. Wodehouse*

BUTTERFLY

> And what's a butterfly? At best,
> He's but a caterpillar, drest.
> *John Gay*

• C •

CABBAGE
A familiar kitchen-garden vegetable about as large and wise as a man's head. *Ambrose Bierce*

CABINET (FILING)
Where papers get lost alphabetically.

CADDIE
A person who can smile when everything around him goes wrong on a golf course.

CAESAR, JULIUS
The complete and perfect man. *Theodor Mommsen*
All the world allows that the emperor was the greatest genius that ever was, and the greatest judge of mankind. *David Hume*
Caesar was a failure. Otherwise he would not have been assassinated. *Napoleon Bonaparte*

CALAMITIES
Calamities are of two kinds: misfortune to ourselves, and good fortune to others. *Ambrose Bierce*

CALAMITY
The perfect glass wherein we truly see and know ourselves. *Sir William D'Avenant*
The test of integrity. *Samuel Richardson*
Calamity is virtue's opportunity. *Seneca*

CALENDAR
Something that goes in one year and out the other.
A method of "reminding us that each day that passes is the anniversary of some perfectly uninteresting event." *Oscar Wilde*

CALIFORNIA
Much like Florida except that part of it isn't for sale. *San Diego Union Tribune*
A fine place to live in—if you happen to be an orange. *Fred Allen*

CALUMNY
A vice of curious constitutions; trying to kill it keeps it alive; leave it to itself and it will die a natural death. *Thomas Paine*

CAMEL
The ship of the desert. *English Phrase*
A race horse designed by a committee.

CANDIDATE
A man who stands for what he thinks the people will fall for.

CANDID CAMERA FAN
> A person who takes the worst view of everything. Synonym: pessimist.

CANDOR
> Candor is a proof of both a just frame of mind, and of a good tone of breeding. It is a quality that belongs equally to the honest man and to the gentleman. *James Fenimore Cooper*

CANNON
> The last argument of kings. *Engraved on French Cannon by Decree of Louis XIV*

CANOE
> An object that acts like a small boy: it behaves better when paddled from the rear.

CAPITAL
> Dead labor that, vampire-like, lives only by sucking living labor, and lives the more, the more labor it sucks. *Karl Marx*

> That part of wealth which is devoted to obtaining further wealth. *Alfred Marshall*

> Capital is that part of the wealth of a country which is employed in production, and consists of food, clothing, tools, raw materials, machinery, etc., necessary to give effect to labor. *David Ricardo*

> A result of labor, and is used by labor to assist it in further production. Labor is the active and initial force, and labor is therefore the employer of capital. *Henry George*

CAPITAL PUNISHMENT
> When the government taxes you to get capital, in order to go into business in competition with you, and then taxes the profits on your business in order to pay its losses.

CAPITALIST
> One who lives on the wealth of brains—his father's or his own.

CAR SICKNESS
> The feeling you get when the monthly installment comes due.

CARDS
> Cards are the Devil's books. *English Proverb*

CARE
> Care keeps his watch in every old man's eye,
> And where care lodges, sleep will never lie.
> > *Shakespeare*

> An enemy to life. *Shakespeare*

CAREFUL DRIVER
The fellow who has made the last payment on his car.

CARICATURE
The tribute that mediocrity pays to genius. *Oscar Wilde*

CARLYLE, THOMAS
Carlyle is a poet to whom nature has denied the faculty of verse. *Alfred Tennyson*

CARNALITY
To be carnally minded is death. *Rom. 8:6*
The carnal mind is enmity against God. *Rom. 8:7*

CARNEGIE, ANDREW
There was no secret about his success; he was an idealist. . . . Here was a man who represented American ideals. *Calvin Coolidge*

CARPENTER
A skilled workman who keeps a straight face while he repairs a do-it-yourself project.

CARPENTER (AMATEUR)
A carpenter who resembles lightning. He never strikes twice in the same place.

CASH
Cash is virtue. *Lord Byron*

CASTLES IN THE AIR
Houses that "cost a vast deal to keep up." *Edward Bulwer-Lytton*

CAT
A lion to a mouse.
A pygmy lion who loves mice, hates dogs, and patronizes human beings. *Oliver Herford*
An indestructible automaton provided by nature to be kicked when things go wrong in the domestic circle. *Ambrose Bierce*

CAULIFLOWER
Cauliflower is nothing but cabbage with a college education. *Mark Twain*

CAUTION
What we call cowardice in others. *Oscar Wilde*
The confidential agent of selfishness. *Woodrow Wilson*
The eldest child of wisdom. *Victor Hugo*
A valuable asset, especially to a fish.

CELEBRITY
A man who works all his life to become famous enough to be recognized—then goes around in dark glasses so no one will know who he is. *Earl Wilson*

CEMETERY

A place filled with people who thought the world couldn't get along without them.

A place which "receives all without asking questions." *English Proverb*

CENSURE

The tax a man pays to the public for being eminent. *Jonathan Swift*

CEREMONY

The superstition of good-breeding, as well as of religion; but yet, being an outwork to both, should not be absolutely demolished. *Earl of Chesterfield*

The invention of wise men to keep fools at a distance. *Richard Steele*

CERTAINTY

The only certainty is that nothing is certain. *Pliny the Elder*

CHAMPAGNE

One of "those bottled windy drinks that laugh in a man's face and then cut his throat." *Thomas Adams*

Here's to champagne, the drink divine
That makes us forget our troubles;
It's made of a dollar's worth of wine
And three dollar's worth of bubbles.
Anonymous

CHANCE

Chance is a word devoid of sense; nothing can exist without a cause.

CHANGE

Change is an easy panacea. It takes character to stay in one place and be happy there. *Elizabeth Dunn*

CHAOS

A normal condition in the world.

The wrecks of matter and the crash of worlds. *Joseph Addison*

CHARACTER

Like a tree and reputation like its shadow. The shadow is what we think of it; the tree is the real thing. *Abraham Lincoln*

What you are in the dark. *Dwight L. Moody*

Character is that which can do without success. *Ralph Waldo Emerson*

A by-product; it is produced in the great manufacture of daily duty. *Woodrow Wilson*

What God and the angels know of us; reputation is what
men and women think of us. *Horace Mann*

The spiritual body of the person. *E. P. Whipple*

Character is moral order seen through the medium of an
individual nature. *Ralph Waldo Emerson*

Character is that which reveals moral purpose, exposing the
class of things a man chooses or avoids. *Aristotle*

The measure of a man's real character is what he would
do if he knew he would never be found out. *Thomas B.
Macaulay*

CHARITY

A thing that begins at home, and usually stays there.
Elbert Hubbard

Generosity which begins at home and generally dies from
lack of out-of-door exercise; sympathy travels abroad ex-
tensively.

A bone to the dog is not charity. Charity is the bone shared
with the dog, when you are just as hungry as the dog.
Jack London

Preferring to store your money in the stomachs of the
needy rather than hide it in a purse. *Adapted from St.
Jerome*

The sterilized milk of human kindness. *Oliver Herford*

Another of the old virtues, is usually looked upon as a short
cut to heaven. But too often it is a road paved with
human misery, a disguise for the injustice that we mete
out to our fellow men. *I. A. R. Wylie*

The perfection and ornament of religion. *Joseph Addison*

Charity suffereth long and is kind; charity envieth not;
charity vaunteth not itself, is not puffed up. *I. Cor.13:4*

CHARM

Nothing but rich undiluted flattery, laid on with a trowel,
but springing honestly from the heart.

The ability to make some one else feel he is as wonderful
as you are.

CHARMING PEOPLE

Persons who "are spoiled; it is the secret of their attraction."
Oscar Wilde

CHASTITY

The cement of civilization and progress. *Mary Baker Eddy*

CHAUFFEUR

The power behind the thrown.

CHECKBOOK

A book that often has an unhappy ending.

CHECKING ACCOUNT (JOINT)
A handy little device that permits your wife to beat you to the draw.

CHEEK
A drip-pan for tears.

CHEESE
> Cheese it is a peevish elf,
> It digests all things but itself.
> *English Proverb*

CHESS
A foolish expedient for making idle people believe they are doing something very clever, when they are only wasting their time. *George Bernard Shaw*

CHICAGO
Of all the places in the world, the one which from its literary societies sends me the most intelligent and thoughtful criticism upon my poetry is Chicago. *Robert Browning*

Hog butcher for the world,
Tool maker, stacker of wheat,
Player with railroads and the nation's freight handler;
Stormy, husky, brawling,
City of the big shoulders.
> *Carl Sandburg*

CHICKEN
A fowl which will help you to tell the vegetables from the weeds in your garden.

CHICKEN CONSOMMÉ
The result of passing a small piece of chicken through hot water quickly.

CHILD
A loud noise with a dirty neck.
The second chance for a parent.
A beam of sunlight from the Infinite and Eternal, with possibilities of virtue and vice—but as yet unstained. *Lyman Abbott*

> You are the trip I did not take;
> You are the pearls I cannot buy;
> You are my blue Italian lake;
> You are my piece of foreign sky.
> *Anne Campbell*

The child is father of the man. *William Wordsworth*
A curly, dimpled lunatic. *Ralph Waldo Emerson*

CHILDHOOD

The time of life when all you need to do to lose weight is to bathe.

The age without pity. *Jean de la Fontaine*

CHILDREN

Natural mimics—they act like their parents in spite of every attempt to teach them good manners.

A great comfort in your old age—and they help you to reach it faster, too. *Lionel M. Kaufman*

Expensive, time-consuming, patience-taxing additions to the family, but the sacrifices they demand are trivial to what they give. *Chad Walsh*

Additions to the family that hold a marriage together by keeping the parents so busy they haven't time to argue with each other.

What you know how to bring up when you don't have any.

The anchors that hold a mother to life. *Sophocles*

Lo, children are a heritage of the Lord: and the fruit of the womb is his reward. As arrows are in the hand of a mighty man, so are children of the youth. Happy is the man that hath his quiver full of them. *Ps. 127:3–5*

God's apostles, day by day sent forth to preach of love and hope and peace. *James Russell Lowell*

Children are poor men's riches. *English Proverb*

Children in a family are like flowers in a bouquet: there's always one determined to face in an opposite direction from the way the arranger desires. *Marcelene Cox*

Children are a torment, and nothing else. *Leo Tolstoy*

CHIMPANZEE

An ape that "yearns for a tail." *West African Proverb*

CHINA

A country that colors all seas that wash her shores. *Mme. Chiang Kai-shek*

CHINESE PUZZLE

China.

CHIROPODIST

A person who, when given an inch, will take a foot.

A man who is down at the heel even when he is prosperous.

CHIVALRY

A thing which must be courteously and generously conceded, and must never be pettishly claimed. *A. C. Benson*

CHOPIN, F. F.

Hats off, gentlemen—a genius! *Robert Schumann*

CHRIST
> Christ is the prototype of a humanity that is yet to be; not the great exception but the great example. *George Seaver*
> This is my beloved Son, in whom I am well pleased. *Matt. 17: 5*
> There is . . . one mediator between God and men, the man Christ Jesus. *I Tim. 2: 5*

CHRISTIAN
> A person who "is like the ripening corn; the riper he grows the more lowly he bends his head." *Guthrie*
> A sinful man who has put himself to school to Christ for the honest purpose of becoming better. *Henry Ward Beecher*
> A Christian is God Almighty's gentleman. *J. C. and A. W. Hare*
> The Christians do not commit adultery. They do not bear false witness. They do not covet their neighbor's goods. They honor father and mother. They love their neighbors. They judge justly. They avoid doing to others what they do not wish done to them. They do good to their enemies. They are kind. *St. Aristides*
> To be like Christ is to be a Christian. *William Penn*

CHRISTIANITY
> A religion that "has not been tried and found wanting; it has been found difficult and not tried." *G. K. Chesterton*
> The companion of liberty in all its conflicts, the cradle of its infancy, and the divine source of its claims. *De Tocqueville*
> Not the religion of Jesus; it is that of the worshipers of Jesus. *Maurice Goguel*
> Christianity does not remove you from the world and its problems; it makes you fit to live in it, triumphantly and usefully. *Charles Templeton*
> Christianity is the highest perfection of humanity. *Samuel Johnson*

CHRISTMAS
> The day into which we try to crowd all "the long arrears of kindliness and humanity of the whole year." *Adapted from David Grayson*

> Let nothing you dismay,
> For Jesus Christ, our Saviour,
> Was born upon this day.
> *Anonymous Old Carol*

CHURCH

Not a club of saints; it is a hospital for sinners. *George Craig Stewart*

This is God's House; but 'tis to be deplor'd
More come to see the House than serve its Lord.

CICERO

A journalist in the worst sense of the word. *Theodor Mommsen*

CIGARETTE

The perfect type of pleasure; it is exquisite and it leaves one unsatisfied. *Oscar Wilde*

CIRCLE (SEWING)

A group of women who darn husbands.

CIRCUMSTANCES

The rulers of the weak; they are but the instruments of the wise. *Samuel Lover*

CIRCUS

An entertaining performance in competition with the human race.

A great show if it is half as good as it smells. *Adapted from Fred Allen*

CIRRHOSIS (OF THE LIVER)

The occupational disease of the reporter. *Stanley Walker*

CITIZEN

A person who only wants better highways, better parks, better schools, and more service from government, with lower taxes.

CITY

The place where men are constantly seeking to find their door and where they are doomed to wandering forever. *Thomas Wolfe*

Has always been the fireplace of civilization, whence light and heat radiated out into the dark. *Theodore Parker*

Millions of people being lonesome together. *Henry David Thoreau*

A great city, a great solitude. *Latin Proverb*

A large number of persons striving to avoid being hit by an automobile.

Cities are the abyss of the human species. *Jean-Jacques Rousseau*

CIVILITY

A desire to be civilly treated "and to be accounted well bred." *La Rochefoucauld*

CIVILIZATION
Just a slow process of creating more needs to supply. *Roanoke World-News*

The end of the human race will be that it will eventually die of civilization. *Ralph Waldo Emerson*

The degree of a nation's disregard for the necessities of existence. *W. Somerset Maugham*

Society sufficiently developed to mistake respectability for character.

A state of human development that moves a man to pay the laundry for destroying his shirts.

A slow process of getting rid of our prejudices. *Macon News*

A coat of paint that washes away when the rain falls. *Auguste Rodin*

A society based upon the opinion of civilians. It means that violence, the rule of warriors and despotic chiefs, the conditions of camps and warfare, of riot and tyranny, give place to parliaments where laws are made, and independent courts of justice in which over long periods those laws are maintained. *Winston Churchill*

Order and freedom promoting cultural activity. . . . Civilization begins with order, grows with liberty and dies with chaos. *Will Durant*

A system under which a man pays a quarter to park his car so he won't be fined a dollar while spending a dime for a nickel cup of coffee.

A slow process of learning to be kind.

A constant quest for nonviolent means of solving conflicts; it is a common quest for peace. *Max Ascoli*

Civilization is like a skin above bottomless waters. *Jacquetta Hawkes*

Mankind's struggle upwards, in which millions are trampled to death, that thousands may mount on their bodies. *Clara L. Balfour*

CIVILIZED
When you take a bath. When you don't take a bath, you are cultured. *Lin Yutang*

CIVILIZED NATION
One that is horrified by other civilized nations.

CLARINET
An ill wood wind that nobody blows good.

CLARITY
So clearly one of the attributes of truth that very often it passes for truth. *Joseph Joubert*

CLASSIC
> Something that everybody wants to have read and no-body wants to read. *Mark Twain*

CLEANLINESS
> A physical condition that is said to be next to godliness. For a small boy it is also next to impossible.

CLERGY
> We are ambassadors for Christ, as though God did beseech you by us. *II Cor. 5: 20*

CLERICALISM
> The pursuit of power, especially political power, by a religious hierarchy, carried on by secular methods and for purposes of social dominations. *Dr. John A. Mackay*

CLEVERNESS
> Cleverness is not wisdom. *Euripides*

CLIMATE
> A theory. Weather is a condition. *Oliver Herford*

CLIMBER (SOCIAL)
> One who has a hearty taste for exactly the right sports. *H. L. Mencken*

CLOCK
> Indicates the moment—but what does eternity indicate? *Walt Whitman*

CLOSET
> A place that makes a skeleton terribly restless. *John Barrymore*

CLOTHES
> An expression of the social life of the time. *Elizabeth Hawes*
> The intellect of the dandy. *Josh Billings*

CLUB
> An assembly of good fellows, meeting under certain conditions. *Samuel Johnson*

CLUB (FAN)
> A group of people who tell an actor he's not alone in the way he feels about himself. *Jack Carson*

COAL
> Coal is a portable climate. *Ralph Waldo Emerson*

COCK
> The trumpet of the morn. *Shakespeare*

COCKTAIL
> Cocktails have all the disagreeability, without the utility, of a disinfectant. *Shane Leslie*

> A cocktail is a pleasant drink:
> Mild and harmless—I don't think.
>
> *Anonymous*

COEDS
College students who sign up for the romance languages.

COFFEE
A drink that "has two virtues: it is wet and warm." *Dutch Proverb*

COFFIN
The one article about which no one says, "I can get it for you wholesale."

COLD
A pain "in the head" that "causes less suffering than an idea." *Jules Renard*

A physical ailment that "is both positive and negative; sometimes the eyes have it and sometimes the nose." *William Lyon Phelps*

COLD FEET
The ailment you get when you know what the consequences are going to be.

COLD WAR
A period when nations flex their missiles.

COLLECTIVE IDEOLOGISTS
Those professional intellectuals who revel in decimals and polysyllables. *Winston Churchill*

COLLEGE
Similar to a laundry. You get out of it just what you sent—but you would never recognize it.

The land of the midnight sons.

An educational institution in which any person competent with a pigskin (football) is assured of a sheepskin.

An educational institution where the professors don't recognize ability and the students don't possess it.

An institution where young people are sent when they don't have sense enough to do other things well.

A place where fools are not made but are sometimes developed. *Adapted from Horace Lorimer*

COLLEGE (COEDUCATIONAL)
A match factory.

COLLEGE EDUCATION
A form of training which does not hurt you provided you study and work hard after graduation.

Shows a man how little other people know. *Thomas C. Haliburton*

COLLEGE ENGLISH DEPARTMENT
The chamber of commas.

COLLEGE GRADUATE
A graduate of an institution of higher learning who finishes college and his father at about the same time.

One who gets a liberal education while his dad is getting an education in liberality.

COLLEGE PROFESSOR
A man who is paid to study sleeping conditions among students.

COLONEL
A male resident of Kentucky. *Gideon Wurdz*

COLONIES
All colonies are oppressed peoples. *Nikolai Lenin*

COLOR
Colors are the smiles of nature. *Leigh Hunt*

COLUMBUS
The man who discovered America at an alleged cost of only $7,250, but it must be remembered he did not have to live in it after he had discovered it.

COLUMNISTS
Perfectionists, and impatient when the neat pattern of their typed pages fails to congeal a nation . . . to instant docility. *Charles Fisher*

COMEDIAN
A fellow who finds other comedians too humorous to mention. *Jack Herbert*

One who is no better than his script. *Louis R. Reid*

COMFORT
The happiness of the indolent, while pleasure is the comfort of the unhappy.

COMIC
Tragedy viewed from the wings. *Elbert Hubbard* (*The Roycroft Dictionary*)

COMMENDATION
Praise attained by merit or by wealth. *Samuel Johnson*

The tribute that we pay to achievements that resemble, but do not equal, our own. *Ambrose Bierce*

COMMERCE
The great civilizer. We exchange ideas when we exchange fabrics. *Robert G. Ingersoll*

The equalizer of the wealth of nations. *William Gladstone*

COMMITTEE

A cul-de-sac to which ideas are lured and then quietly strangled. *John A. Lincoln*

A group of men who, individually, can do nothing, but collectively can meet and decide that nothing can be done.

A group of persons organized to delay decision and hamper progress.

The most effective method of killing an idea. The absence of a committee made it possible for the Israelites to leave Egypt.

A group of persons who follow a long and tortuous route to an obvious conclusion.

A group of the unfit, appointed by the unwilling, to do the unnecessary. *Henry Cooke*

A group which succeeds in getting something done only when it consists of three members, one of whom happens to be sick and another absent. *Hendrik W. Van Loon*

A group of men who keep minutes and waste hours.

COMMON SENSE

The knack of seeing things as they are, and doing things as they ought to be done. *C. E. Stowe*

What the world calls wisdom. *Samuel Taylor Coleridge*

The ability to detect values.

Instinct, and enough of it is genius. *Josh Billings*

COMMUNISM

The theory of communism may be summed up in one sentence: Abolish all private property. *Karl Marx and Friedrich Engels*

The exploitation of the strong by the weak. In communism, inequality springs from placing mediocrity on a level with excellence. *Pierre J. Proudhon*

A system that is based on the belief that man is so weak and inadequate that he is unable to govern himself, and therefore requires the rule of strong masters. *Harry S. Truman*

The devil's imitation of Christianity. *A. W. Tozer*

The theory which teaches that the labor and the income of society should be distributed equally among all its members by some constituted authority. *Sir R. H. Inglis Palgrave*

COMMUNIST

A person who labors under the impression that everybody wants to die poor.

> What is a Communist? One who hath yearnings
> For equal division of unequal earnings.
> Idler or bungler, or both, he is willing,
> To fork out his copper and pocket your shilling.
>
> *Ebenezer Elliott* (1831)

A person who feels disloyal when he catches himself thinking.

A person who says everything is perfect in Soviet Russia but stays here because he likes to rough it.

A man who has given up hope of becoming a capitalist.

A person who stands on his constitutional rights when he hasn't a leg to stand on.

A Socialist without a sense of humor. *George Barton Cutten*

A Socialist in a violent hurry. *G. W. Gough*

A Marxman.

A person who wants your pot so he can cook your goose.

A person who has nothing and is eager to share it with others.

COMMUTER

> Commuter—one who spends his life
> In riding to and from his wife;
> A man who shaves and takes a train,
> And then rides back to shave again.
>
> *E. B. White*

COMPENSATION

To find that a detour has no billboards.

COMPETITION

The life of trade, but the death of profit.

The keen cutting edge of business, always shaving away at costs. *Henry Ford II*

The life of trade, and the death of the trader. *Elbert Hubbard* (*The Roycroft Dictionary*)

COMPLACENCY

He's all buttoned up in an impenetrable little coat of complacency. *Ilka Chase*

The feeling of persons "who have the happy conviction that they are not as other men." *Margery Allingham*

COMPLAINT

The largest tribute heaven receives and the sincerest part of our devotion. *Jonathan Swift*

COMPLIMENT

Something like a kiss through a veil. *Victor Hugo*

Only lies in court clothes.

COMPROMISE
> The sacrifice of one right or good in the hope of retaining another, too often ending in the loss of both. *Tryon Edwards*
>
> The English spirit of compromise tempts us to believe that injustice, when it is halved, becomes justice. *Viscount Samuel*
>
> A temporary expedient, often wise in party politics, almost sure to be unwise in statesmanship. *James Russell Lowell*
>
> It means "if you can't lick 'em, join 'em." *American Political Proverb*

CONCEIT
> An idea that "causes more conversation than wit." *La Rochefoucauld*
>
> God's gift to little men. *Bruce Barton*
>
> Being a little country bounded on the north, south, east, and west by yourself. *Adapted from Martha Ostenso*
>
> A personal quality that makes an ignoramus satisfied with himself.
>
> The father who tries for twenty years to make his child just what he is.
>
> The first armor a man can wear. *Jerome K. Jerome*
>
> Conceited persons are those who "carry their comfort about with them." *George Eliot*

CONCENTRATION
> The secret of strength in politics, in war, in trade, in short in all management of human affairs.

CONDOLENCE
> Of all cruelties, those are the most intolerable that come under the name of condolence and consolation. *Walter Savage Landor*

CONDUCTOR
> One who tells everyone where to get off.
>
> > This backward Man, this view obstructor,
> > Is known to us as the Conductor.
> > > *Laurence McKinney*

CONEY ISLAND
> Where the surf is one-third water and two-thirds people. *John Steinbeck*

CONFERENCE
> A meeting where no grand idea is ever born, but a lot of foolish ideas die there. *Adapted from F. Scott Fitzgerald*

A place where you talk about doing something instead of doing it.

A place where conversation is substituted for the dreariness of labor and the loneliness of thought.

The confusion of the loudest talking person multiplied by the number present.

A gathering of important people who singly can do nothing, but together can decide that nothing can be done. *Fred Allen*

CONFESSION

Confession is the first step of repentance. *English Proverb*

CONFIDENCE

The feeling that makes one believe a man, even when one knows that one would lie in his place. *H. L. Mencken*

The feeling you have before you know better.

That feeling by which the mind embarks in great and honorable courses with a sure hope and trust in itself. *Cicero*

The thing that enables you to eat raspberry jam on a picnic without looking to see if the seeds move.

CONFORMITY

The virtue most in request in society. Self-reliance is its aversion. *Adapted from Ralph Waldo Emerson*

Conformity gives comeliness to things. *Robert Herrick*

CONGRESS

A great deliberative body, but many business conferences run it a close second.

CONGRESSMAN

Reader, suppose you were an idiot. And suppose you were a member of Congress. But I repeat myself. *Mark Twain*

CONQUEST

The acquiring of the right of sovereignty by victory. *Thomas Hobbes*

CONSCIENCE

The sixth sense that comes to our aid when we are doing wrong and tells us that we are about to get caught.

Merely your own judgment of the right or wrong of our actions, and so can never be a safe guide unless enlightened by the word of God. *Tryon Edwards*

The thing that aches when everything is feeling good.

An inner voice that warns us somebody is looking. *H. L. Mencken*

The sum of all inhibitions of a religious and ethical character. *Wilhelm Stekel*

The voice that says you shouldn't have done something after you did it.

A sacred sanctuary where God alone may enter as judge. *F. R. Lamennais*

The guardian in the individual of the rules which the community has evolved for its own preservation. *W. Somerset Maugham*

God's presence in man. *Emanuel Swedenborg*

A small voice that keeps interrupting when money is talking.

The still small voice that tells you what other people should do.

God's vice-regent on earth . . . a divine voice in the human soul. *Francis Bowen*

Conscience tells us that we ought to do right, but it does not tell us what right is—that we are taught by God's word. *H. C. Trumbull*

The soft whispers of the God in man. *Young*

Conscience does make cowards of us all. *Shakespeare*

>
> Conscience is but a word that cowards use,
> Devised at first to keep the strong in awe.
> *Shakespeare*

Conscience is but the pulse of reason. *Samuel Taylor Coleridge*

CONSCIENCE (AND COWARDICE)

Really the same things. Conscience is the trade name of the firm. *Oscar Wilde*

CONSERVATION

The wise use of the earth and its resources for the lasting good of men. *Gifford Pinchot*

CONSERVATISM

A state of mind resulting from a good job.

Conservatism defends those coercive arrangements which a still-lingering savageness makes requisite. *Herbert Spencer*

What is conservatism? Is it not adherence to the old and tried, against the new and untried? *Abraham Lincoln*

CONSERVATIVE

A man who will not look at the new moon, out of respect for that ancient institution, the old one. *Douglas Jerrold*

A statesman who is enamored of existing evils, as distinguished from the liberal, who wishes to replace them with others. *Ambrose Bierce*

A man who is too cowardly to fight and too fat to run. *Elbert Hubbard*

A man with two perfectly good legs who has never learned to walk. *Franklin D. Roosevelt*

A man who just sits and thinks, mostly sits. *Woodrow Wilson*

A person who wears both belt and suspenders.

A person who can't see any difference between radicalism and an idea.

A person who thinks a rich man should have a square deal.

A person who has learned to love the new order forced upon him by radicals.

A person who says that a radical may sometimes be right, but when he is, he is right for the wrong reasons.

A man who does not think that anything should be done for the first time. *Frank Vanderlip*

Men "when they are least vigorous, or when they are most luxurious. They are conservatives after dinner." *Ralph Waldo Emerson*

CONSIDERATE MOTORIST

One who will give a woman half of the road if he knows which half she wants.

CONSISTENCY

The last refuge of the unimaginative. *Oscar Wilde*

A paste jewel that only cheap men cherish. *William Allen White*

CONSTANCY

Constancy is but a dull sleepy quality at best. *George Farquhar*

It is as absurd to say that a man can't love one woman all the time as it is to say that a violinist needs several violins to play the same piece of music. *Honoré de Balzac*

There are two kinds of constancy in love: one arises from continually discovering in the loved person new subjects for love, the other arises from our making a merit of being constant. *La Rochefoucauld*

CONSTITUTION

The Constitution is what the judges say it is. *Charles Evans Hughes*

A means of assuring that depositories of power cannot misemploy it. *J. S. Mill*

The Constitution is not a mere lawyer's document; it is a vehicle of life, and its spirit is always the spirit of the age. *Woodrow Wilson*

The Constitution was essentially an economic document based upon the concept that the fundamental rights of private property are anterior to government and morally beyond the reach of popular majorities. *Charles H. Beard*

The American Constitution—the most wonderful work ever struck off at a given time by the brain and purpose of man. *William E. Gladstone*

CONSULT

To seek another's approval of a course already decided on. *Ambrose Bierce*

CONSULTANT

A man who knows less about your business than you do and gets more for telling you how to run it than you could possibly make out of it even if you ran it right instead of the way he tells you.

An executive who can't find another job. *Henry W. Platt*

CONTEMPT

A kind of gangrene, which if it seizes one part of a character corrupts all the rest. *Samuel Johnson*

The subtlest form of revenge. *Boltasar Gracian*

Contempt is egotism in ill humor. *Samuel Taylor Coleridge*

The sharpest reproof.

CONTENTMENT

A warm sty for eaters and sleepers. *Eugene O'Neill*

The contented mind is the only riches, the only quietness, the only happiness. *George Pettie*

Content is the philosopher's stone, which turns all it touches into gold. *Thomas Fuller*

Contentment iz a kind of moral laziness; if thare want ennything but kontentment in his world, man wouldn't be any more of a suckcess than an angleworm iz. *Josh Billings*

CONTRALTO

A female singer who makes a low sort of music.

CONTRAST

Evermore in the world is this marvelous balance of beauty and disgust, magnificence, and rats. *Ralph Waldo Emerson*

CONVERSATION

An art in which a man has all mankind for his competitors. *Ralph Waldo Emerson*

> Conversation is but carving!
> Give no more to every guest
> Than he's able to digest.
> Give him always of the prime,
> And but little at a time.
> Carve to all but just enough,
> Let them neither starve nor stuff,
> And that you may have your due,
> Let your neighbor carve for you.
> *Jonathan Swift*

The slowest form of human communication. *Don Herold*

Conversation is the image of the mind. As the man is, so is his talk. *Publius Syrus*

CONVICTION

A viewpoint you can explain without getting angry. Antonym: prejudice.

That commendable quality in ourselves which we call bullheadedness in others.

The conscience of the mind. *Mrs. Humphrey Ward*

Convictions are the mainsprings of action, the driving powers of life. What a man lives are his convictions. *Bishop Francis C. Kelly*

Opinions which circumstances have temporarily backed. *Henry S. Haskins*

Often the most "dangerous enemies of truth." *F. W. Nietzsche*

What an employee has after he knows what the boss thinks.

Mortgages on the mind.

COOKERY

The art of poisoning mankind, by rendering the appetite still importunate, when the wants of nature are supplied. *François Fénelon*

COPERNICUS, NICOLAUS

A distinguished astronomer. "Copernicus . . . did not publish his book until he was on his deathbed. He knew how dangerous it is to be right when the rest of the world is wrong." *Thomas B. Reed*

COQUETTE

A woman without any heart, who makes a fool of a man that hasn't got any head. *Mme. Deluzy*

A young lady of more beauty than sense, more accomplishments than learning, more charms of person than graces of mind, more admirers than friends, more fools than wise men for attendants. *Henry Wadsworth Longfellow*

CORPORATION
> Corporations are invisible, immortal, and have no soul. *Ascribed to Roger Manwood*

CORROBORATION
> . . . detail, intended to give artistic verisimilitude to an otherwise bold and unconvincing narrative. W. S. *Gilbert*

CORRUPTION
> The most infallible symptom of constitutional liberty. *Edward Gibbon*

COUGH
> A convulsion of the lungs, vellicated by some sharp serosity. *Samuel Johnson*

COUNTRY
> It is a kind of healthy grave. *Sydney Smith*
>
> Our country is the world—our countrymen are mankind. *William Lloyd Garrison*
>
> God made the country, and man made the town. *William Cowper*

COURAGE
> A perfect sensibility of the measure of danger, and a mental willingness to endure it. *General W. T. Sherman*
>
> Not simply one of the virtues but the form of every virtue at the testing point, which means at the point of highest reality. *C. S. Lewis*
>
> A quality which few persons have enough of to admit that they haven't got it.
>
> Almost a contradiction in terms. It means a strong desire to live taking the form of readiness to die. *G. K. Chesterton*
>
> It is not freedom from fear; it is being afraid and going on.
>
> Grace under pressure. *Ernest Hemingway*
>
> Knowing what not to fear. *Socrates*
>
> Courage is rightly esteemed the first of human qualities, because . . . it is the quality which guarantees all others. *Winston Churchill*
>
> True courage is like a kite; a contrary wind raises it higher. *J. Petit-Senn*
>
> Courage is a virtue only so far as it is directed by prudence. *François Fénelon*

COURT
> An assembly of noble and distinguished beggars. *Charles Maurice de Talleyrand*

COURTESY
> What keeps you pleasant when you visit with someone you wish would leave.

Smiling while your departing guest holds the screen door open and lets the flies in.

COURTSHIP

The period during which the girl decides whether or not she can do better.

A number of quiet attentions, not so pointed as to alarm, nor so vague as not to be understood. *Lawrence Sterne*

A man pursuing a woman until she catches him.

COVETOUSNESS

Covetousness has for its mother unlawful desire, for its daughter injustice, and for its friends violence. *Arab Proverb*

COW

A new milk-cow is stepmother to every man's baby. *Josh Billings*

COWARD

One who in a perilous emergency thinks with his legs. *Ambrose Bierce*

One in whom the instinct of self-preservation is normal.

COWARDICE

Protection against temptation. *Mark Twain*

CREDIT

A person who can't pay, gets another person who can't pay, to guarantee that he can pay. *Charles Dickens*

Not merely a term in business; it is a condition of human relationships. It binds the future to the present by the confidence we have in the integrity of those with whom we deal. *James T. Shotwell*

Applied faith.

The life blood of industry, and the control of credit is the control of all society. *Upton Sinclair*

CREDITOR

A person who has a better memory than a debtor. *Adapted from Benjamin Franklin*

The creditors are a superstitious sect, great observers of set days and times. *Benjamin Franklin*

A body without a soul in contrast to an angel which is a soul without a body.

A creditor is worse than a master; for a master owns only your person, a creditor owns your dignity, and can belabor that. *Victor Hugo*

CREDULOUS

One "who knows nothing" and "doubts nothing." *George Herbert*

CRICKET
An antidote to Bolshevism and degeneracy.

CRIME
Merely a name for the most obvious, extreme, and directly
dangerous forms of . . . departure from the norm in
manners and customs. *Havelock Ellis*

CRIMINAL
One who does by illegal means what all the rest of us do
legally. *Elbert Hubbard (The Roycroft Dictionary)*

A person with predatory instincts who has not sufficient
capital to form a corporation. *Howard Scott*

A person who gets caught in contrast to the rest of us.

CRISIS
Crises refine life. In them you discover what you are. *Allan
Knight Chalmers*

CRITIC
A man who expects miracles. *James Gibbons Huneker*

A legless man who teaches running. *Channing Pollock*

A man whose watch is five minutes ahead of other people's watches. *Charles Augustin Sainte-Beuve*

A necessary evil, and criticism is an evil necessity. *Carolyn
Wells*

An artist who has failed. *Adapted from Logan Pearsall
Smith*

A person who speaks for an audience of book and play lovers
he destroys.

One who has "failed in literature and art." *Benjamin Disraeli*

Brushers of noblemen's clothes. *George Herbert*

They who write ill, and they who ne'er durst write,
Turn critics out of mere revenge and spite.

John Dryden

Cut-throat bandits in the paths of fame. *Robert Burns*

Venomous serpents that delight in hissing. *W. B. Daniel*

The critic takes a book in one hand, and uses the other to
paint himself with. When his work is done, we may
fail to find the book in it, but we are sure to find him.
J. G. Holland

Men who quarrel over the motive of a book that never had
any. *Elbert Hubbard (The Roycroft Dictionary)*

Sentinels in the grand army of letters, stationed at the
corners of newspapers and reviews to challenge every
new author. *Henry Wadsworth Longfellow*

CRITIC (DRAMATIC)

A newspaperman whose sweetie ran away with an actor. *Walter Winchell*

A person who is given a seat on the aisle in a theater, but prefers to sit on the author, the cast, the scenery and the producers. Motto: The flay's the thing.

A man who gives the best jeers of his life to the theater.

A person who surprises the playwright by informing him what he meant. *Wilson Mizner*

CRITICISM

A study by which men grow important and formidable at very small expense. *Samuel Johnson*

A process of which, "while an author is yet living, we estimate his powers by his worst performance; and when he is dead, we rate them by his best." *Samuel Johnson*

What we say about other people who don't have the same faults we have.

As it is practiced by most poets and novelists, it is a sort of indirect self-exhibition. *Paul Rosenfeld*

The most agreeable of all amusements. *H. H. Kames*

Criticism is above all a gift, an intuition, a matter of tact and flair; it cannot be taught or demonstrated—it is an art. *H. F. Amiel*

CROQUETTE

Hash that has come to a head. *Irvin S. Cobb*

CROSBY, BING

A man who sounds like everyone else thinks they sound in the bath. *Dinah Shore*

CROWD

A device for indulging ourselves in a kind of temporary insanity by all going crazy together.

CRUELTY

The child of ignorance. *Clarence Darrow*

Cruelty is the first attribute of the Devil. *Proverb*

CRYING

The refuge of plain women, but the ruin of pretty ones. *Oscar Wilde*

CUCUMBER

A vegetable that "should be well sliced, and dressed with pepper and vinegar, and then thrown out, as good for nothing." *Samuel Johnson*

CULTURE

To know the best that has been said and thought in the world. *Matthew Arnold*

What your butcher would have if he were a surgeon. *Mary Pettibone Poole*

The love of perfection; it is a study of perfection. *Matthew Arnold*

CUNNING

The dark sanctuary of incapacity. *Lord Chesterfield*

A short blanket—if you pull it over your face, you expose your feet.

The dwarf of wisdom. *W. R. Alger*

CUPID

A blind gunner. *George Farquhar*

CURIOSITY

The direct incontinency of the spirit. *Jeremy Taylor*

In great and generous minds, the first passion and the last. *Samuel Johnson*

The greatest virtue of man. *Anatole France*

One of the permanent and certain characteristics of a vigorous mind. *Samuel Johnson*

The reason why most of us haven't committed suicide long ago.

Curiosity is only vanity. Most frequently we wish not to know, but to talk. We would not take a sea voyage for the sole pleasure of seeing without hope of ever telling. *Blaise Pascal*

CURSE

To pray to the Devil. *German Proverb*

CUSTOM

The plague of wise men and the idol of fools. *Thomas Fuller*

CUT (TAX)

The kindest cut of all.

CYNIC

A blackguard whose faulty visions sees things as they are, and not as they ought to be. *Ambrose Bierce*

A man who knows the price of everything, and the value of nothing. *Oscar Wilde*

A man who, when he smells flowers, looks around for a coffin. *H. L. Mencken*

A man who looks at the world with a monocle in his mind's eye. *Carolyn Wells*

A man who looks both ways before crossing a one-way street.

One who never sees a good quality in a man, and never fails to see a bad one. He is the human owl, vigilant in darkness, and blind to light, mousing for vermin, and never seeing noble game. *Henry Ward Beecher*

One who looks down on those above him.

CYNICISM

The anticipation of the historical perspective. *Russell Green*

Intellectual dandyism. *George Meredith*

● D ●

DACHSHUND

An animal that is half a dog high and a dog and a half long.

DAMNATION

A passage broad,
Smooth, easy, inoffensive, down to Hell.
John Milton

DANCING

Wonderful training for girls; it's the first way you learn to guess what a man is going to do before he does it. *Christopher Morley*

The art of pulling your feet away faster than your partner can step on them.

A public revelation of the secrets of the subconscious mind and its revelations are often disastrous. *Gelett Burgess*

DANDY

A dandy is a clothes-wearing man, a man whose trade, office, and existence consists in the wearing of clothes. *Thomas Carlyle*

DARLING

The popular form of address used in speaking to a person of the opposite sex whose name you cannot at the moment recall. *Oliver Herford*

DAWN

The friend of the Muses. *Latin Proverb*

The time when men of reason go to bed. *Ambrose Bierce*

DAY

A miniature Eternity. *Ralph Waldo Emerson*

The confluence of two eternities. *Thomas Carlyle*

A little space of time ere time expires. *Algernon C. Swinburne*

DEACONS

Must be grave, not double-tongued, not given to much wine, not greedy of filthy lucre, holding the mystery of the faith in a pure conscience. *I Tim. 3: 8–9*

DEAF AND DUMB COUPLE
> The only married people who can settle a quarrel at night by turning out the lights.

DEAN
> A person who is not smart enough to be a university professor but is too smart to be a university president. *A Canadian University Dean*

DEATH
> A punishment to some, to some a gift, and to many a favor. *Seneca*
>
> A cessation from the impression of the senses, the tyranny of the passions, the errors of the mind, and the servitude of the body. *Marcus Aurelius*
>
> To stop sinning suddenly. *Elbert Hubbard*
>
> The sole equality on earth. *Philip J. Bailey*
>
> More universal than life; everyone dies but not everyone lives. *A. Sachs*
>
> A law, not a punishment. *Jean-Baptiste Dubos*
>
>> The undiscover'd country, from whose bourne
>> No traveler returns.
>>> *Shakespeare*
>
> The ugly fact which nature has to hide, and she hides it well. *Alexander Smith*
>
>> Death, a thing which makes men weep,
>> And yet a third of life is passed in sleep.
>>> *Lord Byron*
>
> The most beautiful adventure in life. *Charles Frohman*
>
> Death—the last sleep? No, it is the last final awakening. *Sir Walter Scott*
>
> Death levels all things. *Claudius Claudianus*

DEATH VALLEY
> The distance in a street from curb to curb.

DEBATE
> The death of conversation. *Emil Ludwig*

DEBT
> The only thing that doesn't become smaller when it is contracted.
>
> The wages of war.
>
> The easiest thing for any one to run into.
>
> The worst poverty.
>
> Debt, grinding debt, whose iron face the widow, the orphan, and the sons of genius fear and hate; debt, which consumes so much time, which so cripples and dis-

heartens a great spirit with cares that seem so base, is a preceptor whose lessons cannot be foregone, and is needed most by those who suffer from it most. *Ralph Waldo Emerson*

A bottomless sea. *Thomas Carlyle*

The fatal disease of republics, the first thing and the mightiest to undermine governments and corrupt the people. *Wendell Phillips*

Like any other trap, easy enough to get into, but hard enough to get out of. *Josh Billings*

DEBT (PUBLIC)

Public credit means the contracting of debts which a nation never can pay. *William Cobbett*

As I believe it is a national curse, my vow shall be to pay the national debt. *Andrew Jackson*

DECATHLON

Any combination of ten athletic events, such as painting the garage and falling off the ladder.

DECENCY

Decency is indecency's conspiracy of silence. *George Bernard Shaw*

DECLARATION OF INDEPENDENCE

This holy bond of our Union. *Thomas Jefferson*

DECORATION

The first spiritual want of a barbarous man. *Thomas Carlyle*

DEEDS

Deeds are facts, and are forever and ever. *Thomas B. Reed*

DEFEAT

A school in which truth always grows strong. *Henry Ward Beecher*

Nothing but education, nothing but the first step to something better. *Wendell Phillips*

It is defeat that turns bone to flint; it is defeat that turns gristle to muscle; it is defeat that makes men invincible. *Henry Ward Beecher*

DEFERENCE

The most complicated, the most indirect, and the most elegant of all compliments. *William Shenstone*

DEFICIT

What the government has when it hasn't as much as if it had nothing.

One of the few things that is permanent in government.

DEFICITIZENS

The present and coming generation of citizens.

DELEGATE-AT-LARGE

A man who goes to a convention without his wife.

DELICATESSEN OPERATOR

A man who has women eat out of his hand.

DELINQUENCY (JUVENILE)

A product of sickness in society. It is largely an urban phenomenon and its most fertile breeding place is in the slums of the great cities. *Life*

DEMAGOGUE

One who preaches doctrines he knows to be untrue to men he knows to be idiots. *H. L. Mencken*

The demagogue is usually sly, a detractor of others, a professor of humility and disinterestedness, a great stickler for equality as respects all above him, a man who acts in corners, and avoids open and manly exposition of his course, calls blackguards gentlemen, and gentlemen folks, appeals to passions and prejudices rather than to reason, and is in all respects a man of intrigue and deception, of sly cunning and management. *James Fenimore Cooper*

A wise fellow who is also worthless always charms the rabble. *Euripides*

A man of loose tongue, intemperate, trusting to tumult, leading the populace to mischief with empty words. *Euripides*

DEMOCRACY

A form of government that "gives every man the right to be his own oppressor." *James Russell Lowell*

A government of bullies tempered by editors. *Ralph Waldo Emerson*

Government that "substitutes election by the incompetent many for appointment by the corrupt few." *George Bernard Shaw*

Simply the bludgeoning of the people, by the people, for the people. *Oscar Wilde*

Encourages the nimble charlatan at the expense of the thinker, and prefers the plausible wizard with quack remedies to the true statesman. *Sir James Jeans*

Having the right to complain when there is nothing to complain about. Dictatorship is a government in which you have no right to complain when there is everything to complain about.

An attempt to apply the principles of the Bible to a human society. *Wallace C. Speers*

A method of our getting ahead without leaving any of us behind. *T. V. Smith*

Democracy arose from men thinking that if they are equal in any respect they are equal in all respects. *Aristotle*

A form of government by popular ignorance. *Elbert Hubbard* (*The Roycroft Dictionary*)

President Lincoln defined democracy to be "the government of the people, by the people, for the people." This is a sufficiently compact statement of it as a political arrangement. Theodore Parker said that "Democracy meant not 'I'm as good as you are,' but 'You're as good as I am.'" And this is the ethical conception of it, necessary as a complement of the other. *James Russell Lowell*

A country where "you say what you like and do what you're told." *Gerald Berry*

Means government of the mentally unfit by the mentally mediocre tempered by the saving grace of snobbery. *Saki*

A country in which everyone has an equal right to feel superior to the other fellow.

Democracy means that the aggregate of mankind shall be so organized as to create for each man the maximum opportunity of growth in accordance with the dictates of his own genius and aspiration. *Ralph Barton Perry*

The government of the people, by the people, for the people. *Abraham Lincoln*

Direct, self-government, over all the people, for all the people, by all the people. *Theodore Parker*

A democracy is a state which recognizes the subjection of the minority to the majority, that is, an organization for the systematic use of violence by one class against the other, by one part of the population against another. *Nikolai Lenin*

DENTIST

A collector of old issues of magazines.

A man who runs a filling station.

A person who always looks down in the mouth.

The only person who can tell a woman to open or close her mouth and get away with it.

One who pulls out the teeth of others to obtain employment for his own.

One who believes people enjoy pain if they pay for it.

DENUNCIATION OF THE YOUNG
> A necessary part of the hygiene of older people, and greatly assists the circulation of their blood. *Logan Pearsall Smith*

DEPRESSION
> A period when people do without the things their parents never had.

DESERTION
> The poor man's method of divorce. *A. G. Hays*

DESIRE
> Perhaps the greatest feature which distinguishes man from animals. *William Osler*

DESK
> A wastebasket with drawers.

DESPAIR
> A great incentive to honorable death. *Quintus Curtius Rufus*
> The conclusion of fools. *Benjamin Disraeli*

DESTINY
> Destiny is not a matter of chance, it is a matter of choice; it is not a thing to be waited for, it is a thing to be achieved. *William Jennings Bryan*

DETOUR
> The longest distance between two driven points.
> The roughest distance between two points.
> "Something that lengthens your mileage, diminishes your gas, and strengthens your vocabulary." *Oliver Herford*

DEVIL
> A gentleman who never goes where he is not welcome. *John A. Lincoln*
> The father of lies, but he neglected to patent the idea, and the business now suffers from competition. *Josh Billings*

DIAGNOSIS
> A preface to an autopsy.

DIAMOND
> A woman's idea of a stepping stone to success.

DIAPER
> An article of apparel that gets less thanks out of life than anything else and does more good.

DIAPHRAGM
> A muscular partition separating disorders of the chest from disorders of the bowels. *Ambrose Bierce*

DIARY
> To see one's self as no one else cares to see us. *Elbert Hubbard (The Roycroft Dictionary)*

DICTATORS
> Rulers who always look good until the last ten minutes. *Jan Masaryk*

DICTATORSHIP
> A form of government in which only one pronoun is needed in the language.
>
> Always merely an aria, never an opera. *Emil Ludwig*
>
> Like a great beech tree, nice to look at, but nothing grows under it. *Stanley Baldwin*

DICTIONARY
> A malevolent literary device for cramping the growth of a language and making it hard and inelastic. *Ambrose Bierce*

DIET
> A plan, generally hopeless, for reducing your weight, which tests your will power but does little for your waistline.

DIETING
> A grueling task.

DIFFICULT
> That which can be done immediately; the impossible, that which takes a little longer. *George Santayana*
>
> The nurse of greatness. *William Cullen Bryant*

DIFFICULTIES
> God's errands and trainers, and only through them can one come to the fullness of manhood. *Henry Ward Beecher*
>
> Things that show what men are. *Epictetus*

DIFFICULTY
> The excuse history never accepts. *Samuel Grafton*

DIGESTION
> The great secret of life. *Sydney Smith*

DIGNIFIED
> One who "never unbuttons himself." *Said of Robert Peel*

DIGNITY
> The capacity of man to despise himself. *George Santayana*
>
> A mask we wear to hide our ignorance. *Elbert Hubbard (The Roycroft Dictionary)*
>
> One thing that can't be preserved in alcohol. *Graeme and Sarah Lorimer*
>
> A veil between us and the real truth of things. *E. P. Whipple*

DILEMMA
> A politician trying to save both his faces at once. *John A. Lincoln*
>
> In front a precipice, behind a wolf. *Latin Proverb*

DILIGENCE
The mother of good luck. *Benjamin Franklin*

DIME
A dollar with all taxes deducted.

DIMPLE
Hollows which love made. *Adapted from Shakespeare*

DINNER
A time when "one should eat wisely but not too well, and talk well but not too wisely." *W. Somerset Maugham*

DIPLOMACY
Lying in state. *Oliver Herford*

The art of letting someone have your way. *Daniele Vare*

The business of handling a porcupine without disturbing the quills.

The ability to take something and make the other fellow believe he is giving it away.

Diplomacy is to do and say the nastiest thing in the nicest way. *Isaac Goldberg*

The patriotic art of lying for one's country. *Ambrose Bierce*

The art of being able to say, "nice doggie," until you have time to pick up a rock.

A disguised war, in which states seek to gain by barter and intrigue, by the cleverness of arts, the objectives which they would have to gain more clumsily by means of war. *Randolph Bourne*

The atmosphere of accredited mendacity. *Lord Acton*

DIPLOMAT
An honest man sent abroad to lie for his country. *Henry Wooton*

A man who knows what it isn't safe to laugh at.

A man who convinces his wife that a woman looks stout in a mink coat.

A person who counts his fingers after shaking hands with another diplomat.

A person who straddles or dodges issues.

A person who goes both ways when he comes to the parting of the ways.

A person who puts his cards on the table but still has a few up each sleeve.

A person who can make his country's greed seem like altruism.

A man who remembers a lady's birthday but forgets her age.

One who thinks twice before saying nothing.

DIRECTORY (TELEPHONE)
> The only books without obscenity. *Adapted from George Bernard Shaw*

DIRT
> Matter in the wrong place. *Lord Palmerston*

DISADVANTAGE
> Having too many advantages in life. *Elbert Hubbard (The Roycroft Dictionary)*

DISAPPOINTMENT
> The nurse of wisdom. *Sir Boyle Roche*
> Parent of despair. *John Keats*

DISCONTENT
> Something that "follows ambition like a shadow." *Henry H. Haskins*
> The mainspring of progress. *Elbert Hubbard (The Roycroft Dictionary)*
> The starting-point in every man's career. *Elbert Hubbard (The Roycroft Dictionary)*
> The first step in the progress of a man or a nation. *Oscar Wilde*
> The first necessity of progress. Show me a thoroughly satisfied man—and I will show you a failure. *Thomas A. Edison*
> Discontent is the want of self-reliance; it is infirmity of will. *Ralph Waldo Emerson*

DISCRETION
> The thing "called cunning in animals." *Alphonse de Lamartine*
> When you are sure you are right and then ask your wife.
> The better part of valor. *English Proverb*
> Impotence.

DISCUSSION
> A method of confirming others in their errors. *Ambrose Bierce*
> One of the most important things in the world, for it is almost our only arena of thinking. Without discussion intellectual experience is only an exercise in a private gymnasium. *Randolph Bourne*

DISEASE
> A physical process that "generally begins that equality which death completes." *Samuel Johnson*
> A retribution of outraged Nature. *Hosea Ballou*
> An experience of so-called mortal mind. It is fear made manifest on the body. *Mary Baker Eddy*

DISILLUSIONMENT

What takes place when your son asks you to help him with his algebra.

DISK JOCKEY

A person who lives on spins and needles.

DISOBEDIENCE

The rarest and most courageous of the virtues, is seldom distinguished from neglect, the laziest and most common of the vices. *George Bernard Shaw*

DISSIPATION

Stupidity in despair.

DISTANCE

A great promoter of admiration. *Denis Diderot*

The thing that lends enchantment to most television and radio sopranos.

DISTANT RELATIVES

The best kind, and the further the better. *Frank McKinney Hubbard*

DISTINCTION

The consequences, never the object, of a great mind. *Washington Allston*

DOCTOR

One who gets no pleasure out of the health of his friends. *Michel de Montaigne*

A person who has his appendix, tonsils, and gall bladder.

A practitioner of the art of medicine of which there are two types: (1) the specialist who has his patients trained to become ill only in his office hours; and (2) the general practitioner who may be called off the golf course at any time.

A person who has inside information.

The person who takes the fee after God cures. *Adapted from Benjamin Franklin*

Not infrequently death's pilot-fish. *G. D. Prentice*

Two sorts: "those who practice with their brains, and those who practice with their tongues." *William Osler*

Persons who pour drugs of which they know little, to cure diseases of which they know less, into human beings of whom they know nothing. *Voltaire*

DOCTOR (BUSY)

A doctor who has so many patients that when there is nothing the matter with you, he will tell you so.

DOCTRINE

The skin of truth set up and stuffed. *Henry Ward Beecher*

DOG

The only thing on this earth that loves you more than he loves himself. *Josh Billings*

An animal to whom "every man is Napoleon; hence the constant popularity of dogs." *Aldous Huxley*

The filthiest of the domestic animals. For this he makes up in a servile, fawning attitude towards his master. *Thorstein Veblen*

An animal that teaches fidelity. *Adapted from John Horneck*

DOGMATISM

Puppism come to its full growth. *Douglas Jerrold*

DOING GOOD

Like patriotism, a favorite device of persons with something to sell. *H. L. Mencken*

DOLLAR

A soldier that does your bidding. *Vincent Astor*

That great object of universal devotion throughout our land. *Washington Irving*

DOORKNOB

A thing a revolving door goes around without. *Colonel I. Q. Stoopnagle*

DOSTOEVSKY, F.

The Rembrandt of fiction. *J. A. T. Lloyd*

DOUBLE JEOPARDY

When your doctor calls in a consulting physician.

DOUBT

A pain too lonely to know that faith is his twin brother. *Kahlil Gibran*

What gets you an education. *Wilson Mizner*

Modest doubt is call'd
The beacon of the wise.
Shakespeare

DOUGH

A misnomer for money; dough sticks to your fingers.

DRAW

A term used to describe the result of a battle between a dentist and a patient.

DRAWING

Drawing is "speaking to the eye, talking is painting to the ear." *Joseph Joubert*

DREAMER

One who gazes at the stars and is "at the mercy of the puddles on the road." *Adapted from Alexander Smith*

DRINK

> A drink does not drown care, but waters it, and makes it grow faster. *Benjamin Franklin*

DRUG STORE

> A place that carries things you can't find in the dictionary, atlas, or encyclopedia.

DRUNKARD

> A person who was willing to try something once—too often.

> Like a whisky bottle, all neck and belly and no head. *Austin O'Malley*

> The drunken man is a living corpse. *St. John Chrysostom*

DRUNKENNESS

> Not a mere matter of intoxicating liquors; it goes deeper— far deeper. Drunkenness is the failure of a man to control his thoughts. *David Grayson*

> A pair of spectacles to see the devil and all his works.

> Temporary suicide: the happiness that it brings is merely negative, a momentary cessation of unhappiness. *Bertrand Russell*

> Voluntary madness. *Seneca*

DUCK (LAME)

> A defeated political candidate who is never so lame he can't waddle as far as a new government job.

DULLNESS

> Dullness is the coming of age of seriousness. *Oscar Wilde*

DUNKING

> Shows "bad taste but tastes good." *Franklin P. Adams*

DUTY

> What one expects from others. *Oscar Wilde*

> That which sternly impels us in the direction of profit, along the line of desire. *Ambrose Bierce*

> The thing that leads a few to virtue and the rest to discontent.

> Something we look forward to with distaste, do with reluctance, and boast about forever after.

> A pleasure which we try to make ourselves believe is a hardship. *Elbert Hubbard (The Roycroft Dictionary)*

> That action which will cause more good to exist in the universe than any possible alternative. *G. E. Moore*

DYING

> Something ghastly, as being born is something ridiculous. *George Santayana*

> Receive death with gladness, as one of the things that nature wills. *Marcus Aurelius*

DYSPEPTIC

A man that can eat his cake and have it too. *Austin O'Malley*

● E ●

EARLY TO BED AND EARLY TO RISE

An adage whose practice will result in your missing a great deal that doesn't go on in the daytime.

EARNESTNESS

Enthusiasm tempered by reason. *Blaise Pascal*

The devotion of all the faculties. *C. N. Bovee*

The salt of eloquence. *Victor Hugo*

EARTH

It is a bawdy planet. *Shakespeare*

The lunatic asylum of the solar system. *S. Parkes Cadman*

This earth, a spot, a grain, an atom. *John Milton*

EASTER

The story of the fundamental fight between life and death, between hope and despair. *Heywood Broun*

EASY STREET

Always a dead end street or a blind alley.

ECCENTRIC

A characteristic of intelligent people.

ECONOMICS

The science of the production, distribution and use of wealth, best understood by college professors on half-rations. *Elbert Hubbard* (*The Roycroft Dictionary*)

Like theology, and unlike mathematics, economics deals with matters which men consider very close to their lives. *John Kenneth Galbraith*

The laws of economics are statements of tendencies expressed in the indicative mood, and not ethical precepts in the imperative. *Alfred Marshall*

What we might call by way of eminence, the dismal science. *Thomas Carlyle*

ECONOMIST

A person who forecasts business conditions after they have happened.

A person who says we move in cycles instead of running around in circles.

One who is uncertain about the future and hazy about the present.

An individual who knows all the answers but doesn't understand the questions.

A person who knows all about money but has none. *J. Marvin Peterson*

A man who advises what should be done with the money someone else made.

One whose forecasts are forgotten by the time circumstances prove them wrong.

A person who is academically trained in the art of guessing the future wrong with confidence.

One who is "engaged in defeating the last slump." *Adapted from Stuart Chase*

ECONOMY

Going without something you do want, in case you should some day want something which you probably won't want. *Anthony Hope*

EDIBLE

Good to eat, and wholesome to digest, as a worm to a toad, a toad to a snake, a snake to a pig, a pig to a man, and a man to a worm. *Ambrose Bierce*

EDINBURGH

Pompous the boast, and yet a truth it speaks:
A modern Athens—fit for modern Greeks.
James Hannay

EDISON, THOMAS

The man who did not invent the first talking machine. He invented the first one you could turn off.

EDITOR

A person employed on a newspaper, whose business it is to separate the wheat from the chaff, and to see that the chaff is printed. *Elbert Hubbard (The Roycroft Dictionary)*

EDUCATED MAN

One who gets his thinks from someone else, but an intelligent man works out his own thinks. *New Zealand Newspaper*

A well-trained mind is made up, so to speak, of all the minds of past ages; only a single mind has been educated during all that time. *Bernard de Fontenelle*

EDUCATION

It is a painful, continual and difficult work to be done by kindness, by watching, by warning, by precept, and by praise, but above all—by example. *John Ruskin*

An admirable thing, but it is well to remember from time to time that nothing that is worth knowing can be taught. *Oscar Wilde*

It is the great end of education to raise ourselves above the vulgar. *Richard Steele*

What remains when we have forgotten all that we have been taught. *George Saville*

Learning what to do with a living after you earn it.

Being afraid at the right time. *Angelo Patri*

The cheap defense of nations. *Edmund Burke*

Learning a great deal about how little you know.

A better safeguard of liberty than a standing army. *Edward Everett*

Education makes a people easy to lead, but difficult to drive; easy to govern, but impossible to enslave. *Lord Brougham*

A kind of continuing dialogue, and a dialogue assumes, in the nature of the case, different points of view. *Robert M. Hutchins*

An educated man is one who can entertain a new idea, entertain another person and entertain himself. *Sydney Herbert Wood*

Education is dynamic and is tested by what the educated man does in the world. It was the tragedy of the Middle Ages that the scholar, the man with the cultivated mind, found the world intolerable and withdrew from it. The obligation of the educated man is quite the contrary. The characteristic of a free society is that there is no privilege that is not to be counterbalanced by an appropriate responsibility. Unhappily there are men who all their lives plow the fields and take the crops from the soil of freedom and make no effort to restore the fertility . . . education is a privilege . . . it involves the responsibility of leadership. *Clarence B. Randall*

Education is a thing of which only the few are capable; teach as you will only a small percentage will profit by your most zealous energy. *George Gissing*

The process of driving a set of prejudices down your throat. *Martin H. Fischer*

That which discloses to the wise and disguises from the foolish their lack of understanding. *Ambrose Bierce*

A ladder to gather fruit from the tree of knowledge, not the fruit itself.

A slow process of training the mind which would save half a million lives if we ever were enough educated to read traffic signs.

A form of training which pays unless you decide to become an educator.

The inculcation of the incomprehensible into the ignorant by the incompetent. *Sir Josiah Stamp*

The only thing a man is willing to pay for, and hopes he doesn't get.

Makes one rogue cleverer than another. *Oscar Wilde*

Shows a man how little other people know. *Thomas C. Haliburton*

Teaches you to walk alone. *Trader Horn*

What some persons get without going to school and some get after going to school.

A process that "has produced a vast population able to read but unable to distinguish what is worth reading." *George M. Trevelyan*

Teaching people to behave as they do not behave. *John Ruskin*

The only interest worthy the deep, controlling anxiety of the thoughtful man. *Wendell Phillips*

Education is leading human souls to what is best, and no crime can destroy, no enemy can alienate, no despotism can enslave. At home a friend, abroad an introduction, in solitude a solace, and in society an ornament. It chastens vice, it guides virtue, it gives at once grace and government to genius. Without it, what is man? A splendid slave, a reasoning savage. *Joseph Addison*

EFFICIENCY
Using instant coffee to dawdle away an hour.

EGG
A potential chicken.

EGGHEAD
One who stands firmly on both feet in mid-air on both sides of an issue. *Homer Ferguson*

EGO
The only thing that can grow without nourishment.

EGOTISM
A measure of the importance with which a person holds himself.

A drug that enables some people to live with themselves.

Usually just a case of mistaken nonentity. *Barbara Stanwyck*

Self-confidence searching for trouble.

EGOTIST
A person of low taste, more interested in himself than in me. *Ambrose Bierce*

A man who thinks that a woman will marry him for himself alone.

A person who thinks he knows as much as you do. *Ambrose Bierce*

One who brazenly tells the world that he thinks as much of himself as you silently think of yourself.

An I specialist.

One who thinks that if he hadn't been born, people would wonder why.

A man who talks so much about himself that he gives me no time to talk about myself. *H. L. Wayland*

EGYPT
There sits drear Egypt, mid beleaguering sands,
Half woman and half beast,
The burnt-out torch within her moldering hands
That once lit all the East.

James Russell Lowell

EIFFEL TOWER
An American skyscraper after taxes.

ELBOW GREASE
Elbow grease is the best polish. *English Proverb*

ELECTION
When good candidates receive the solid backing of all the good people who don't vote.

A procedure by which you find that different sections of the country are mad about different things.

ELECTRICIAN
A man who wires for money.

ELEPHANT
A useful animal with a vacuum cleaner in front and a rug beater at the back.

ELOPEMENT
Getting married without presents.

To elope is cowardly; it is running away from danger; and danger has become so rare in modern life. *Oscar Wilde*

ELOQUENCE
The power to translate a truth into language perfectly intelligible to the person to whom you speak. *Ralph Waldo Emerson*

What you think you have after five drinks.

The child of knowledge. *Benjamin Disraeli*

Eloquence is the painting of thought. *Blaise Pascal*

Eloquence is logic on fire.

He is an eloquent man who can treat subjects of a humble

nature with delicacy, lofty things impressively, and moderate things temperately. *Cicero*

EMINENCE

He who surpasses or subdues mankind. *Lord Byron*

EMOTION

Emotion is not something shameful, subordinate, second-rate; it is a supremely valid phase of humanity at its noblest and most mature. *Joshua Loth Liebman*

ENDURANCE

Patience concentrated. *Thomas Carlyle*

The prerogative of woman, enabling the gentlest to suffer what would cause terror to manhood. *Christopher M. Wieland*

ENEMIES

Those who "come nearer the truth in their opinions of us than we do in our opinion of ourselves." *La Rochefoucauld*

The friend who stings you into action. *Elbert Hubbard* (*The Roycroft Dictionary*)

Any one who tells the truth about you. *Elbert Hubbard* (*The Roycroft Dictionary*)

ENGAGEMENT

In war, a battle. In love, the salubrious calm that precedes the real hostilities. *Gideon Wurdz*

The period during which they both wonder if they could have done better.

ENGLAND

A nation "never so great as in adversity." *Benjamin Disraeli*

A nation in which "there are only two classes in good society: the equestrian classes and the neurotic classes." *George Bernard Shaw*

A nation where we don't bother much about dress and manners, because, as a nation we don't dress well and we've no manners. *George Bernard Shaw*

England is the mother of parliaments. *John Bright*

A nation of shopkeepers. *Napoleon Bonaparte*

ENGLAND (AND AMERICA)

Two countries separated by the same language. *George Bernard Shaw*

ENGLISH

A people that "instinctively admire any man who has no talent and is modest about it." *James Agate*

A people who have "sixty different religions, and only one sauce." *Francesco Caraccioli*

ENGLISHMAN

Not only England, but every Englishman is an island. *Friedrich von Hardenberg*

One who does everything on principle: he fights you on patriotic principles; he robs you on business principles; he enslaves you on imperial principles. *George Bernard Shaw*

A person who "thinks he is moral when he is only uncomfortable." *George Bernard Shaw*

A man who has never been able to tell a lie about others and who is never willing to face the truth about himself. *Michael Arlen*

A strong being who takes a cold bath in the morning and talks about it for the rest of the day. *Ellen Wilkinson*

A man who lives on an island in the North Sea governed by Scotsmen. *Philip Guedalla*

A person who laughs last.

One who "has all the qualities of a poker except its occasional warmth." *Daniel O'Connell*

ENGLISH NOVELS

The only relaxation of the intellectually unemployed. *Oscar Wilde*

ENOUGH

Just a little more than the neighbors have.

Enough is abundance to the wise. *Euripides*

What would satisfy us if the neighbors didn't have more.

ENTERPRISE (PRIVATE)

Consists of harnessing men, money, and ideas, and the genius of investors and technologists with the savings of the thousands. *Malcolm Muir*

ENTHUSIASM

Always exaggerates the importance of important things and overlooks their deficiencies. *Hugh Stevenson Tigner*

The best protection in any situation. Wholeheartedness is contagious. Give yourself, if you wish to get others. *David Seabury*

Unmistakable evidence that you're in love with your work.

Nothing but moral inebriety. *Lord Byron*

ENVY

The sincerest form of flattery. *John Churton Collins*

Almost the only vice which is practicable at all times, and in every place; the only passion which can never lie quiet from want of irritation. *Samuel Johnson*

The basis of democracy. *Bertrand Russell*

A pain of mind that successful men cause their neighbors. *Onasander*

Envy, the meanest of vices, creeps on the ground like a serpent. *Ovid*

The adversary of the fortunate. *Epictetus*

A kind of praise. *John Gay*

EPIGRAM

Only a wisecrack that's played Carnegie Hall. *Oscar Levant*

A solemn platitude gone to a masquerade ball. *Lionel Strachey*

Striking a verbal match on the seat of your intellectual pants. *John A. Lincoln*

Truth on a "binge". *John A. Lincoln*

> What is an epigram? A dwarfish whole,
> Its body brevity, and wit its soul.
> *Samuel Taylor Coleridge*

A quick quip or a flip quip.

> Three things must epigrams, like bees, have all,
> A sting, and honey, and a body small.
> *Latin Distich*

> He misses what is meant by epigram
> Who thinks it only frivolous flim-flam.
> *Martial*

Half truth so stated as to irritate the person who believes the other half. *Shailer Mathews*

> An epigram is but a feeble thing
> With straw in trail, stuck there by way of sting.
> *William Cowper*

EPITAPH

A belated advertisement for a line of goods that has been permanently discontinued. *Irvin S. Cobb*

Postponed compliments. *Elbert Hubbard* (*The Roycroft Dictionary*)

EPITHETS

The arguments of malice. *Robert G. Ingersoll*

EQUALITY

That which we only desire with our superiors. *Adapted from Henry Becque*

Equality is the share of every one at their advent upon earth; and equality is also theirs when placed beneath it. *Enclos*

The only real equality is in the cemetery. *German Proverb*

EQUIVOCATION
> Equivocation is halfway to lying, as lying is the whole way to Hell. *William Penn*

ERROR (TYPOGRAPHICAL)
> A misstatement. Illustration: A newspaper carried the notice that John Doe was a "defective" on the police force. This was a typographical error. It should have said, "Mr. John Doe is a detective on the police farce."

ESCAPE
> A legitimate function of genuine literature, escape from the provincial into the universal, from the here to the there, from today to yesterday. *Halford E. Luccock*

ESKIMO
> A perfect host. He never lets callers who have dropped in for the evening guess that the last few months of their stay are beginning to drag a little. . . .

ESTATE (POOR)
> An estate so small "there are few grave legal questions involved." *Edgar W. Howe*

ETC.
> A sign used to make people believe you know more than you are telling them.

ETERNITY
> The Sunday of time. *Elbert Hubbard* (*The Roycroft Dictionary*)
> The sum of all sums is eternity. *Lucretius*

ETHICS
> The science of human duty. *David Swing*
> The art of living well and happily. *Henry More*

ETHNOLOGY
> The science that treats of the various tribes of man, as robbers, thieves, swindlers, dunces, lunatics, idiots, and ethnologists. *Ambrose Bierce*

ETIQUETTE
> Learning to yawn with your mouth closed.
> The noise you must not swallow your soup with.

EULOGY
> Praise of a person who has either the advantages of wealth and power, or the consideration to be dead. *Ambrose Bierce*
> Lavish praise too late to be helpful.

EUROPEAN
> An inhabitant of New York City. *Elbert Hubbard* (*The Roycroft Dictionary*)

EUROPEANS
> People who cannot understand our foreign policy; and this makes us even.

EUROPEAN TRIP
> A trip you enjoy after you have rested a month at home.

EVENTS
> Only the shells of ideas. *E. H. Chapin*

EVERYBODY
> The square root of zero. *Elbert Hubbard (The Roycroft Dictionary)*
>
> Nobody in toto. *Elbert Hubbard (The Roycroft Dictionary)*

EVIL
> That which one believes of others. It is a sin to believe evil of others, but it is seldom a mistake. *H. L. Mencken*
>
> Fire, water, storms, robbers, rulers—these are the five great evils. *Burmese Saying*
>
> Whatever springs from weakness. *F. W. Nietzsche*

EVOLUTION
> Dress, $9.75; frock, $19.98; gown, $65; creation, $225.

EXACTNESS
> The sublimity of fools.

EXAGGERATION
> Truth that has lost its temper. *Kahlil Gibran*
>
> A blood relation to falsehood and nearly as blamable. *Hosea Ballou*
>
> A department of lying. *Baltasar Gracian*

EXAMINATIONS
> When the foolish ask questions that the wise cannot answer. *Oscar Wilde*

EXAMPLE
> Example is not the main thing in life—it is the only thing. *Albert Schweitzer*
>
> Example is the school of mankind, and they will learn at no other. *Edmund Burke*
>
> The best sermon.

EXCHANGE OF ACTORS BETWEEN NATIONS
> Hams across the sea.

EXCLUSIVENESS
> A characteristic of recent riches, high society, and the skunk. *Austin O'Malley*

EXECUTIVE
> One who has the faculty of earning his bread by the work of other people.

A man who can go directly from an unwarranted assumption to a preconceived conclusion.

One who hires others to do what he is hired to do.

If a man has an office with a desk on which there is a buzzer, and if he can press that buzzer and have somebody come dashing in response—then he's an executive. *Elmer Frank Andrews*

A man who can make quick decisions and is sometimes right. *Elbert Hubbard* (*The Roycroft Dictionary*)

A man who sets up an organization that can run efficiently without him.

A person who would take two hours for luncheon if he had time and didn't have ulcers.

EXERCISE

Like a cold bath. You think it does you good because you feel better when you stop it. *Robert Quillen*

A poor substitute for proper diet. *Blake Clark*

EXPEDITE

A business term meaning to confound confusion with commotion.

EXPERIENCE

Experience is the child of Thought, and Thought is the child of Action. We cannot learn men from books. *Benjamin Disraeli*

One thing you can't get for nothing. *Oscar Wilde*

The name we give our mistakes. It demonstrates that the future will be the same as the past. *Oscar Wilde*

A revelation in the light of which we renounce our errors of youth for those of age. *Ambrose Bierce*

A jewel that I have purchased at an infinite rate. *Thomas Ford*

A dear school, but fools will learn in no other. *Benjamin Franklin*

A parent never wakes up the second baby just to see it smile. *Grace Williams*

The one perpetual best seller.

One thing you can't buy on the easy payment plan.

Teaches us that experience teaches us nothing. *André Maurois*

Increases our wisdom but doesn't reduce our follies. *Josh Billings*

A good teacher but not many pupils bring her bright red apples.

A hard teacher—no graduates, degrees, survivors.

Not only a dear teacher, but by the time you get through going to her school, life is over.

The best of schoolmasters, only the school-fees are heavy. *Thomas Carlyle*

The name men give to their follies or their sorrows. *Alfred de Musset*

A good school, but the fees are high. *Heinrich Heine*

In that all our knowledge is founded; and from that it ultimately derives itself. *John Locke*

The only prophecy of wise men. *Alphonse de Lamartine*

A school where a man learns what a big fool he has been. *Josh Billings*

Experience is remolding us every moment, and our mental reaction on any given thing is really a resultant of our experience of the whole world up to that date. *William James*

The extract of suffering. *Arthur Helps*

The fool's best teacher; the wise do not need it. *Welsh Proverb*

EXPERIMENT
That which we call sin in others. *Ralph Waldo Emerson*

EXPERT
An ordinary man away from home giving advice. *Oscar Wilde*

A person who avoids the small errors as he sweeps on to the grand fallacy. *Benjamin Stolberg*

One who knows more and more about less and less. *Ambrose Bierce*

A person who takes ideas we understand and makes them sound confusing.

EXTRAVAGANCE
Anything you buy that is of no earthly use to your wife. *Franklin P. Jones*

EYE
The light of the body is the eye. *Matt. 6:22*

These lovely lamps, these windows of the soul. *Guillaume Salluste Du Bartas*

● F ●

FABLE
The story a husband thinks his wife believes.

FACE
The image of the soul. *Cicero*

Often only a smooth impostor. *Pierre Corneille*

Books in which not a line is written, save perhaps a date. *Henry Wadsworth Longfellow*

FACT

Stubborn things. *Tobias Smollett*

A fact in itself is nothing. It is valuable only for the idea attached to it, or for the proof which it furnishes. *Claude Bernard*

FAILURE

A man who has blundered but is not able to cash in the experience. *Elbert Hubbard*

The path of least persistence.

The line of least persistence.

Only the opportunity to begin again, more intelligently. *Henry Ford*

FAITH

Not contrary to reason, but rather "reason grown courageous." *Sherwood Eddy*

Faith is courage; it is creative while despair is always destructive. *D. S. Muzzey*

Faith is not a human dream or illusion. Faith is God's work within us. It transmutes us and makes for our rebirth in God. It kills the old Adam and makes us different, recreating our heart, courage, understanding, and all other forces, and it carries with it the holy spirit. There is a power and life about faith that makes it impossible not to do the good. Faith does not inquire whether there are good works to be done, but even before asking questions, faith has done these works already. *Martin Luther*

Faith has to do with things that are not seen, and hope with things that are not in hand. *Thomas Aquinas*

The continuation of reason. *William Adams*

To believe what we do not see; and the reward of this faith is to see what we believe. *St. Augustine*

An outward and visible sign of an inward and spiritual grace. *Book of Common Prayer*

The substance of things hoped for, the evidence of things not seen. *Heb. 11:1*

The force of life. *Leo Tolstoy*

FAME

We speak of fame as the reward of genius, whereas in truth genius, the imaginative dominion of experience, is its own reward, and fame is but a foolish image by which its worth is symbolized. *George Santayana*

When the million applaud, you ask yourself what harm you

have done; when they censure you, what good. *Charles Caleb Colton*

The advantage of being known to those who do not know us. *Nicholas Chamfort*

A matter of dying at the right time.

A hundred autograph collectors after one man. *Toledo Blade*

To have your name paged . . . in a fashionable hotel. *Elbert Hubbard (The Roycroft Dictionary)*

The spirit of a man surviving himself in the minds and thoughts of other men. *William Hazlitt*

Fame is the spur that the clear spirit doth raise
(That last infirmity of noble mind)
To scorn delights, and live laborious days.
                              John Milton

Fame is the scentless sunflower,
With gaudy crown of gold;
But friendship is the breathing rose,
With sweets in every fold.
                    Oliver Wendell Holmes

Fame is a fickle food
Upon a shifting plate.
                    Emily Dickinson

The perfume of heroic deeds. *Socrates*

Fame is that parasite of pride, ever scornful to meekness, and ever obsequious to insolent power. *John Quincy Adams*

Fame is but wind. *Thomas Coryate*

What's fame after all? 'Tis apt to be what someone writes on your tombstone. *F. P. Dunne*

Fame is proof that people are gullible. *Ralph Waldo Emerson*

Fame, we may understand, is no sure test of merit, but only a probability of such. *Thomas Carlyle*

Fame is but the breath of the people, and that often unwholesome. *Thomas Fuller*

What is fame? An empty bubble. *James Grainger*

FAMILIARITY

A magician that is cruel to beauty, but kind to ugliness. *Ouida*

FAMILY

Too often a commonwealth of malignants. *Alexander Pope*

The family is a society limited in numbers, but nevertheless a true society, anterior to every state or nation, with rights and duties of its own, wholly independent of the commonwealth. *Pope Leo XIII*

FAMILY ALBUM

A book of pictures that convinces one that the truth is a terrible thing.

FAMILY TREE

The one tree that invariably produces some nuts.

A tree in which the branches are so uninteresting that they are forced to brag about the roots.

FANATICISM

Consists in redoubling your effort when you have forgotten your aim. *George Santayana*

The child of false zeal and of superstition, the father of intolerance and of persecution. *J. W. Fletcher*

Fanaticism is always the child of persecution. *Napoleon Bonaparte*

FANCY

Fancy is a willful, imagination a spontaneous act; fancy, a play as with dolls and puppets which we choose to call men and women; imagination, a perception and affirming of a real relation between a thought and some material fact. Fancy amuses; imagination expands and exalts us. *Ralph Waldo Emerson*

FANTASY

Weak serious drama filtered through a poetic imagination into beauty. *George Jean Nathan*

FARCE

Comedy in its cups. *George Jean Nathan*

FARM

A neglected body of land surrounded by national prosperity.

An old word formerly used to describe what is now "a magnificent tract for subdivision."

FARMER

A person who visits the city occasionally to see where his sons and his profits went.

A man who can make money if he can sell his farm to a golf club.

A man who moves to the city in order to solve his problems.

A person who gets up at 5 A.M. and hurries through his work so he can read a farm paper about how to make money by farming more intensively.

A man who believes in the eight-hour day, eight hours in

the forenoon and eight in the afternoon. *Worcester Gazette*

A man who is outstanding in his field.

Those who labor in the earth are the chosen people of God; if He ever had a chosen people, whose breasts He has made His peculiar deposit for substantial and genuine virtue. *Thomas Jefferson*

FARMER (GENTLEMAN)

A farmer who has more hay in the bank than in the barn.

FARMING

An occupation that "looks nice—from a car window." *Kin Hubbard*

A senseless pursuit, a mere laboring in a circle. You sow that you may reap, and then you reap that you may sow. Nothing ever comes of it. *Johannes Stobaeus*

FASHION

Gentility running away from vulgarity, and afraid of being overtaken. *William Hazlitt*

The means whereby "the fantastic becomes for a moment universal." *Oscar Wilde*

A despot whom the wise ridicule and obey. *Ambrose Bierce*

A form of ugliness so intolerable that we have to alter it every six months. *Oscar Wilde*

Fashion is what one wears oneself. What is unfashionable is what other people wear. *Oscar Wilde*

The tax which the industry of the poor levies on the vanity of the rich. *Nicholas Chamfort*

That which "wears out more apparel than the man." *Shakespeare*

A barricade behind which men hide their nothingness. *Elbert Hubbard (The Roycroft Dictionary)*

The most powerful of all tyrants.

The attempt to realize art in living forms and social intercourse. *Oliver Wendell Holmes*

FASTIDIOUSNESS

The ability to resist a temptation in the hope that a better one will come along. *John A. Lincoln*

Only another form of egotism. *James Russell Lowell*

FASTING

Fasting is a medicine. *St. John Chrysostom*

FAT MAN

A jolly fellow everybody loves, unless he sits down with you in a bus.

FATHER

A kin they love to touch.

Fathers should be neither seen nor heard. That is the only proper basis for family life. *Oscar Wilde*

A father is a banker provided by nature. *French Proverb*

One father is more than a hundred schoolteachers. *George Herbert*

FATHER'S BIRTHDAY

The quietest day of the year.

FATIGUE

Fatigue is the best pillow. *Hindu Proverb*

FEAR

Nature's warning signal to get busy. *Henry C. Link*

The offspring of ignorance.

A kind of bell . . . it is the soul's signal for rallying. *Henry Ward Beecher*

Fear is a basic emotion, part of our native equipment, and like all normal emotions has a positive function to perform. Comforting formulas for getting rid of anxiety may be just the wrong thing. Books about "peace of mind" can be bad medicine. To be afraid when one should be afraid is good sense. *Dorothy Fosdick*

Fear is pain arising from the anticipation of evil. *Aristotle*

Fear is the foundation of safety. *Tertullian*

Fear gives intelligence even to fools. *French Proverb*

FEAR (OF SELF)

The greatest of all terrors, the deepest of all dread, the commonest of all mistakes. From it grows failure. Because of it, life is a mockery. Out of it comes despair. *David Seabury*

FEBRUARY

February brings the rain,
Thaws the frozen lake again.
Sara Coleridge

FEELING

The ennobling difference between one man and another,—between one animal and another,—is precisely in this, that one feels more than another. *John Ruskin*

FEELING (SINKING)

How an overweight person feels when he steps on a scale.

FELLOW (SMART)

A man who says what he thinks, provided of course he agrees with us.

FELLOWSHIP

The virtue of pigs in a litter which lie close together to keep each other warm. *Henry David Thoreau*

Fellowship is Heaven, and lack of fellowship is Hell; fellowship is life, and lack of fellowship is death. *William Morris*

FERN

A plant that you're supposed to water once a day, but when you don't it dies, but if you do it dies anyway, only not so soon. *Colonel L. Q. Stoopnagle*

FICTION

The world of our dreams come true. *Courtney Riley Cooper*

The criticism of life's implausibility; it teaches good manners to destiny. *Anthony Abbott*

FIDDLER

He was a fiddler, and consequently a rogue. *Jonathan Swift*

FIFTH AVENUE

The widow's chance. *Elbert Hubbard (The Roycroft Dictionary)*

The underworld of the upper world. *Elbert Hubbard (The Roycroft Dictionary)*

FIGHTING

It is the ignorant and childish part of mankind that is the fighting part. Idle and vacant minds want excitement, as all boys kill cats. *Ralph Waldo Emerson*

When a man fights it means that a fool has lost his argument. *Chinese Proverb*

FILLING STATION

Along with the skyscraper a distinctive form of American architecture.

FINANCIAL SENSE

Knowing that certain men will promise to do certain things, and fail. *E. W. Howe*

FINANCIER

A pawnbroker with imagination. *Arthur Wing Pinero*

FINLAND

A country which sophisticated Europeans even today barely consider civilized, especially for its queer custom of paying its debts. *E. T. Bell*

FIREMAN

A person who has a burning ambition to get ahead.

A man who will "spoil a house to save a town." *Robert Herrick*

FISH

Monsters of the bubbling deep. *Cotton Mather*

FISHING

A delusion entirely surrounded by liars in old clothes. *Don Marquis*

A pastime in which a jerk at one end of the line waits for a jerk on the other.

FISHING ROD

A stick with a hook at one end and a fool at the other. *Samuel Johnson*

A pole with a loafer at one end and a worm at the other.

FLAG

The emblem of our unity, our power, our thought and purpose as a nation. *Woodrow Wilson*

FLATTERER

One who extremely exaggerates in his opinion of your qualities so that it may come nearer to your opinion of them. *Oscar Wilde*

A friend who is your inferior, or pretends to be so. *Aristotle*

FLATTERY

When a woman demands equal rights.

Never comes up to the expectancy of conceit.

Like cologne water, to be smelt of, not swallowed. *Josh Billings*

Something that is obnoxious to all except the flattered.

Telling the other person what he thinks of himself.

Just praise is only a debt, but flattery is a present. *Samuel Johnson*

Flattery corrupts both the receiver and the giver. *Edmund Burke*

FLAW

What the Harvard graduate thinks you walk on in a house.

FLEA

An insect that is "good for a dog; it keeps him from brooding over being a dog." *Edward Noyes Westcott*

An insect that knows for a certainty that all of his children will go to the dogs. *Annapolis Log*

FLIRTATION

A circulating library in which we seldom ask twice for the same volume. *C. N. Bovee*

Attention without intention.

FLORIDA

A state which requires you to catch a sailfish and go to

the expense of having it mounted. *Adapted from Frank McKinney Hubbard*

FLOWER

The sweetest thing that God ever made, and forgot to put a soul into. *Henry Ward Beecher*

Love's truest language. *P. Benjamin*

FLUENT TONGUE

The only thing a mother doesn't like her daughter to resemble her in. *Richard B. Sheridan*

FLUTE

An ill wind that nobody blows good.

FOLK SONG

A song that nobody ever wrote.

FOLLY

The foolishness of fools is folly. *Prov. 14: 24*

The prettiest word in the language. *William Shenstone*

The direct pursuit of happiness and beauty. *George Bernard Shaw*

The common curse of mankind,—folly and ignorance. *Shakespeare*

FOOD

Part of the spiritual expression of the French, and I do not believe that they have ever heard of calories. *Beverley Baxter*

FOOL

A person whom no advice will help.

A person whom gray hairs ill become. *Adapted from Shakespeare*

One who expects things to happen that never can happen. *George Eliot*

One who "always finds one still more foolish to admire him." *Nicolas Boileau*

What everyone is at least occasionally.

FOOL AND HIS MONEY

A combination that frequently winds up in college.

A combination soon invited to parties.

FOOLS

"There are two kinds: One says, 'This is old, therefore it is good'; the other says, 'This is new, therefore it is better.'" *William Ralph Inge*

FOOTBALL

A sport that makes a nation hardy. It builds up a lot of strong resistance by requiring people to sit on a cold concrete seat in rain or snow.

Rather . . . a friendly kind of fight than a play or recreation. *Philip Stubbes*

One of the last great strongholds of genuine, old-fashioned American hypocrisy. *Paul Gallico*

FOOTNOTES

An abomination. *Huger Elliott*

FORBEARANCE

To forgive an enemy who has been shorn of power. *Elbert Hubbard* (*The Roycroft Dictionary*)

Knowing when to forego an advantage. *Benjamin Disraeli*

FORCE

Force rules the world, and not opinion; but opinion is that which makes use of force. *Blaise Pascal*

The vital principle and immediate parent of despotism. *Thomas Jefferson*

FORECAST

To observe that which has passed, and guess it will happen again. *Elbert Hubbard* (*The Roycroft Dictionary*)

FOREHEAD

The dome of thought. *Lord Byron*

FOREIGN RELATIONS

An open book—generally a checkbook. *Will Rogers*

FORETHOUGHT

To dig a well before you are thirsty. *Chinese Proverb*

FORGER

A man who makes a name for himself.

One who gives a check a bad name.

FORGIVENESS

Man's deepest need and highest achievement. *Horace Bushnell*

FORGOTTEN

Unminded, unmoaned. *Proverb*

FORGOTTEN MAN

He is the clean, quiet, virtuous, domestic citizen, who pays his debts and his taxes and is never heard of out of his little circle. *W. G. Sumner*

FORTITUDE

That quality of mind which does not care what happens so long as it does not happen to us. *Elbert Hubbard* (*The Roycroft Dictionary*)

FORTUNE

That which "is always on the side of the largest battalions." *Mme. de Sévigné*

What you make by buying low and selling too soon. *Baron Rothschild*

Fortune is like glass—the brighter the glitter, the more easily broken. *Publius Syrus*

FORTY

The old age of youth; fifty is the youth of old age. *Victor Hugo*

FOUNTAIN PEN

An instrument that writes, and having writ, blots.

FOX HUNTER

The unspeakable in full pursuit of the uneatable. *Oscar Wilde*

FRAILTY

Frailty, thy name is woman! *Shakespeare*

FRANCE

A nation without a national sport except taking tourists, although some maintain this is a business and not a sport.

An absolute monarchy tempered by songs. *Anonymous Frenchman*

A despotism tempered by epigrams. *Thomas Carlyle*

FRANKLIN, BENJAMIN

The greatest man and ornament of the age and country in which he lived. *Thomas Jefferson*

A philosophical Quaker full of mean and thrifty maxims. *John Keats*

FRATERNITY (COLLEGE)

A rooming and boarding house where only the most discerning person knows whose clothes he is wearing.

FRAUD

It would be honesty itself if it could only afford it. *Lord Macnaghten*

FRECKLES

A suntan which didn't get together.

FREE ADVICE

Advice that costs you nothing unless you act upon it.

FREE COUNTRY

One in which there is no particular individual to blame for the existing tyranny.

FREEDOM

That faculty which enlarges the usefulness of all other faculties. *Immanuel Kant*

To be merely free is not much. To be able to do whatever you want to do does not in itself produce a good life or a fine character. All you can say is that without freedom the real problem of a good life cannot even begin. *Gilbert Murray*

An indivisible word. If we want to enjoy it, and fight for it, we must be prepared to extend it to everyone, whether they are rich or poor, whether they agree with us or not, no matter what their race or the color of their skin. *Wendell L. Willkie*

Is freedom anything but the right to live as we wish? Nothing else. *Epictetus*

That faculty of man by which he is able to determine his being through history. *Paul Tillich*

The intense claim to obey no one but reason. *Heinrich Mann*

The supremacy of human rights everywhere. *Franklin D. Roosevelt*

An achievement by men, and, as it was gained by vigilance and struggle, it can be lost by indifference and supineness. *H. F. Byrd*

Freedom means mastery of our world. Fear and greed are common sources of bondage. We are afraid, beset by anxiety. We do not know what tomorrow will bring. We seem so helpless over against the forces that move on without apparent thought for men. And our inner freedom is destroyed by greed. We think that if we only had enough goods we should be free, happy, without care. And so there comes the lust for money, and slavery to the world of things. The world can enslave; it can never make us free. *H. F. Rall*

FREEDOM (OF THE PRESS)

The staff of life for any vital democracy. *Wendell L. Willkie*

One of the greatest bulwarks of liberty. *George Mason*

FREE ENTERPRISE

An economy open to new ideas, new products, new jobs, new men. *William B. Benton*

FREE SPEECH

The right to argue about issues you don't understand.

FREE THINKERS

Generally those who never think at all. *Laurence Sterne*

FRENCH

A people who "are wiser than they seem," whereas "the Spaniards seem wiser than they are." *Francis Bacon*

The French are a fickle nation. *Napoleon Bonaparte*

FRIEND

One who knows all about you and loves you just the same. *Elbert Hubbard*

One who dislikes the same people that you dislike.

A person who excuses you when you have made a fool of yourself.

Someone who forgives your defects. If he is very fond of you, he doesn't see any.

A person who doesn't buy your children a drum for Christmas.

One who can't understand how you got there, but still doesn't knock you.

A person with whom I may be sincere. *Ralph Waldo Emerson*

A true friend unbosoms freely, advises justly, assists readily, adventures boldly, takes all patiently, defends courageously, and continues a friend unchangeably. *William Penn*

One who runs interference for you in your pursuit of happiness.

Friendship is almost always the union of a part of one mind with a part of another; people are friends in spots *George Santayana*

The thermometers by which we may judge the temperature of our fortune. *Countess of Blessington*

Those relations that one makes for onself! *Emile Deschamps*

FRIENDSHIP

Among women only a suspension of hostilities. *Comte de-Rivarol*

A strong and habitual inclination in two persons to promote the good and happiness of one another. *Eustace Budgell*

Consists in forgetting what one gives, and remembering what one receives. *Alexander Dumas the Younger*

Only a little more honor among rogues. *Henry David Thoreau*

A tacit agreement between two enemies to work together for common swag. *Elbert Hubbard (The Roycroft Dictionary)*

A word the very sight of which in print makes the heart warm. *Augustine Birrell*

Friendship is nothing else than an accord in all things, human and divine, conjoined with mutual good will and affection. *Cicero*

A union of spirits, a marriage of hearts, and the bond thereof virtue. *William Penn*

The magnanimous art of overlooking shortcomings.

A condition that exists "when each friend thinks he has a slight superiority over the other." *Honoré de Balzac*

A sweet responsibility, never an opportunity. *Kahlil Gibran*

Only a reciprocal conciliation of interests, and an exchange of good offices; it is a species of commerce out of which self-love always expects to gain something. *La Rochefoucauld*

The only cement that will ever hold the world together. *Woodrow Wilson*

One soul in two bodies. *Pythagoras*

The highest degree of perfection in society. *Michel de Montaigne*

A plant of slow growth, and must undergo and withstand the shocks of adversity before it is entitled to the appellation. *George Washington*

FROG

The only living thing that has more lives than a cat. It croaks every night.

FRUGALITY

Frugality is a handsome income. *Desiderius Erasmus*
Tacitus

FUNERAL

An event at which "we are apt to comfort ourselves with the happy difference that is betwixt us and our dead friend." *Thomas Wilson*

FURNITURE (ANTIQUE)

Furniture found in the homes of the rich and in homes with a number of children.

A piece of furniture that is paid for.

FUTILITY

To spend life doing nothing.

Two baldheaded men fighting over a comb. *Russian Saying*

FUTURE

Where you will spend the rest of your life.

An unwelcome guest. *Edmund Gosse*

• G •

GADGETS

The modern inconveniences. *Mark Twain*

GAIETY

Often the reckless ripple over depths of despair. *E. H. Chapin*

GAIT

The proper gait is one in which there is an appearance

of authority, weight, dignity, and tranquillity. *St. Ambrose*

GALLANT

To give up your seat in a car to a woman, and tread on your neighbor's foot to get even. *Elbert Hubbard (The Roycroft Dictionary)*

To do a perfectly unselfish act from selfish motives. *Elbert Hubbard (The Roycroft Dictionary)*

Gallantry consists in saying empty things in an agreeable manner. *La Rochefoucauld*

GALLOWS

The place where "everyone is a preacher." *Dutch Proverb*

GAMBLING

Promises the poor what property performs for the rich—something for nothing. *George Bernard Shaw*

A disease of barbarians superficially civilized. *Dean Inge*

A revolt against boredom. *Stuart Chase*

The child of avarice, the brother of iniquity, and the father of mischief. *George Washington*

Gambling is the child of avarice and the father of despair. *French Proverb*

GARAGE MECHANIC

A person who is not finicky. He would just as soon wipe his hands on a cheap seat cover as on a costly one.

GARDEN

The purest of human pleasures. *Francis Bacon*

A thing of beauty and a job forever.

A garden is a lovesome thing. *T. E. Browne*

GARDENING

An activity that requires "a cast-iron back, with a hinge in it." *Charles D. Warner*

GARRULITY

Conversation "marked by its happy abundance." *Mary Godwin Shelley*

GENEALOGIST

One who traces back your family as far as your money will go.

GENEALOGY

An account of one's descent from an ancestor who did not particularly care to trace his own. *Ambrose Bierce*

GENERAL

The proper arts of a general are judgment and prudence. *Tacitus*

I am the very pattern of a modern major general.
I've information vegetable, animal and mineral;
I know the kings of England,
   and I quote the fights historical,
From Marathon to Waterloo, in order categorical.
W. S. Gilbert

Generals always die in bed. *Saying of English Soldiers*

GENERALITY

A lifesaver in most conversations, particularly a vague generality. *Adapted from George Ade*

GENEROSITY

Giving more than you can, and pride is taking less than you need. *Kahlil Gibran*

Generosity goes with good birth. *Pierre Corneille*

Usually only the vanity of giving. *La Rochefoucauld*

The virtue of a man. *Adam Smith*

GENIUS

A promontory jutting out into the infinite. *Victor Hugo*

Persons who "are not seen with the eyes, but with the mind; that is enough." *Blaise Pascal*

Genius is patience. *George de Buffon*

Genius is reason made sublime. *M. J. de Chenier*

A supreme capacity for taking trouble. . . . It might be more fitly described as a supreme capacity for getting its possessors into trouble of all kinds. *Samuel Butler*

A person that the dunces are all in confederacy against. *Adapted from Jonathan Swift*

A perception of the obvious which nobody else sees.

An infinite capacity for taking life by the scruff of the neck. *Christopher Quill*

A person who finds the whole world determined to destroy him and his ideas.

Anyone "up to the age of ten." *Aldous Huxley*

"One per cent inspiration and ninety-nine per cent perspiration." *Thomas Alva Edison*

The introduction of a new element into the intellectual universe. *William Wordsworth.*

That power which dazzles mortal eyes, is oft but perseverance in disguise. *Henry W. Austin*

One who offends his time, his country and his relatives; hence, any person whose birthday is celebrated throughout the world about one hundred years after he has been crucified, burned, ostracized or otherwise put to death. *Elbert Hubbard (The Roycroft Dictionary)*

The talent of a man who is dead. *Edmond de Goncourt*

An infinite capacity for giving pains. *Don Herold*

The man whom God wills to slay in the struggle of life He first individualizes. *Henrik Ibsen*

Genius is mainly an affair of energy, and poetry is mainly an affair of genius; therefore a nation characterized by energy may well be eminent in poetry. *Matthew Arnold*

Genius may be almost defined as the faculty of acquiring poverty. *E. P. Whipple*

GENTILITY

Gentility is nothing but ancient riches. *George Herbert*

GENTLEMAN

One who never hurts anyone's feelings unintentionally. *Oliver Herford*

One who never strikes a woman without provocation. *H. L. Mencken*

One who "never heard the story before." *Austin O'Malley*

One who has "respect for those who can be of no possible service to him." *William Lyon Phelps*

A man who can disagree without being disagreeable.

A person who is polite even when he isn't asking favors.

Any man who wouldn't hit a woman with his hat on. *Fred Allen*

One who is always as nice as he sometimes is.

The product of four generations of training or one good guess in the stock market.

Here (in Kentucky) is the old idea, somewhat current still in England, that the highest mark of the gentleman is not cultivation of mind, not intellect, not knowledge, but elegant living. *James Lane Allen*

Gentlemen are those who neither "envy the great, nor do the low despise." *Shakespeare*

Manners and money make a gentleman. *Thomas Fuller*

One who never inflicts pain. *J. H. Newman*

A person who has had the same operation but says nothing.

GEOLOGY

Popularly conceived as the study of rocks and minerals, metallic and non-metallic ores, fuels and water-supplies, fossil animals and plants. It is all that and more, for it is nothing less than the history of the earth and its inhabitants. *Kirtley F. Mather*

GEOMETRY

The purest realization of human reason; but Euclid's axioms

cannot be proved. He who does not believe in them sees the whole building crash. *Arthur Koestler*

GERMANS
A race to whom work is not "the painful obligation and punishment which it often is to others . . . they go into it with their whole heart, as if yielding to a powerful mania, and fall back into work as others fall back into sin." *Jacques Rivière*

GHOST
The outward and visible sign of an inward fear. *Ambrose Bierce*

GIFT
A precious stone in the eyes of him that hath it. *Prov.* 17:8

Gifts are like fish-hooks. *Martial*

The gift bindeth the wise, and perverteth the words of the righteous. *Exod.* 23: 8

Whatever a man has is in the end only a gift. *C. M. Wieland*

GIFT (ANONYMOUS)
A donation by someone who hopes everyone will find out without his telling them.

GIRAFFE
An animal that must get up at six in the morning if it wants to have its breakfast in its stomach by nine. *Samuel Butler*

GIRL
Innocence playing in the mud, Beauty standing on its head, and Motherhood dragging a doll by the foot. *Allan Beck*

GIRL (BACHELOR)
A girl looking for a bachelor.

GIRL (SMART)
One who can refuse a kiss without being deprived of it.

GIVING
The business of the rich. *J. W. von Goethe*

GLADSTONE, W. E.
A sophistical rhetorician, inebriated with the exuberance of his own verbosity. *Benjamin Disraeli*

The grand old man. *W. Vernon Harcourt*

GLORY
Glory is the shadow of virtue. *Latin Proverb*

Glory is a torch to kindle the noble mind. *Silius Italicus*

A viewpoint that depends on "the estimation of lookers-on.

When lookers-on perish as countless generations have done, glory perishes, as countless glories have done." *Henry S. Haskins*

GLUTTON
A poor man who eats too much, as contradistinguished from a gourmand, who is a rich man who "lives well." *Elbert Hubbard (The Roycroft Dictionary)*

One who digs his grave with his teeth. *French Proverb*

GOAT
A lamb who kidded himself into believing he knew Wall Street.

GOD
Not a cosmic bellboy for whom we can press a button to get things. *Harry Emerson Fosdick*

God is love; and he that dwelleth in love dwelleth in God, and God in him. *I John 4: 16*

The one great employer, thinker, planner, supervisor. *Henry Ward Beecher*

God is the I of the Infinite. *Victor Hugo*

> A mighty fortress is our God,
> A bulwark never failing,
> Our helper he amid the flood
> Of mortal ills prevailing.
> *Martin Luther*

God is our refuge and strength, a very present help in trouble. *Ps. 46: 1*

The King eternal, immortal, invisible, the only wise God *I Tim. 1: 17*

God is the ruler of all. *Tacitus*

GO-GETTER
A person who walks seven blocks to the place where he parked his car.

GOLD
Gold is a living god. *Percy Bysshe Shelley*

Gold is a wonderful clearer of the understanding; it dissipates every doubt and scruple in an instant, accommodates itself to the meanest capacities, silences the loud and clamorous, and brings over the most obstinate and inflexible. *Joseph Addison*

GOLD DIGGER
A woman after all.

GOLDEN AGE
The Golden Age never was the present age. *Thomas Fuller*

GOLDEN RULE

All things whatsoever ye would that man should do to you, do ye even so to them; for this is the law and the prophets. *Matt.* 7: 12

GOLDFISH

A fish without privacy. Synonym: husband.

GOLF

An activity consisting mostly of walking with regular intervals of disappointment and bad arithmetic.

The only thing that depreciates above par.

The most useless outdoor game ever devised to waste the time and try the spirit of man. *Westbrook Pegler*

A funny game. If there is any larceny in a man, golf will bring it out. *Paul Gallico*

A game in which you drive hard to get to the green and then wind up in the hole.

A game in which you "claim the privileges of age, and retain the playthings of childhood." *Samuel Johnson*

GOLF BALL

A small, indented, round object that remains on the tee while a perspiring person fans it violently with a large club.

GOLF PLAYER

A person who can drive seventy miles an hour in traffic with perfect ease, but blows up on a two-foot putt if somebody coughs.

A person who just putters around.

The man who moves heaven and earth to play golf.

GOOD

Good has two meanings: it means both that which is good absolutely and that which is good for somebody. *Aristotle*

The enemy of the best. *English Proverb*

Good is when I steal other people's wives and cattle; bad is when they steal mine. *Hottentot Proverb*

GOOD ADVICE

One of those injuries which a good man ought, if possible, to forgive, but at all events to forget at once. *Horace Smith*

GOOD BEHAVIOR

The last refuge of mediocrity. *Henry S. Haskins*

GOOD BOOK

The precious life-blood of a master-spirit. *John Milton*

GOOD BREEDING

Surface Christianity. *Oliver Wendell Holmes*

GOOD LISTENER
> A person who "is not only popular everywhere, but after a while he knows something." *Wilson Mizner*

GOOD NEIGHBOR
> A fellow who smiles at you over the back fence but doesn't climb over it. *Arthur (Bugs) Baer*

GOOD SERMON
> One that goes over your head—and hits one of your neighbors.

GOOD WILL
> The one and only asset that competition cannot undersell or destroy. *Marshall Field*

GOODNESS
> A special kind of truth and beauty. It is truth and beauty in human behavior. *Harry A. Overstreet*

> The only investment that never fails. *Henry David Thoreau*

GOSSIP
> Vice enjoyed vicariously—the sweet, subtle satisfaction without the risk. *Elbert Hubbard*

> What no one claims to like but everybody enjoys. *Joseph Conrad*

> The art of saying nothing in a way that leaves practically nothing unsaid. *Walter Winchell*

> Social sewage. *George Meredith*

> The lack of a worthy theme. *Elbert Hubbard (The Roycroft Dictionary)*

> Anything that goes in one ear and over the back fence or that goes in one ear and out of the mouth.

> A person with a keen sense of rumor.

> What people say behind your back is your standing in the community. *E. W. Howe*

> A personal confession either of malice or imbecility. *J. G. Holland*

> Cutting honest throats by whispers. *Sir Walter Scott*

> Foul whisperings. *Shakespeare*

GOSSIPER
> A professional athlete—of the tongue. *Aldous Huxley*

> Sociologists on a mean and petty scale. *Woodrow Wilson*

GOUT
> Gout is the distemper of a gentleman; whereas the rheumatism is the distemper of a hackney-coachman or chairman, who is obliged to be out in all weathers and at all hours. *Lord Chesterfield*

GOVERNMENT

The very essence of a free government consists in considering offices as public trusts, bestowed for the good of the country, and not for the benefit of an individual or a party. *John C. Calhoun*

A contrivance of human wisdom to provide for human wants. *Edmund Burke*

A cruel trade; good-nature is a bungler in it. *Lord Halifax*

Mainly an expensive organization to regulate evildoers and tax those who behave; government does little for fairly respectable people except annoy them. *Edgar W. Howe*

In theory, is simply a device for supplying a variable series of common needs and the men constituting it (as all ranks of them are so fond of saying) are only public servants; but in fact its main purpose is not service at all but exploitation, and the men constituting it are as little moved by concepts of public duty and responsibility as, say, the corps of advertising agents, or that of stockbrokers, or that of attorneys. *H. L. Mencken*

A scoundrel. In its relations with other governments it resorts to frauds and barbarities that were prohibited to privatemen by the Common Law of civilization so long ago as the reign of Hammurabi, and in its dealings with its own people it not only steals and wastes their property and plays a brutal and witless game with their natural rights, but regularly gambles with their very lives. *H. L. Mencken*

Apathy at the circumference and apoplexy at the center.

An institution through which sound travels faster than light.

A kind of legalized pillage. *Elbert Hubbard (The Roycroft Dictionary)*

Government is a trust, and the officers of the government are trustees; and both the trust and the trustees are created for the benefit of the people. *Henry Clay*

Government is an association of men who do violence to the rest of us. *Leo Tolstoy*

Government, even in its best state, is but a necessary evil; in its worst state, an intolerable one. *Thomas Paine*

Government is not reason, it is not eloquence—it is force. *George Washington*

Government is itself an art, one of the subtlest of the arts.

It is the art of making men live together in peace and with reasonable happiness. *Felix Frankfurter*

GRACE

A quality which "is to the body what reason is to the mind." *La Rochefoucauld*

The outward expression of the inward harmony of the soul. *William Hazlitt*

GRADE CROSSING

A place where headlights and light heads meet.

GRADUATE

One who completes a college course and "is presented with a sheepskin to cover his intellectual nakedness." *Robert M. Hutchins*

GRAFT

An agrarian expression first used by Ali Baba. *Elbert Hubbard (The Roycroft Dictionary)*

GRAFTING

A process by which some family trees are started.

GRAMMAR

The logic of speech, even as logic is the grammar of reason. *Richard C. Trench*

The grave of letters. *Elbert Hubbard (The Roycroft Dictionary)*

GRANDCHILDREN

Those who will have to pay for the good times we didn't have.

GRANDMOTHER

An old lady who keeps your mother from spanking you.

GRAPEFRUIT

A lemon that had a chance and took advantage of it.

A fruit that succeeds in getting into the public eye.

GRASS

Grass is the forgiveness of nature—her constant benediction. Fields trampled with battle, saturated with blood, torn with the ruts of the cannon, grow green again with grass, and carnage is forgotten. Forests decay, harvests perish, flowers vanish, but grass is immortal. *John James Ingalls*

GRATITUDE

A strong and secret hope of greater favors. *La Rochefoucauld*

A lively sense of future favors. *Sir Robert Walpole*

The memory of the heart. *J. B. Massieu*

A duty which ought to be paid, but which none have a right to expect. *Jean-Jacques Rousseau*

One of those things that cannot be bought. It must be born with men, or else all the obligations in the world will not create it. *Lord Halifax*

Next to ingratitude, the most painful thing to bear. *Henry Ward Beecher*

One of the least articulate of the emotions, especially when it is deep. *Felix Frankfurter*

The fairest blossom which springs from the soul. *Henry Ward Beecher*

A fruit of great cultivation; you do not find it among gross people. *Samuel Johnson*

Gratitude is not only the greatest of virtues, but the parent of all the others. *Cicero*

GRAVE

Such a quiet place. *Edna St. Vincent Millay*

"A piece of churchyard" which "fits everybody." *George Herbert*

The grave is the general meeting place. *Thomas Fuller*

The grave itself is but a covered bridge,
Leading from light to light, through a brief darkness.
                          Henry Wadsworth Longfellow

GRAVITY

The bark of wisdom's tree, but it preserves it. *Confucius*

A trick of the body devised to conceal deficiencies of the mind. *La Rochefoucauld*

GREATNESS

A quality with which some men are born, others achieve and still others thrust upon themselves.

A spiritual condition worthy to excite love, interest, and admiration; and the outward proof of possessing greatness is, that we excite love, interest, and admiration. *Matthew Arnold*

Greatness, after all, in spite of its name, appears to be not so much a certain size as a certain quality in human lives. It may be present in lives whose range is very small. *Phillips Brooks*

To have no talent and to be modest about it. *Adapted from James Agate*

So often a courteous synonym for great success. *Philip Guedalla*

Great men are meteors designed to burn so that the earth may be lighted. *Napoleon Bonaparte*

He is great who . . . never reminds us of others. *Ralph Waldo Emerson*

GREEK SCHOLARS

Privileged men; few of them know Greek, and most of them know nothing else. *George Bernard Shaw*

GRIEF

A species of idleness. *Samuel Johnson*

Grief is itself a medicine. *William Cowper*

The overtones in all joy. *Elbert Hubbard* (*The Roycroft Dictionary*)

The pleasure that lasts the longest. *Elbert Hubbard* (*The Roycroft Dictionary*)

Great grief is a divine and terrible radiance which transfigures the wretched. *Victor Hugo*

GROWTH INDUSTRY

One that produces a product which can be manufactured for ten cents and sold for a dollar, while being not only patentable but also habit forming.

GROWTH (METROPOLITAN)

Means more and more of worse and worse. *Professor Geddes*

GUESSWORK

A shallow depression, pit, or cavity in the consciousness of an editorial writer when he is warning the people. *Elbert Hubbard* (*The Roycroft Dictionary*)

GUEST TOWEL

A towel you look at but never use.

GUILLOTINE

The first real cure for dandruff.

A machine that "will take off a head in a twinkling, and the victim will feel nothing but a sense of refreshing coolness. We cannot make too much haste, gentlemen, to allow the nation to enjoy this advantage." *J. I. Guillotin*

GUILT

Guilt is the source of sorrow, 'tis the fiend,
Th' avenging fiend, that follows us behind
With whips and stings.

Nicholas Rowe

The guilty is he who merely meditates a crime. *Vittorio Alfieri*

GUILTY CONSCIENCE

The mother of invention. *Carolyn Wells*

GUITAR
> A musical instrument that has moonlight in it. *James M. Cain*

GUNPOWDER
> A black substance much employed in marking the boundary lines of nations. *Gideon Wurdz*

GYPSY
> Gypsies . . . tell men of losses, and the next time they look for their purses they find their words true. *Wye Saltonstall*

> One who "tells the truth once in his life and immediately repents." *Russian Proverb*

• H •

HABEAS CORPUS
> The most stringent curb that ever legislation imposed on tyranny. *Thomas B. Macaulay*

HABIT
> Habit is habit and not to be flung out of the window by any man, but coaxed downstairs a step at a time. *Mark Twain*

> A cable; we weave a thread of it every day, and at last we cannot break it. *Horace Mann*

> The enormous flywheel of society, its most precious conservative agent. *William James*

> To the soul what the veins and arteries are to the blood, the courses in which it moves. *Horace Bushnell*

> Habits are the things that make one person different from another.

> Habit is a shirt made of iron. *Czech Proverb*

HAIR (GRAY)
> Gray hair is a sign of age, not of wisdom. *Greek Proverb*
> The hoary head is a crown of glory. *Prov. 16:31*
> Gray hairs are death's blossoms. *English Proverb*

HAMBURGER
> The last roundup.

HAMILTON, ALEXANDER
> Hamilton was an honest man, but, as a politician, believed in the necessity of either force or corruption to govern man. *Thomas Jefferson*

> He smote the rock of the national resources, and abundant streams of revenue gushed forth. He touched the dead corpse of public credit, and it sprung upon its feet. *Daniel Webster*

HANDEL, G. F.

Handel is the greatest composer who ever lived. I uncover my head and kneel at his grave. *Ludwig von Beethoven*

HANGING

The worst use man can be put to. *Henry Wotton*

A necktie party. *American Saying*

HANGOVER

The thing that occupies the head you didn't use the night before.

HAPPINESS

Happiness is not a destination. It is a method of life. *Burton Hillis*

True happiness is of a retired nature, and an enemy to pomp and noise; it arises, in the first place, from the enjoyment of one's self; and, in the next from the friendship and conversation of a few select companions. *Joseph Addison*

An experience "not found in self-contemplation; it is perceived only when it is reflected from another." *Samuel Johnson*

The only sanction of life; where happiness fails, existence remains a mad and lamentable experiment. *George Santayana*

A delicate balance between what one is and what one has. *J. H. Denison*

Something man ought to pursue, although they seldom do. *George Santayana*

A good bank account, a good cook, and a good digestion. *Jean-Jacques Rousseau*

The perpetual possession of being well deceived. *Jonathan Swift*

No laughing matter. *Richard Whately*

Like jam—you can't spread even a little without getting some on yourself.

A statement of enjoyment, but one cannot be really happy unless one is enjoying the realities as well as the frivolities of life. *Edward Bulwer-Lytton*

The most powerful of tonics. *Herbert Spencer*

To admire without desiring. And that is not happiness. *Dr. F. H. Bradley*

A form of courage. *Holbrook Jackson*

A sunbeam which may pass through a thousand bosoms without losing a particle of its original ray; nay, when it strikes on a kindred heart, like the converged light on a mirror, it reflects itself with redoubled brightness. It is not perfected till it is shared. *Jane Porter*

The result of being too busy to be miserable.

Forgetting self in useful effort. *Elbert Hubbard (The Roycroft Dictionary)*

A wine of the rarest vintage, and seems insipid to a vulgar taste. *Logan Pearsall Smith*

Essentially a state of going somewhere, wholeheartedly, one-directionally, without regret or reservation. *William H. Sheldon*

Happiness, to some elation, is to others, mere stagnation. *Amy Lowell*

HARD WORK

An accumulation of easy things you didn't do when you should have.

HARVARD UNIVERSITY

A college at Cambridge, about four miles from Boston, where divinity, mathematics, philosophy, and the oriental languages are taught. *Patrick M'Roberts* (1775)

HAS-BEEN

Any man who thinks he has arrived. *Elbert Hubbard (The Roycroft Dictionary)*

HAT

Something the average man covers his head with, the beggar passes around, the statesman throws into the ring and the politician talks through.

A creation that will never go out of style; it will just look ridiculous year after year. *Fred Allen*

A hat is the *ultimatum moriens* of respectability. *Oliver Wendell Holmes*

A new hat for a woman is her Declaration of Independence.

HATRED

The coward's revenge for being intimidated. *George Bernard Shaw*

Hatred is by far the longest pleasure;
Men love in haste, but they detest at leisure.
Lord Byron

We must hate—hatred is the basis of Communism. Children must be taught to hate their parents if they are not Communists. *Nikolai Lenin*

HAVE-NOTS

Those who demand a place in the sun, or in more vulgar language, a share in the loot. *Aldous Huxley*

HAY
> Grass à la mowed.

HEAD
> The dome of thought, the palace of the soul. *Lord Byron*

HEADLESS HORSEMAN
> A myth in contrast to the headless motorist, a stark reality.

HEALTH
> The first wealth. *Ralph Waldo Emerson*

HEARSE
> Father Time's delivery van.

HEART
> The heart of man is the place the Devil dwells in. *Thomas Browne*
>
> Out of the heart proceed evil thoughts, murders, adulteries, fornications, thefts, false witness, blasphemies. *Matt.* 15:19
>
> The heart is the most noble of all the members of our body. *St. John Chrysostom*

HEART (MOTHER'S)
> The child's schoolroom. *Henry Ward Beecher*

HEAVEN
> Heaven is the presence of God. *Christina Rosetti*
> To be one with God. *Confucious*

> There is a land of pure delight,
> Where saints immortal reign;
> Infinite day excludes the night,
> And pleasures banish pain.
> *Isaac Watts*
> Heaven is our heritage
> Earth but a player's stage.
> *Thomas Nashe*

HEIR
> One whose tears are masked laughter. *Publius Syrus*

HELL
> Hell is a city much like London. *Percy Bysshe Shelley*
> Self-love and the love of the world. *Emanuel Swedenborg*
> Hell is paved with good intentions. *Samuel Johnson*
> Hell is full of the ungrateful. *Spanish Proverb*

HEMINGWAY, ERNEST
> An author whose characters do not produce children, although, between drinks, they long for them.

HEN
> Only an egg's way of making another egg. *Samuel Butler*
> A bird that can lay around and make money.

HENPECKED
> When "the hens crow, and the cock holds his peace." *John Florio*

HEREDITY
> An omnibus in which all our ancestors ride, and every now and then one of them puts his head out and embarrasses us. *Oliver Wendell Holmes*
>
> The thing a child gets from the other side of the family. *Marceline Cox*

HERESY
> What the minority believe; it is the name given by the powerful to the doctrine of the weak. *Robert G. Ingersoll*

HERO
> The beginning of a bore.
>
> One who "becomes a bore at last." *Ralph Waldo Emerson*
>
> One who is brave five minutes longer than an ordinary man. *Adapted from Ralph Waldo Emerson*
>
> One who kindles a great light in the world, who sets up blazing torches in the dark streets of life for men to see by. The saint is the man who walks through the dark paths of the world, himself a light. *Felix Adler*
>
> A person whom good fortune makes.

HEROISM
> When the will defies fear, when duty throws the gauntlet down to fate, when honor scorns to compromise with death—this is heroism. *Robert G. Ingersoll*
>
> Heroism, the Caucasian mountaineers says, is endurance for one moment more. *George Kennan*
>
> Heroism is the brilliant triumph of the soul over the flesh: that is to say, over fear: fear of poverty, of suffering, of calumny, of sickness, of isolation, and of death. *H. F. Amiel*

HIDE AND SEEK
> A game played on any ocean liner by a large number of the passengers.

HIGH CIVILIZATION
> A pyramid: it can stand only on a broad base; its primary prerequisite is a strong and soundly consolidated mediocrity. *F. W. Nietzsche*

HIGHBROW
> He is a man who has found something more interesting than women. *Edgar Wallace*
>
> A person educated beyond his intelligence. *Brander Matthews*

The kind of person who looks at a sausage and thinks of
  Picasso. *A. P. Herbert*

HIGHWAY INTERSECTION
The place where the bodies are found.

HIPPOPOTAMUS
The ugliest of the works of God. *Thomas B. Macaulay*

HISTORIAN
A prophet in retrospect. *August W. von Schlegel*
A person who may lie in contrast to history which doesn't.
Persons who relate "not so much what is done, as what they
  would have believed." *Benjamin Franklin*
One who looks backward and in the end believes backward.
  F. W. Nietzsche

HISTORY
Walter Bagehot rightly argued that much history is of
  slender value—"the mere scum of events." *Rogert Fulford*
A distillation of rumor. *Thomas Carlyle*
A fable agreed upon. *Napoleon Bonaparte*
A lie! *Sir Robert Walpole*
In essence a history of ideas. *H. G. Wells*
A pattern of timeless moments. *T. S. Eliot*
An account mostly false, of events unimportant, which are
  brought about by rulers mostly knaves, and soldiers
  mostly fools. *Ambrose Bierce*
A record of the past which could not be written if it had to
  be true.
What enables each nation to use the other fellow's past
  record as an alibi.
Little else than a picture of human crimes and misfortunes.
  Voltaire
Little more than the register of the crimes, follies, and
  misfortunes of mankind. *Edward Gibbon*
Lies agreed upon.
Sin writes histories, goodness is silent. *J. W. von Goethe*
A collection of epitaphs. *Elbert Hubbard (The Roycroft
  Dictionary)*
Gossip well told. *Elbert Hubbard (The Roycroft Dic-
  tionary)*
The evil that men do. *Gideon Wurdz*
The record of a man in quest of his daily bread and butter.
  Hendrik van Loon
The record of the periodical crusades for or against some
  bogey which believing men have evolved out of their
  credulity or fear. *Ernest Boyd*

The propaganda of the victorious. *Ernest Toller*

The art of giving meaning to the meaningless.

Merely gossip.

History is bunk. *Henry Ford*

The record of the follies of the majority. *Lindsay Rogers*

Clarified experience. *James Russell Lowell*

A kind of Newgate calendar, a register of the crimes and miseries that man has inflicted on his fellow man. *Washington Irving*

The biography of great men. *Thomas Carlyle*

History is something that never happened, written by a man who wasn't there.

HITCHHIKER

The only person who could be completely incapacitated by the loss of his thumb.

HOBBY

Hard work you wouldn't do for a living.

HOLDING COMPANY

A thing where you hand an accomplice the goods while the policeman searches you. *Will Rogers*

HOLE

Nothing at all, but you can break your neck in it. *Austin O'Malley*

HOLIDAY (PERPETUAL)

A good working definition of hell. *George Bernard Shaw*

HOLLAND

A country naturally cold, moist, and unpleasant. *William Petty*

Where the broad ocean leans against the land. *Oliver Goldsmith*

God made the ocean, but the Dutch made Holland. *Dutch Proverb*

The very cockpit of Christendom. *James Howell* (1642)

HOLLYWOOD

Full of people that learned to write but evidently can't read. *Will Rogers*

A place where "one can get along quite well by knowing two words of English—swell and lousy." *Vicki Baum*

A place where you spend more than you make, on things you don't need, to impress people you don't like. *Ken Murray*

Ten million dollars' worth of intricate and highly ingenious machinery functioning elaborately to put skin on boloney. *George Jean Nathan*

The town where inferior people have a way of making superior people feel inferior. *Dudley Field Malone*

A place where people from Iowa mistake each other for movie stars. *Fred Allen*

A place where you can see many a famous movie star skate down Sunset Boulevard on a pair of sports cars.

Just Bridgeport with palm trees! *Edward MacNamara*

A place where the inmates are in charge of the asylum. *Laurence Stallings*

A sewer with service from the Ritz Carlton. *Wilson Mizner*

HOME

The place most persons have to leave in order to appreciate good food and good beds.

The place where you don't have to engage reservations in advance.

The place where, when you have to go there, they have to take you in. *Robert Frost*

The place where a man can say anything he pleases because no one pays the slightest attention to him.

Where a woman puts up with her husband.

The abode of the heart. *Elbert Hubbard (The Roycroft Dictionary)*

Where we love is home, home that our feet may leave, but not our hearts. *Oliver Wendell Holmes*

Where half the family waits for the other half to come back with the car.

Where the mortgage is.

What is home? A roof to keep out the rain. Four walls to keep out the wind. Floors to keep out the cold. Yes, but home is more than that. It is the laugh of a baby, the song of a mother, the strength of a father. Warmth of living hearts, light from happy eyes, kindness, loyalty, comradeship. Home is first school and first church for young ones, where they learn what is right, what is good and what is kind. Where they go for comfort when they are hurt or sick. Where joy is shared and sorrow eased. Where fathers and mothers are respected and loved. Where children are wanted. Where the simplest food is good enough for kings because it is earned. Where money is not so important as loving-kindness. Where even the teakettle sings from happiness. That is home. God bless it. *Ernestine Schumann-Heink*

The place where the great are small and the small are great.

Where "hearts are of each other sure." *John Keble*

HOME (TO THE SMALL BOY)
Merely a filling station.

HOME OWNER
One who is always on his way to a hardware store.

HONEST PERSON
An honest person is one who has traveled in every continent and hasn't any idea of how to save the world.

An honest man's the noblest work of God. *Alexander Pope*

HONESTY
The best policy, but he who is governed by that maxim is not an honest man. *Richard Whately*

A cowardly attempt to establish a safe precedent.

The thing that keeps you from turning to the end of the book to see how the story ends.

The rarest wealth anyone can possess, and yet all the honesty in the world ain't lawful tender for a loaf of bread. *Josh Billings*

HONEYMOON
The period during which the bride trusts the bridegroom's word of honor.

HONOR
Honor is but an itch in youthful blood
Of doing acts extravagantly good.
Samuel Howard

The spur that pricks the princely mind. *George Peele*

That name, that idle name of wind, that empty sound called honor. *Samuel Daniel*

Honor is a baby's rattle. *Thomas Randolph*

Honor's the moral conscience of the great. *William D'Avenant*

Honor is best an empty bubble. *John Dryden*

HOPE
A species of happiness, and perhaps, the chief happiness which this world affords. *Samuel Johnson*

Generally a wrong guide, though it is very good company by the way. *Lord Halifax*

A pathological belief in the occurrence of the impossible. *H. L. Mencken*

The only universal liar who never loses his reputation for veracity. *Robert G. Ingersoll*

The only good that is common to all men; those who have nothing else possess hope still. *Thales*

Hope is a very thin diet. *Thomas Shadwell*

Hope! of all ills that men endure,
The only cheap and universal cure.
Abraham Cowley

The gay, skylarking pajamas we wear over yesterday's bruises. *Benjamin De Casseres*

The poor man's bread. *George Herbert*

We speak of hope; but is not hope only a more gentle name for fear? *L. E. Landon*

The struggle of the soul, breaking loose from what is perishable, and attesting her eternity. *Herman Melville*

Hope is grief's best music. *Proverb*

HOPELESS
Like the setting of the sun. The brightness of our life is gone. *Henry Wadsworth Longfellow*

HOROSCOPE
The blue-ribbon exhibit of the misuse of intelligence. *Joseph Jastrow*

HORS DE COMBAT
A war horse.

HORSE AND BUGGY DAYS
When you lived until you died and not until you were just run over. *Will Rogers*

HORSE SENSE
What keeps horses from betting on what people will do. *Oscar Wilde*

HORSESHOE
A symbol of good luck when it's on the right horse.

HOSPITAL
A place where people who are run down, wind up.

HOSPITALITY
The virtue which induces us to feed and lodge certain persons who are not in need of food and lodging. *Ambrose Bierce*

Hospitality consists in a little fire, a little food, and an immense quiet. *Ralph Waldo Emerson*

HOST
The man who sits in the lowest place, and who is always industrious in helping everyone. *David Hume*

HOURGLASS
A reminder not only of time's quick flight, but also of the dust to which we must at last return. *G. C. Lichtenberg*

HOUSE
A great source of happiness. It ranks immediately after health and a good conscience. *Sydney Smith*

HOUSEHOLD
> The household is a school of power. *Ralph Waldo Emerson*

HOUSE OF LORDS
> That hospital of incurables, the House of Lords. *Lord Chesterfield*

HOUSEWARMING
> The final call for those who haven't sent a wedding present.

HUCKSTER
> A good name for an advertising man. A huckster with a station wagon instead of a pushcart. *Frederic Wakeman*

HUG
> A roundabout way of expressing affection. *Gideon Wurdz*

HUMAN BEINGS
> The only animals of which I am thoroughly and cravenly afraid. *George Bernard Shaw*

> The greatest of the earth's parasites. *Martin Henry Fischer*

HUMAN SPECIES
> Two distinct races: the men who borrow, and the men who lend. *Charles Lamb*

HUMANITY
> The children of God.

HUMBLENESS
> Humbleness is always grace, always dignity. *James Russell Lowell*

HUMILITY
> A virtue all men preach, none practice, and yet everybody is content to hear. The Master thinks it's good Doctrine for his Servants, the Laity for the Clergy, and the Clergy for the Laity. *John Selden*

> The first of the virtues—for other people. *Oliver Wendell Holmes*

> Preached by the clergy, but practised only by the lower classes. *Bertrand Russell*

> The highest virtue, mother of them all. *Alfred Tennyson*

> That low, sweet root, from which all heavenly virtues shoot. *Thomas Moore*

> The solid foundation of all the virtues. *Confucius*

> The first test of a truly great man. *John Ruskin*

> A state of mind appropriate to perception of the truth of things. A soul that has not attained humility is not prepared to grasp the truth of the world in its fullness. *Jakob Klatzkin*

> Pride in God. *Austin O'Malley*

> To make a right estimate of one's self. *C. H. Spurgeon*

Humility, like darkness, reveals the heavenly lights. *Henry David Thoreau*

HUMOR

One of the very best articles of dress one can wear in society. *William Makepeace Thackeray*

A peerless weapon of the British when dealing with foreign countries. *Walter Starkie*

Demands a measure of serenity and a pretty confident stance in life—attributes that are not too widely encountered nowadays. *J. Donald Adams*

Nothing but grown-up play. *Max Eastman*

The sunshine of the mind. *Edward Bulwer-Lytton*

The harmony of the heart. *Douglas Jerrold*

HUMOR-IN-ADVERTISING

We Welcome Complaints.

We Trust You.

Home Cooking.

HUMORIST

The person who called installments "easy payments."

One who perceives "simultaneously, the comic and the tragic sides of life." *Luigi Pirandello*

A type that pioneer society required in order to maintain its physic equilibrium. *Van Wyck Brooks*

Cannot be primarily a cynic, nor even an atheist. *Leonard Feeney*

HUNGER

An instinct placed in man to make certain that he will work.

It breeds madness, and all the ugly distempers that make an ordered life impossible. *Woodrow Wilson*

The ability to eat in some restaurants.

A condition in which you find no fault with the cook.

Hunger is the best cook. *Latin Proverb*

HUNTER

A man who will sit in a swamp all day waiting to shoot a duck, but who will complain if dinner is ten minutes late when he gets home.

HUNTERS (FOX)

The unspeakable in full pursuit of the uneatable. *Oscar Wilde*

HUNTING

The sport of kings. *William Somerville*

HURRICANE SEASON

The one time of the year when a citizen of Florida doesn't do any blowing.

HURRY

Hurry is the weakness of fools. *Baltasar Gracian*

Hurry is slow. *Latin Proverb*

HUSBAND

What is left of the lover after the nerve has been extracted. *Helen Rowland*

A man who just listens when he talks to his wife on the telephone.

A hero in his own home until the company leaves.

A man of few words.

A person who lays down the law to his wife and then accepts all her amendments.

A lover with a two-days' growth of beard, his collar off, and a bad cold in the head. *Ascribed to James Huneker*

A man who wishes he had as much fun when he is out as his wife thinks he does.

A good husband is one who isn't worried when he talks in his sleep.

A master of a house, as I have read,

Must be the first man up, and the last in bed.
                              Robert Herrick

A man who buys his football tickets four months in advance and waits until December 24 to do his Christmas shopping.

A man who often finds that words flail him.

HUSBAND (HENPECKED)

A man who gives his wife the best ears of his life.

HYPOCRISY

The homage which vice renders to virtue. *La Rochefoucauld*

Pretending to be wicked, and being really good all the time. That would be hypocrisy. *Oscar Wilde*

HYPOCRITE

A person who isn't himself on Sundays.

Every man. *Frederick IV*

HYPOTHESIS

An inference based on knowledge which is insufficient to prove its high probability. *Frederick Barry*

● I ●

ICELAND

A country which is so cold that most of the inhabitants have to live somewhere else.

IDEA

An incitement. It offers itself for belief and if believed it is acted on unless some other belief outweighs it or some failure of energy stifles the movement at its birth. *Oliver Wendell Holmes, Jr.*

IDEAL WIFE

Any woman who has an ideal husband. *Booth Tarkington*

IDEALISM

Standard of perfection that "increases in direct proportion to one's distance from the problem." *John Galsworthy*

IDEALIST

A person who helps other people to be prosperous. *Henry Ford*

Idealists give invaluable service, they give the distant view, which makes progress, as it makes a walk, exhilarating. *Canon S. Barnett*

IDEALS

Our better selves. *A. B. Alcott*

IDLENESS

To do nothing at all is the most difficult thing in the world, the most difficult and the most intellectual. *Oscar Wilde*

An appendix to nobility. *Robert Burton*

The stupidity of the body, and stupidity is the idleness of the mind. *Johann G. Seume*

Emptiness: the tree in which the sap is stagnant remains fruitless. *Hosea Ballou*

A rust that attaches itself to the most brilliant metals. *Voltaire*

The holiday of fools. *Lord Chesterfield*

Idleness is disgrace. *Hesiod*

The mother of vices. *John Lydgate*

The nurse of sin. *Edmund Spenser*

IGNORANCE

The only thing more expensive than education.

The thing that causes a lot of interesting arguments.

Ignorance gives a sort of eternity to prejudice, and perpetuity to error. *Robert Hall*

The night of the mind, but a night without moon or star. *Confucius*

The wet-nurse of prejudice. *Josh Billings*

The mother of fear. *Henry Home*

Ignorance is a voluntary misfortune. *Nicholas Ling*

The parent of happiness and certainty.

ILLNESS
> A great leveler. At its touch, the artificial distinctions of society vanish away. People in a hospital are just people. *Max Thorek*

> Illness tells us what we are. *Italian Proverb*

ILLUSION
> The first of all pleasures. *Voltaire*

IMAGINATION
> A quality "given a man to compensate him for what he is not, and a sense of humor was provided to console him for what he is." *Oscar Wilde*

> What makes a politician think he is a statesman.

> The eye of the soul. *Joseph Joubert*

> Imagination is a sort of faint perception. *Aristotle*

IMBECILITY
> A weakness in men which "is always inviting the impudence of power." *Ralph Waldo Emerson*

IMITATION
> The sincerest (form) of flattery. *Charles Caleb Colton*

IMITATION (GOOD)
> The most perfect originality. *Voltaire*

IMMORALITY
> The morality of those who are having a better time. *H. L. Mencken*

IMMORTALITY
> The glorious discovery of Christianity. *William Ellery Channing*

> "Immortality," said a famous Chinese statesman, "is when a man dies but his words live." *Carl Crow*

> The thought of life that ne'er shall cease. *Henry Wadsworth Longfellow*

IMPATIENCE
> Waiting in a hurry.

IMPERIALISM
> The transition stage from capitalism to Socialism. . . . It is capitalism dying, not dead. *Nikolai Lenin*

IMPIETY
> Your irreverence toward my deity. *Ambrose Bierce*

IMPOSSIBLE
> A word only to be found in the dictionary of fools. *Napoleon Bonaparte*

> A word not recognized by a willing heart.

IMPOSTOR
> A rival aspirant to public honors. *Ambrose Bierce*

IMPRISONMENT
 A worse crime than any of those committed by its victims.
 George Bernard Shaw

IMPROMPTU
 The touchstone of wit. *Jean B. P. Molière*

IMPROPRIETY
 The soul of wit. *W. Somerset Maugham*

IMPROVIDENCE
 Lightly come, lightly go. *English Proverb*

IMPUDENCE
 The worst of all human diseases. *Euripides*

IN THE MONEY
 A condition many men hope for, but only a bank teller
 experiences.

INCOME TAX
 The fine you pay for thriving too fast.

INCONSISTENCY
 The lifebreath of realism. *John Cowper Powys*

INCREDULITY
 The wisdom of a fool. *Josh Billings*

INDEPENDENCE
 An achievement, not a bequest. *Elbert Hubbard (The Roy-
 croft Dictionary)*
 The privilege of the strong. *F. W. Nietzsche*
 Lord of myself, accountable to none. *Benjamin Franklin*

INDIA
 An old nation but a young republic. We, in comparison,
 are a young nation but an old republic. This truth is
 pointed up in the story of a U. S. tourist who visited an
 Indian village. "Have you ever heard of America?" he
 asked an old peasant. The Indian scratched his head.
 "America?" he replied. "Oh, I guess you mean the coun-
 try Columbus found when he was looking for India."
 Senior Scholastic
 The playground of the sons of English capitalists. *Edward
 Carpenter* (1887)

INDIAN
 A stoic of the woods—a man without a fear. *Thomas
 Campbell*
 One who "sees God in clouds, or hears Him in the wind."
 Alexander Pope

INDIANA
 The home of more first-rate second-class men than any
 state in the Union. *Thomas R. Marshall*

INDIGESTION

> An experience that forces morality on the stomach. *Adapted from Victor Hugo*
>
> That inward fate which makes all Styx through one small liver flow. *Lord Byron*

INDIVIDUALISM

> The system in which human stupidity can do the least harm. *J. M. Clark*
>
> Individuality is the sin of political liberty. *James Fenimore Cooper*

INDOLENCE

> A sort of suicide; for the man is effectually destroyed, though the appetites of the brute may survive. *Earl of Chesterfield*
>
> The sleep of the mind. *Luc de Vauvenargues*

INDOMITABLE

> To hope till hope creates from its own wreck the thing it contemplates; never to change, nor falter. *Percy Bysshe Shelley*

INDUSTRY

> Fortune's right hand and frugality her left. *Proverb*

INFERIORITY

> What you enjoy in your best friends. *Adapted from Lord Chesterfield*

INFLATION

> Inflation is repudiation. *Calvin Coolidge*
>
> The first panacea for a mismanaged nation is inflation of the currency; the second is war. Both bring a temporary prosperity; both bring a permanent ruin. *Ernest Hemingway*

INFORMER

> The worst rogue of the two.

INGENUITY

> What you use to get into debt and also to avoid paying it.

INGRATE

> Any person who has got something for nothing, and wants more on the same terms. *Elbert Hubbard (The Roycroft Dictionary)*

INGRATITUDE

> The daughter of pride. *French Proverb*

INHERITANCE

> Wealth you receive which enables you to know too well those with whom you had to divide it.
>
> What you do not leave others if you wish them to mourn.

INITIATIVE

Doing the right thing without being told. *Elbert Hubbard*

INSINCERITY

Merely a method by which we can multiply our personalities. *Oscar Wilde*

INSOMNIA

A contagious disease often transmitted from babies to parents. *Shannon Fife*

A sad condition in which you can't sleep when it's time to get up.

When a lot of innocent sheep are kept jumping over a fence all night because one man can't sleep.

A condition when you can't sleep when you are working. *Adapted from Arthur Baer*

INSOMNIAC

A person who can't sleep because he worries about it and worries about it because he can't sleep. *Franklin P. Adams*

INSPIRATION

Having "a touch of divine afflatus." *Cicero*

INSTINCT

Instinct is action taken in pursuance of a purpose, but without conscious perception of what the purpose is. *Van Hartmann*

Untaught ability. *Alexander Bain*

The nose of the mind. *Mme. de Girardin*

INSTINCTS

The prime movers of all human activity. *William McDougall*

INSTITUTION

The lengthened shadow of one man. *Ralph Waldo Emerson*

INSURANCE

An ingenious modern game of chance in which the player is permitted to enjoy the comfortable conviction that he is beating the man who keeps the table. *Ambrose Bierce*

INSURANCE (LIFE)

A plan that keeps you poor all your life so you can die rich.

INTELLECTUAL

A person who is so smart that he cannot understand the obvious.

INTELLECTUALS

Our most anxious social class is that known by courtesy as the intellectuals. *Frank Moore Colby*

INTELLIGENCE

A luxury, sometimes useless, sometimes fatal. It is a torch

or firebrand according to the use one makes of it. *Caballero*

Intelligence is derived from two words—*inter* and *legere*— *inter* meaning "between" and *legere* meaning "to choose." An intelligent person, therefore, is one who has learned "too choose between." He knows that good is better than evil, that confidence should supersede fear, that love is superior to hate, that gentleness is better than cruelty, forbearance than intolerance, compassion than arrogance and that truth has more virtue than ignorance. *J. Martin Klotsche*

INTEMPERANCE
Of all calamities this is the greatest. *Thomas Jefferson*

INTERNATIONALISM
A luxury which only the upper classes can afford; the common people are hopelessly bound to their native shores. *Benito Mussolini*

INTOLERANCE
A form of egoism, and to condemn egoism intolerantly is to share it. *George Santayana*

INTUITION
Reason in a hurry. *Holbrook Jackson*
The strange instinct that tells a woman she is right, whether she is or not. *Oscar Wilde*

INTUITION (WOMAN'S)
Nothing more than man's transparency. *Adapted from George J. Nathan*

I OWE IT ALL TO
An expression commonly used in connection with one's wife, landlord, or pawn broker.

IRELAND
A country in which the probable never happens and the impossible always does. *John Pentland Mahaffy*
The Emerald Isle

IRISH
A fair people; they never speak well of one another. *Samuel Johnson*
An imaginative race, and it is said that imagination is too often accompanied by somewhat irregular logic. *Benjamin Disraeli*

IRISHMAN
One who "can be worried by the consciousness that there is nothing to worry about." *Austin O'Malley*

An Irishman, before answering a question, always asks another. *P. W. Joyce*

IRONY

To give father a billfold for Christmas.

The cactus-plant that sprouts over the tomb of our dead illusions. *Elbert Hubbard (The Roycroft Dictionary)*

An insult conveyed in the form of a compliment. *E. P. Whipple*

Jesting hidden behind gravity. *John Weiss*

ISOLATION

Short pants for a grown-up United States. *Henry A. Wallace*

ITALY

Only a geographical expression. *Clemens von Metternich*

A nation made by the Creator "from designs by Michael Angelo." *Mark Twain*

• J •

JACK

The thing that lifts a car and keeps it going.

JAIL

I think a jail a school of virtue is,

A house of study, and of contemplation:

A place of discipline and reformation.

John Taylor

JANITOR

A man who never puts out any excess hot air.

JANUARY

January brings the snow,

Makes our feet and fingers glow.

Sara Coleridge

JAYWALKER

Synonym for the deceased.

JAYWALKING

A bad habit that may give you that run-down feeling.

JAZZ

American folk music. *George Gershwin*

The folk-music of the machine age. *Paul Whitman*

May be a thrilling communion with the primitive soul; or it may be an ear-splitting bore. *Winthrop Sargeant*

JAZZ BAND

A group of musicians that put the din in dinner and take the rest out of restaurant.

JEALOUSY

The fear or apprehension of superiority; envy, our uneasiness under it. *William Shenstone*

The mark of a man embittered. *John Keats*

More self-love than love. *La Rochefoucauld*

One of the consequences of love; you may like it, or not, at pleasure, but there it is. *Robert Louis Stevenson*

An awkward homage which inferiority renders to merit. *Mme. de Puisieux*

Jealousy is the great exaggerator. *J. C. F. Schiller*

Magnifier of trifles. *J. C. F. Schiller*

JEFFERSON, THOMAS

A gentleman of thirty-two who could calculate an eclipse, survey an estate, tie an artery, plan an edifice, try a case, break a horse, dance a minuet and play the violin. *James Parton*

A man of proud ambition and violent passions. *Alexander Hamilton*

JEOPARDY (DOUBLE)

When a man with a two pants suit discovers both pairs need to be replaced.

JEST

Jesting is often only indigence of intellect. *Jean de La Bruyère*

JESUS CHRIST

Christ is God clothed with human nature. *Benjamin Whichcote*

Jesus the Savior of Men. *Latin phrase usually written I.H.S.*

JEWELRY

Orators of love. *Samuel Daniel*

Infinite riches in a little room. *Christopher Marlowe*

JEWELRY (CHRISTMAS)

The first thing to turn green in the spring. *Kin Hubbard*

JIMMY

An implement employed by men of acquisitive natures. *Gideon Wurdz*

JOHN THE BAPTIST

He was a burning and a shining light. *John 5: 35*

JOHNSON, SAMUEL

A man who was willing to love all mankind except an American.

A great wit who "gives you a forcible hug, and shakes laughter out of you, whether you will or no." *Ascribed to David Garrick*

JOKE

The cayenne of conversation, and the salt of life. *Paul Chatfield*

A joke's a very serious thing. *Charles Churchill*

"Sport to one" but "death to another." *William Hazlitt*

JONSON, BEN

A great borrower from the works of others. *William Hazlitt*

The greatest man after Shakespeare in that age of dramatic genius. *Samuel Taylor Coleridge*

JOURNALISM

A profession whose business it is to explain to others what it personally does not understand. *Lord Northcliffe*

Consists largely in saying "Lord Jones Dead" to people who never knew that Lord Jones was alive. *G. K. Chesterton*

Organized gossip. *Edward Eggleston*

Consists in buying white paper at two cents a pound and selling it at ten cents a pound. *Charles A. Dana*

A news sense is really a sense of what is important, what is vital, what has color and life—what people are interested in. That's journalism. *Burton Rascoe*

The first power in the land. *Adapted from Samuel Bowles*

JOY

Joy is the life of man's life. *Benjamin Whichcote*

All great joys are serious. *Alexander Smith*

JOY RIDER

Someone who is riding while we are walking and a jaywalker is someone who is walking while we are riding. *Pittsburgh Sun*

JUDGE

A law student who marks his own examination papers. *H. L. Mencken*

One who learns law from lawyers and is excluded from the game, getting his in honors. *Elbert Hubbard (The Roycroft Dictionary)*

The judge is nothing but the law speaking. *Benjamin Whichcote*

Judges are apt to be naive, simple-minded men. *Oliver Wendell Holmes, Jr.*

There are no more reactionary people in the world than judges. *Nikolai Lenin*

JUDGMENT DAY

Day of wrath. *Thomas of Celano*

Every day.

The day when God looks you over not "for medals, degrees or diplomas, but for scars." *Elbert Hubbard*

JUNE

The month of weddings and cooing. The billing comes in July.

The month for weddings—when you have perfect daze.

> June brings tulips, lilies, roses,
> Fills the children's hands with posies.
> *Sara Coleridge*
>> It is the month of June,
>> The month of leaves and roses,
>> When pleasant sights salute the eyes,
>> And pleasant scents the noses.
>> *N. P. Willis*

JUNK

Anything that has outlived its usefulness. *Oliver Herford*

JURY

A group of twelve people of average ignorance. *Herbert Spencer*

The stupidity of one brain multiplied by twelve. *Elbert Hubbard* (*The Roycroft Dictionary*)

Twelve "good men and true." *Shakespeare*

JUST

By the just we mean that which is lawful and that which is fair and equitable. *Aristotle*

JUSTICE

A commodity which in a more or less adulterated condition the State sells to the citizen as a reward for his allegiance, taxes and personal service. *Ambrose Bierce*

Truth in action. *Joseph Joubert*

Half religion. *Turkish*

A system of revenge where the State imitates the criminal. *Elbert Hubbard* (*The Roycroft Dictionary*)

Justice is the firm and continuous desire to render to everyone that which is his due. *Justinian*

The arithmetic of love. *Thomas Masaryk*

The great interest of man on earth. *Daniel Webster*

The tolerable accommodation of the conflicting interests of society. *Learned Hand*

Justice is the end of government. It is the end of civil society. It ever has been and ever will be pursued until it be obtained, or until liberty be lost in the pursuit. *Alexander Hamilton*

There is no such thing as justice—in or out of court. *Clarence Darrow*

Justice is the insurance which we have on our lives and property. Obedience is the premium which we pay for it. *William Penn*

Justice is the crowning glory of the virtues. *Cicero*

Justice is what is established. *Blaise Pascal*

Justice is the sum of all moral duty. *William Godwin*

The name we give the verdict when the court agrees with us.

• K •

KANGAROO

Nature's first abortive effort to produce a cheer leader.

A large economy size grasshopper.

KANSAS

A state of the Union, but it is also a state of mind, a neurotic condition, a psychological phase, a symptom, indeed, something undreamt of in your philosophy, an inferiority complex against the tricks and manners of plutocracy—social, political, and economic. *William Allen White*

KEATS, JOHN

One of the noblest specimens of the workmanship of God. *Percy Bysshe Shelley*

The kind of man that Keats was gets ever more horrible to me. *Thomas Carlyle*

KEPLER, JOHANN

Galileo was a great genius, and so was Newton; but it would take two or three Galileos and Newtons to make one Kepler. *Samuel Taylor Coleridge*

KIBITZER

A person with an inferiority complex.

KINDERGARTEN TEACHER

One who knows how to make the little things count.

KINDNESS

A language which the dumb can speak, the deaf can understand. *C. N. Bovee*

The golden chain by which society is bound together. *J. W. von Goethe*

Loving people more than they deserve. *Joseph Joubert*

An act which "disagrees with very proud stomachs." *William Makepeace Thackeray*

Kindness is the beginning and the end of the law. *Hebrew Proverb*

KING

One who has "few things to desire and many things to fear." *Francis Bacon*

> Kings are like stars—they rise and set, they have
> The worship of the world, but no repose.
> > *Percy Bysshe Shelley*

The least independent man in his dominions. *J. C. and A. W. Hare*

Kings is mostly rapscallions. *Mark Twain*

KISS

The sincerest form of flattery.

A peculiar preposition. Of no use to one, yet absolute bliss to two. The small boys gets it for nothing, the young man has to lie for it, and the old man has to buy it. The baby's right, the lover's privilege, and the hypocrite's mask. To a young girl, faith; to a married woman, hope; and to an old maid, charity. *V. P. I. Skipper*

> A kiss, when all is said, what is it?
> A rosy dot placed on the "i" in loving;
> 'Tis a secret told to the mouth instead of to the ear.
> > *Edmond Rostand*

> What is a kiss? Why this, as some approve:
> The sure, sweet cement, glue, and lime of love.
> > *Robert Herrick*

> What is a kiss? Alacke! at worst,
> A single dropp to quenche a thirst,
> Tho' oft it proves in happy hour
> The first sweet dropp of one long shower.
> > *Leland*

Soul meets soul on lovers' lips. *Percy Bysshe Shelley*

KITCHENETTE

An apartment so small you can't tell whether you are listening to your neighbor's radio or yours.

An apartment designed by the man who made the telephone booth.

KLEPTOMANIAC

A person who takes things from you before you lose them.

KNOWLEDGE

Power, if you know it about the right person. *Ethel Watts Mumford*

A comfortable and necessary retreat and shelter for us in an advanced age; and if we do not plant it while young it will give us no shade when we grow old. *Lord Chesterfield*

The small part of ignorance that we arrange and classify.
Ambrose Bierce

The only fountain, both of the love and the principles of
human liberty. *Daniel Webster*

The foundation and source of good writing. *Horace*

The eye of desire and can become the pilot of the soul.
Will Durant

The amassed thought and experience of innumerable minds.
Ralph Waldo Emerson

> Ignorance is the curse of God,
> Knowledge the wing wherewith we fly to heaven.
> *Shakespeare*

Knowledge and human power are synonymous. *Francis
Bacon*

All knowledge is remembrance. *Thomas Hobbes*

Knowledge is the knowing that we cannot know. *Ralph
Waldo Emerson*

To know that you know nothing.

• L •

LABOR

The workingmen are the basis of all government, for the
plain reason that they are the most numerous. *Abraham
Lincoln*

The workers are the saviors of society, the redeemers of the
race. *Eugene V. Debs*

To labor is to pray. *Motto of the Benedictines*

The duty of all citizens of the republic. *Constitution of the
U. S. S. R. (1924)*

LABORER

The author of all greatness and wealth. *U. S. Grant*

LAKE

The landscape's most beautiful and expressive feature. It is
earth's eye; looking into which the beholder measures the
depth of his own nature. The fluviatile trees next to the
shore are the slender eyelashes which fringe it, and the
wooded hills and cliffs around are its overhanging brows.
Henry David Thoreau

LAMB

An animal that frisks on the farm but is frisked in Wall
Street.

LAMB, CHARLES

A clever fellow, certainly; but full of villainous and abortive puns, which he miscarries of every minute. *Thomas Hood*

An author who "conquered poverty and hereditary madness, and won an imperishable name in English literature, all in silence and with a smile." *William C. Hazlitt*

LAME DUCK

A politician whose goose has been cooked.

LAND

That which gives one position, and prevents one from keeping it up. *Oscar Wilde*

LANDLORD

A person who pays for a house once and then quits.

A gentleman who does not earn his wealth. *David Lloyd George*

LANDSCAPE PAINTING

The obvious resource of misanthropy. *William Hazlitt*

LANGUAGE

The dress of thought. *Samuel Johnson*

The only instrument of science, and words are but the signs of ideas. *Samuel Johnson*

The triumph of human ingenuity, surpassing even the intricacies of modern technology. *Alfred North Whitehead*

Spoken language is merely a series of squeaks. *Alfred North Whitehead*

Not an abstract construction of the learned, or of dictionary-makers, but is something arising out of the work, needs, ties, joys, affections, tastes, of long generations of humanity, and has its bases broad and low, close to the ground. *Walt Whitman*

Human language—after all, is but little better than the croak and cackle of fowls, and other utterances of brute nature—sometimes not so adequate. *Nathaniel Hawthorne*

LAST PARADOX

The split atom that unites the world—anyway what's left of it. *John A. Lincoln*

LAUGHING

The sensation of feeling good all over, and showing it principally in one spot. *Josh Billings*

LAUGHTER

I am sure that, since I have had the full use of my reason, nobody has ever heard me laugh. *Lord Chesterfield*

The corrective force which prevents us from becoming cranks. *Henri Bergson*

Not a bad beginning for a friendship, and it is the best ending for one. *Oscar Wilde*

The sound you always hear when you chase your hat down the street. *Elbert Hubbard (The Roycroft Dictionary)*

Little more than an expression of self-satisfied shrewdness. *G. W. F. Hegel*

In laughter there is always a kind of joyousness that is incompatible with contempt or indignation. *Voltaire*

Caused by the spectacle of a human being responding mechanically to an unexpected situation. *Henri Bergson*

Medicine to weary bones. *Carl Sandburg*

A confession of the sins and silliness of the world, but is also a kind of genial acquiescence in these sins and silliness. *Robert Lynd*

The female of tragedy. *Wyndham Lewis*

Laughter is the mind's intonation. There are ways of laughing which have the sound of counterfeit coins. *Edmond de Goncourt*

One faculty that distinguishes man from all other creatures. *Adapted from Joseph Addison*

LAUGHTER (TOLERANT)
The cruelest form of contempt. *Pearl Buck*

LAW
Laws reflect reform; they never induce reform. Laws that violate or go contrary to the mores of a community never bring about social peace and harmony. *Congressman Noah M. Mason*

A bottomless pit. *John Arbuthonot*

The last result of human wisdom acting upon human experience for the benefit of the public. *Samuel Johnson*

A bum profession. It is utterly devoid of idealism and almost poverty stricken as to any real ideas. *Clarence Darrow*

To define law as an aggregate of rules, is to define human thought as an ensemble of the words in the dictionary. *Henri Levy-Ullman*

A formless mass of isolated decisions. *Morris Cohen*

Merely the expression of the will of the strongest for the time being, and therefore laws have no fixity, but shift from generation to generation. *Charles A. Madison*

The very bulwarks of liberty; they define every man's rights, and defend the individual liberties of all men. *J. G. Holland*

Good law means good order. *Aristotle*

A pledge that the citizens of a state will do justice to one another. *Ascribed to Lycophron*

LAW AND EQUITY

Two things which God hath joined, but which man has put asunder. *Charles Caleb Colton*

LAW (AND THE STAGE)

Both are a form of exhibitionism. *Orson Welles*

LAWS (BAD)

The worst sort of tyranny. *Edmund Burke*

LAWSUIT

A machine which you go into as a pig and come out as a sausage. *Ambrose Bierce*

Generally a matter of dollars and suspense.

Defense, expense, suspense, sentence.

To go to law is for two persons to kindle a fire, at their own cost, to warm others and singe themselves to cinders. *Owen Felltham*

LAWYER

One who protects us against robbery by taking away the temptation. *H. L. Mencken*

A learned gentleman who rescues your estate from your enemies and keeps it himself. *Lord Brougham*

The person who steps in when an irresistible force meets an immovable object.

One whose "opinion is worth nothing unless paid for." *English Proverb*

A member of "a profession which abounds with honorable men, and in which I believe there are fewer scamps than in any other." *George Borrow*

Those who earn a living by the sweat of their browbeating. *James Gibbons Huneker*

Men who hire out their words and anger. *Martial*

The only persons in whom ignorance of the law is not punished. *Jeremy Bentham*

LAZINESS

An overwhelming love for physical calm.

A human characteristic sometimes mistaken for patience.

LEADER

One who never permits his followers to discover that he is as dumb as they are. *Rochester Times-Union*

An ordinary person with extraordinary determination.

The leader is necessarily one who breaks new paths into unfamiliar territory. The man who directs us along the old familiar ways is not a leader; he is a traffic cop—a useful and worthy functionary, but not inspiring. *Gerald W. Johnson*

The final test of a leader is that he leaves behind him in other men the conviction and the will to carry on. . . . The genius of a good leader is to leave behind him a situation which common sense, without the grace of genius, can deal with successfully. *Walter Lippmann*

Reason and judgment are the qualities of a leader. *Tacitus*

A trumpet that does not give an uncertain sound.

LEAN YEARS AHEAD

What every woman hopes for.

LEARNED MAN

An idler who kills time by study. *George Bernard Shaw*

LEARNING

The eye of the mind. *Thomas Draxe*

Learning makes the wise wiser and the fool more foolish. *Proverb*

Nothing but history dully taken up. *John Selden*

Words are but wind; and learning is nothing but words; ergo, learning is nothing but wind. *Jonathan Swift*

LECTURER

One with his hand in your pocket, his tongue in your ear, and his faith in your patience. *Ambrose Bierce*

LEGEND

A lie that has attained the dignity of age.

LEISURE

As the Greeks understood it, was not a condition of vacancy, or a time of "vacation." It was work and play rolled into one, and ennobled by being united. Leisure, like work, was a state of activity; but the activity was the activity of the mind, a "cultivation" of the mind, pursued for itself and its own sake. *Sir Ernest Barker*

Man's one opportunity to satisfy whatever appetites he happens to have. *George Boas*

The time you spend on jobs you don't get paid for.

Leisure is an empty cup. It all depends upon what we put into it. *Raphael Demos*

Leisure in time is like unoccupied floor space in a room. *Shu Paihsiang*

The mother of philosophy. *Thomas Hobbes*

LEND ME YOUR EARS

A phrase used by Marc Antony and by the mothers of ten million six-year olds.

LETTER
> That most delightful way of wasting time. *John Morley*
> In a man's letters his soul lies naked. *Samuel Johnson*
> An unannounced visit. *F. W. Nietzsche*

LETTUCE
> Of all herbs, the best and wholesomest for hot seasons, for young men, and them that abound with choler, and also for the sanguine, and such as have hot stomachs. *Tobias Venner* (1620)

LEVITY
> The soul of wit. *Melville D. Landon*

LIAR
> One who tells an unpleasant truth. *Oliver Herford*
> What no person with a short memory should be.
> A man who won't lie to a woman and so has very little consideration for her feelings.
> A man who gets no credit "even when he speaks the truth." *Cicero*

LIBELOUS
> To be tactless in type. *Elbert Hubbard (The Roycroft Dictionary)*

LIBERAL
> One who has both feet firmly planted in the air.
> A man who is willing to spend somebody else's money. *Carter Glass*
> One who believes in more laws and more jobholders, therefore in higher taxes and less liberty. *Baltimore Evening Sun*
> A person with a high pressure feeling, low pressure thinking and a constant urge to give away what belongs to somebody else.
> I'm liberal . . . I mean, so altruistically moral, I never take my own side in a quarrel. *Robert Frost*

LIBERAL-CONSERVATIVE
> So we may put him (John Dalton) down as a Liberal-Conservative, which perhaps may be defined as a man who thinks things ought to progress, but would rather they remained as they are. *James Fitzjames Stephen*

LIBERALISM
> If liberalism means anything, it means complete and courageous devotion to the freedom of inquiry. *John Dewey*
> Trust of the people tempered by prudence; conservatism, distrust of the people tempered by fear. *William E. Gladstone*

LIBERTY

Means responsibility. That is why most men dread it. *George Bernard Shaw*

A transient grace that lights upon the earth by stealth and at long intervals; . . . but power is eternal. *William Hazlitt*

A condition of mankind that "can neither be got, nor kept, but by so much care, that mankind are generally unwilling to give the price for it." *Lord Halifax*

The Mistress of Mankind, she hath powerful Charms which do so dazzle us that we find Beauties in her which perhaps are not there, as we do in other Mistresses; yet if she was not a Beauty, the World would not run mad for her. *Lord Halifax*

The right to do what the laws allow; and if a citizen could do what they forbid, it would be no longer liberty, because others would have the same powers. *C. L. de Montesquieu*

The only thing you cannot have unless you are willing to give it to others. *William Allen White*

Liberty is the sovereignty of the individual. *Josiah Warren*

Meaningless save in terms of law; and law demands authority and subordination as conditions of its life. *Harold J. Laski*

In the most liberal sense it is the negation of law, for law is restraint, and the absence of restraint is anarchy. *Benjamin N. Cardozo*

It is a thing of the spirit. It is an aspiration on the part of people for not alone a free life but a better life. *Wendell L. Willkie*

Not a means to a higher political end. It is itself the highest political end. *J. E. E. Dalbert*

The right of any person to stand up anywhere and say anything whatsoever that everybody thinks. *Lincoln Steffens*

The fullest opportunity for man to be and do the very best that is possible for him. *Phillips Brooks*

LIBRARY

The diary of the human race. The great consulting room of a wise man is a library. *G. Dawson*

The soul's burial ground. *Henry Ward Beecher*

The land of shadows. *Henry Ward Beecher*

The shrines where all the relics of the ancient saints . . . are preserved and reposed. *Francis Bacon*

A hospital for the mind.

LIE

A last resort with a man; with women, it's First Aid. *Gelett Burgess*

The truth in masquerade. *Lord Byron*

The refuse of fools and cowards. *Earl of Chesterfield*

A fault in a boy, an art in a lover, an accomplishment in a bachelor, and second nature in a married woman. *Helen Rowland*

What all men do.

LIFE

A loom, weaving illusion. *Vachel Lindsay*

> Life is but jest:
> A dream, a doom;
> A gleam, a gloom—
> And then—good rest!
>
> Life is but play;
> A throb, a tear:
> A sob, a sneer;
> And then—good day.
> *Léon de Montenaeken*

Life is the game that must be played:
This truth at least, good friends, we know;
So live and laugh, nor be dismayed
As one by one the phantoms go.
                                         Edwin Arlington Robinson

> Out, out, brief candle!
> Life's but a walking shadow.
>   *Shakespeare*

Life is a game of whist. From unseen sources
The cards are shuffled, and the hands are dealt.
I do not like the way the cards are shuffled,
But yet I like the game and want to play.
                                         Eugene F. Ware

> Our lives are albums written through
> With good or ill, with false or true;
> And as the blessed angels turn
> The pages of our years,
> God grant they read the good with smiles,
> And blot the ill with tears!
>   *John Greenleaf Whittier*

Our lives are songs; God writes the words
And we set them to music at pleasure;
And the song grows glad, or sweet or sad,
As we choose to fashion the measure.
                        Ella Wheeler Wilcox

The childhood of our immortality. *J. W. von Goethe*

For most of us a continuous process of getting used to things we hadn't expected.

Life is a fragment, a moment between two eternities, influenced by all that has preceded, and to influence all that follows. The only way to illumine it is by extent of view. *William Ellery Channing*

A one-way street and we are not coming back.

Life is work, and everything you do is so much more experience. *Henry Ford*

Life's a tough proposition, and the first hundred years are the hardest. *Wilson Mizner*

Life is a series of little deaths, out of which life always returns. *Charles Feidelson, Jr.*

A predicament which precedes death. *Henry James*

The life of every man is a diary in which he means to write one story and writes another; and his humblest hour is when he compares the volume as it is with what he vowed to make. *J. M. Barrie*

Life is the rose's hope while yet unblown. *John Keats*

. . . While, in a word, like gnats above a stagnant pool on a summer evening, man danced up and down without the faintest notion why. *John Galsworthy*

As we get older we find that all life is given us on conditions of uncertainty, and yet we walk courageously on. . . . Life to all of us is a narrow plank placed across a gulf, which yawns on either side, and if we were perpetually looking down into it we should fall. So at last, the possibility of disaster ceased to affright me. *Hale White*

A life spent, however victoriously, in securing the necessaries of life is no more than an elaborate furnishing and decoration of apartments for the reception of a guest who is never to come. *A. E. Housman*

A long lesson in humility. *J. M. Barrie*

A pill which none of us can bear to swallow without gilding. *Samuel Johnson*

A school of probability. *Walter Bagehot*

Strange interlude! *Eugene O'Neill*

Consists in what a man is thinking of all day. *Ralph Waldo Emerson* ———

One long process of getting tired. *Samuel Butler*

The art of drawing sufficient conclusion from insufficient premises. *Samuel Butler*

An experience like playing a violin solo in public and learning the instrument as one goes on. *Samuel Butler*

Not a spectacle or a feast; it is a predicament. *George Santayana*

A foreign language: all men mispronounce it. *Christopher Morley*

Far too important a thing ever to talk seriously about. *Oscar Wilde*

As leaves on the trees, such is the life of man. *Homer*

It is "no brief candle to me. It is a sort of splendid torch that I have got hold of for the moment." *Bernard Shaw*

Like a blanket too short. You pull it up and your toes rebel, and you yank it down and shivers meander about your shoulders; but cheerful folks manage to draw their knees up and pass a very comfortable night. *Marion Howard*

A quarry, out of which we are to mold and chisel and complete a character. *J. W. von Goethe*

The life of man on earth is a warfare. *Job 7:1*

Pythagoras used to say life resembles the Olympic Games; a few men strain their muscles to carry off a prize; others bring trinkets to sell to the crowd for a profit; and some there are (and not the worst) who seek no further advantage than to look at the show and see how and why everything is done. They are spectators of other men's lives in order better to judge and manage their own. *Michel de Montaigne*

Life is a tragedy wherein we sit as spectators for a while and then act our part in it. *Jonathan Swift*

For what is your life? It is even a vapour, that appeareth for a little time, and then vanisheth away. *James 4:14*

Life's a voyage that's homeward bound. *Herman Melville*

> Life a jest, and and all things show it,
> I thought so once, and now I know it.
> *John Gay: Epitaph*

A flame that is always burning itself out, but it catches fire again every time a child is born. *George Bernard Shaw*

> Man's life's a vapor,
> And full of woes;

He cuts a caper,
And down he goes.

Like eating artichokes—you've got to go through so much
to get so little. *T. A. Dorgan*

A surgeon. It wounds, and administers no anesthetic. It cuts
out almost the heart of us sometimes. *Winifred Rhoades*

Consists not simply in what heredity and environment do
to us but in what we make out of what they do to us.
Harry Emerson Fosdick

My college. May I graduate well, and earn some honors!
Louisa May Alcott

This long disease. *Alexander Pope*

A disease; and the only difference between one man and
another is the stage of the disease at which he lives.
George Bernard Shaw

A tragedy for those who feel, and a comedy for those who
think. *Jean de La Bruyère*

A very grim and dangerous contest, relieved . . . by a sense
or by an illusion of pleasure, which is the bait, and the
lure for all in this internecine contest. *Theodore Dreiser*

A march from innocence, through temptation, to virtue or
to vice. *Lyman Abbott*

The interval between the time your teeth are almost through
and you are almost through with your teeth. *Elbert
Hubbard (The Roycroft Dictionary)*

A sweet and joyful thing for one who has some one to love
and a pure conscience. *Leo Tolstoy*

A hospital in which every patient is possessed by the desire
to change his bed. *Pierre Charles Baudelaire*

Perhaps the only riddle that we shrink from giving up.
William S. Gilbert

Sobs, sniffles, and smiles, with sniffles predominating.
O. Henry

The saddest thing, next to death. *Edith Wharton*

Like a cash register, in that every account, every thought,
every deed, like every sale, is registered and recorded.
Fulton J. Sheen

A pulsing turmoil filled with terror and bravery and glory,
and to sit down and paint pictures of bleating sheep or
simpering females is not to show much appreciation of
what is going on about us. *Allen Tucker*

Just a bowl of cherries. *Brown–Henderson*

The one supreme thing that interests us all, because we all have to live it. *I. A. R. Wylie*

A mirror in which you never get out more than you put in.

> Life's perhaps the only riddle,
> That we shrink from giving up.
> *W. S. Gilbert*

Life's a long headache in a noisy street. *John Masefield*

> All life is but a game: then gaily play
> Or sadly learn the penalty to pay.
> *Palladas*

Life is a play! 'Tis not its length, but its performance that counts. *Seneca*

A front door to eternity.

LIFE (USELESS)
An early death. *J. W. von Goethe*

LIFELONG ROMANCE
To love oneself. *Oscar Wilde*

LIGHTHOUSE
A tall building on the seashore in which the government maintains a lamp and the friend of a politician. *Ambrose Bierce*

LIMOUSINE
A car with a glass partition to shut out stupid remarks from the back seat.

LION TAMER
A person of questionable courage who enters a cage where he is at least safe from other men. *Adapted from George Bernard Shaw*

LISTENER
A person who "is not only popular everywhere, but after a while he knows something." *Wilson Mizner*

A listener is a silent flatterer.

A great person.

LITERACY
A dangerous thing unless the common people can have some control over what is given them to read in the press and to hear over the radio. *Adapted from Max Lerner*

A significant yardstick of the development of a nation. *Carlos P. Romulo*

LITERATURE
The immortality of speech. *August W. von Schlegel*

The orchestration of platitudes. *Thornton Wilder*

An investment of genius which pays dividends to all subsequent times. *John Burroughs*

Literature is news that stays news. *Ezra Pound*

Printed nonsense. *August Strindberg*

An avenue to glory ever open for those ingenious men who are deprived of honors or of wealth. *Isaac D. Israeli*

LITERATURE (GREAT)

Simply language charged with meaning to the utmost possible degree. *Ezra Pound*

LITIGANT

A person about to give up his skin for the hope of retaining his bones. *Ambrose Bierce*

LITIGATION

A machine which you go into as a pig and come out of as a sausage. *Ambrose Bierce*

LIVING

An experience which makes one unwilling to die.

To live is to function. That is all there is in living. *Oliver Wendell Holmes, Jr.*

LOAFER

The man who is usually busy keeping some one else from working. *Elbert Hubbard (The Roycroft Dictionary)*

A person who believes the world owes him a living and wants the government to collect it for him.

LOCAL GOVERNMENT

The first line of defense thrown up by the community against our common enemies—poverty, sickness, ignorance, isolation and maladjustment. *Winifred Holtby*

The life-blood of liberty. *John Stuart Mill*

LOGIC

The art of convincing us of some truth. *Jean de La Bruyère*

An instrument used for bolstering a prejudice. *Elbert Hubbard*

The soul of wit, not of wisdom; that's why wit is funny. *Lincoln Steffens*

The anatomy of thought. *John Locke*

Neither a science nor an art, but a dodge. *Benjamin Jowett*

LONDON

In London, that great sea, whose ebb and flow
At once is deaf and loud, and on the shore
Vomits its wrecks, and still howls on for more.
Yet in its depth what treasures.

Percy Bysshe Shelley

This London City, with all its houses, palaces, steam-
engines, cathedrals, and huge immeasurable traffic and
tumult, what is it but a Thought, but millions of
Thoughts made into One—a huge immeasurable Spirit
of a Thought, embodied in brick, in iron, smoke, dust,
Palaces, Parliaments, Hackney Coaches, Katherine Docks,
and the rest of it Not a brick was made but some
man had to think of the making of that brick. *Thomas
Carlyle*

A mighty mass of brick, and smoke, and shipping,
Dirty and dusty, but as wide as eye
Could reach, with here and there a sail just skipping
In sight, then lost amidst the forestry
Of masts; a wilderness of steeples peeping
On tiptoe through their sea-coal canopy;
A huge, dun cupola, like a foolscap crown
On a fool's head—and there is London Town.
                                                   Lord Byron

A nation, not a city. *Benjamin Disraeli*

LONELINESS
A feeling you experience when you are without money
among relatives.

LONGEVITY
One of the more dubious rewards of virtue. *Ngaio Marsh*
Barring hanging and accidents, is largely a matter of hered-
ity. *Howard W. Haggard*

LONGFELLOW, HENRY W.
Longfellow for rich color, graceful forms and incidents—
all that makes life beautiful and love refined. *Walt
Whitman*

LONGITUDE
The direction in which a man's clothes run when he is
young. They run more to latitude as he gets older.

LOS ANGELES
Forty suburbs in search of a city.

LOSER
One who "is always in the wrong." *Spanish Proverb*

LOVE
Love! the surviving gift of Heaven,
The choicest sweet of paradise,
In life's else bitter cup distilled.
                         Thomas Campbell
The delightful interval between meeting a beautiful girl

and discovering that she looks like a haddock. *John Barrymore*

The need to escape from oneself. *Pierre Charles Baudelaire*

A fire. But whether it is going to warm your heart or burn down your house, you can never tell.

The great asker. *D. H. Lawrence*

Love is the most terrible, and also the most generous, of the passions; it is the only one which includes in its dreams the happiness of someone else. *Alphonse Karr*

A tie that binds; matrimony straps them together.

Love is the river of life in this world. Think not that ye know it who stand at the little tinkling rill, the first small fountain. Not until you have gone through the rocky gorges, and not lost the stream; not until you have gone through the meadow, and the stream has widened and deepened until fleets could ride on its bosom; not until beyond the meadow you have come to the unfathomable ocean, and poured your treasures into its depths—not until then can you know what love is. *Henry Ward Beecher*

The hardest lesson in Christianity; but, for that reason, it should be most our care to learn it. *William Penn*

Love is a sickness full of woes, all remedies refusing. *Samuel Daniel*

The wisdom of the fool and the folly of the wise. *Samuel Johnson*

Love in France is a comedy; in England a tragedy; in Italy an opera seria; and in Germany a melodrama. *Marguerite Blessington*

An ocean of emotions, entirely surrounded by expenses. *Lord Dewar*

Like the measles—all the worse when it comes late in life. *Douglas Jerrold*

Something "like the measles; we all have to go through it." *Jerome K. Jerome*

Only one of many passions . . . and it has no great influence on the sum of life. *Samuel Johnson*

An intoxication of the nervous system.

The more subtle form of self-interest. *Holbrook Jackson*

A wonderful thing and highly desirable in marriage. *Rupert Hughes*

A talkative passion. *Thomas Wilson*

Like war: easy to begin but very hard to stop. *H. L. Mencken*

The delusion that one woman differs from another. *H. L. Mencken*

The triumph of imagination over intelligence. *H. L. Mencken*

Woman's eternal spring and man's eternal fall. *Helen Rowland*

A gross exaggeration of the difference between one person and everybody else. *George Bernard Shaw*

The history of a woman's life; it is an episode in man's. *Mme. de Staël*

Like the measles; we can have it but once, and the later in life we have it, the tougher it goes with us. *Josh Billings*

Not altogether a delirium, yet it has many points in common therewith. *Thomas Carlyle*

A man's insane desire to become a woman's meal-ticket. *Gideon Wurdz*

Love is precisely to the moral nature what the sun is to the earth. *Honoré de Balzac*

Love withers under constraint: its very essence is liberty: it is compatible neither with obedience, jealousy, nor fear: it is there most pure, perfect, and unlimited where its votaries live in confidence, equality, and unreserve. *Percy Bysshe Shelley*

A conflict between reflexes and reflections. *Magnus Hirschfeld*

A grave mental disease. *Plato*

The fulfilling of the law. *Rom. 13:10*

Spiritual fire. *Emanuel Swedenborg*

The dawn of marriage, and marriage is the sunset of love.

Love makes all hard hearts gentle. *Proverb*

LOVE AT FIRST SIGHT
The world's greatest time-saver.

LOVE OF HUMANITY
A feeling "instigated by violent dislike of the next-door neighbor." *Alfred North Whitehead*

LOVE SONG
Just a caress set to music. *Sigmund Romberg*

LOVER
A man who tries to be more amiable than it is possible for him to be. *Nicholas Chamfort*

A person without reason.

LOVERS
Unconscious comedians. *Elbert Hubbard (The Roycroft Dictionary)*

LOVING WIFE

One who will do anything for her husband except stop criticizing and trying to improve him. *J. B. Priestley*

LUCK

The thing you have more of the harder you work. *Adapted from Stephen Leacock*

When a man marries a girl who will help cook the meals.

Luck means the hardships and privations which you have not hesitated to endure; the long nights you have devoted to work. Luck means the appointments you have never failed to keep; the trains you have never failed to catch. *Max O'Rell*

What enables one to pass as a wise man.

To own a farm and have your roosters lay eggs.

LUCK (GOOD)

A lazy man's estimate of a worker's success.

LUNATIC

One who "thinks all other men are crazy." *Publius Syrus*

LUNCHEON CLUB

A group of people who meet periodically to eat their way to a solution of the world's problems.

LUNT, ALFRED

An actor who "has his head in the clouds and his feet in the box office." *Noel Coward*

LUST

An appetite of the mind by which temporal goods are preferred to eternal goods. *St. Augustine*

LUST (OF POWER)

The most flagrant of all the passions. *Tacitus*

LUXURY

The eventual ruin of every nation.

Anything a husband needs.

A necessity if you can make the down payment on it.

LYING

Terminological inexactitude. *Winston Churchill*

• M •

MACHINE

A tool is but the extension of a man's hand, and a machine is but a complex tool. He that invents a machine augments the power of a man and the well-being of mankind. *Henry Ward Beecher*

MAIDS

Women who "want nothing but husbands, and when they have them, they want everything." *Shakespeare*

MAINE
> Here's to the state of Maine, the land of the bluest skies, the greenest earth, the richest air, the strongest, and what is best, the sturdiest men, the fairest, and what is best of all, the truest women under the sun. *Thomas B. Reed*

MAJOR GENERAL
> The army officer who has his men behind him before the battle and ahead of him during it.

MAJORITY
> Having all the fools on one side.
>
> One on God's side is a majority. *Wendell Phillips*
>
> One with the law is a majority. *Calvin Coolidge*

MALICE
> A blind mule kicking by guess. *Josh Billings*

MAMMALS
> The lower animals. Man does the classifying.

MAN
> The aloof animal, has deteriorated in everything except mentality. and in that he has done no more than barely hold his own for the past two thousand years. *James Thurber*
>
> A pliable animal, a being who gets accustomed to everything! *Feodor Dostoyevsky*
>
> A reasoning rather than a reasonable animal. *Robert B. Hamilton*
>
> An imitative creature, and whoever is foremost leads the herd. *J. C. F. Schiller*
>
> The merriest species of the creation; all above or below him are serious. *Joseph Addison*
>
> The only animal that plays poker. *Don Herold*
>
> A piece of the universe made alive. *Ralph Waldo Emerson*
>
> A god in ruins. *Ralph Waldo Emerson*
>
> A political animal by nature; he is a scientist by chance or choice; he is a moralist because he is a man. *Hans J. Morgenthau*
>
> A gaming animal. *Charles Lamb*
>
> The artificer of his own happiness. *Henry David Thoreau*
>
> A tool-using animal. *Thomas Carlyle*
>
> Man! Thou pendulum betwixt a smile and tear. *Lord Byron*
>
> The miracle of miracles, the great inscrutable mystery of God. *Thomas Carlyle*
>
> A volume, if you know how to read him. *William Ellery Channing*
>
> The bad child of the universe. *James Oppenheim*
>
> The measure of all things. *Protagoras*

A social animal. *Seneca*

A civic animal. *Aristotle*

A man is the whole encyclopedia of facts. The creation of a thousand forests is in one acorn, and Egypt, Greece, Rome, Gaul, Britain, America, lie folded already in the first man. *Ralph Waldo Emerson*

> Man is of soul and body, formed for deeds
> Of high resolve; on fancy's boldest wing.
> *Percy Bysshe Shelley*

No man is an island entire of itself; every man is part of the main. If a clod be washed away by the sea, Europe is the less, as well as if a promontory were, as well as if a manor of thy friends or thine own were. Any man's death diminishes me because I am involved in mankind, and therefore never send to know for whom the bell tolls; it tolls for thee. *John Donne*

The only animal that laughs and has a state legislature.

The only animal that can remain on friendly terms with the victims he intends to eat until he eats them. *Samuel Butler*

An irrational animal.

Nature's sole mistake. *W. S. Gilbert*

The only animal that deliberately undertakes, while reshaping his outer world, to reshape himself also. *William E. Hocking*

A tiny dot of light amidst the blind fury of the elements; the human mind is the dot of light that is proof against any tempest, and it is the only light we have. *Jules Henri Poincaré*

Has only two primal passions, to get and to beget. *Sir William Osler*

An animal and until his immediate material and economic needs are satisfied, he cannot develop further. *W. H. Auden*

Something that feels happy, plays the piano, likes going for a walk, and, in fact, wants to do a whole lot of things that are really unnecessary. *Karel Chapek*

An animal that makes bargains; no other animal does this —no dog exchanges bones with another. *Adam Smith*

A creature who lives not upon bread alone, but principally by catchwords. *Robert Louis Stevenson*

A human being—that is enough for me; he can't be any worse. *Mark Twain*

A rational animal who always loses his temper when he is called upon to act in accordance with the dictates of reason. *Oscar Wilde*

One who "like an angry ape plays such fantastic tricks before high heaven as make the angels weep. . . ." *Shakespeare*

The only being that can properly be called idle. *Samuel Johnson*

The weakest reed in nature; but he is a thinking reed. *Blaise Pascal*

Merely dust, and woman settles him.

The only animal with brains enough to find a cure for the diseases caused by his own folly.

Like a car. Just so much mileage in him, whether he runs it out in forty years or eighty. *Cedar Falls Record*

An omnibus in which his ancestors ride. *Oliver Wendell Holmes*

A prisoner who has no right to open the door of his prison and run away. . . . A man should wait, and not take his own life until God summons him. *Socrates*

Consists of body, mind, and imagination. His body is faulty, his mind untrustworthy, but his imagination has made him remarkable. In some centuries, his imagination has made life on this planet an intense practice of all the lovelier energies. *John Masefield*

A worm. He comes alone, wiggles a bit, then some chicken gets him.

Half dust, half deity, *Lord Byron*

A sinful, an ignorant, a miserable being. *Joseph Addison*

A make-believe animal—he is never so truly himself as when he is acting a part. *William Hazlitt*

The only animal that can be a fool. *Holbrook Jackson*

The only animal that laughs and weeps; for he is the only animal that is struck with the difference between what things are, and what they ought to be. *William Hazlitt*

A toad-eating animal. The admiration of power in others is as common to men as the love of it in himself; the one makes him a tyrant, the other a slave. *William Hazlitt*

A noble animal, splendid in ashes, and pompous in the grave, solemnizing nativities and deaths with equal lustre, not omitting ceremonies of bravery, in the infamy of his nature. *Sir Thomas Browne*

Biologically considered . . . is the most formidable of all beasts of prey, and, indeed, the only one that preys systematically on its own species. *William James*

An intellectual animal, and therefore an everlasting contradiction to himself. His senses center in himself, his ideas reach to the ends of the universe; so that he is torn in pieces between the two, without a possibility of its ever being otherwise. *William Hazlitt*

We are all monsters, that is, a composition of man and beast. *Sir Thomas Browne*

A dog's ideal of what God should be. *Holbrook Jackson*

The greatest animal in creation, the animal who cooks. *Douglas Jerrold*

Men are but gilded loam or painted clay. *Shakespeare*

Two-legged animal without feathers. *Plato*

One who loses his illusions first, his teeth second, and his follies last. *Helen Rowland*

One who snatches the first kiss, pleads for the second, demands the third, takes the fourth, accepts the fifth—and endures all the rest. *Helen Rowland*

MAN-ABOUT-TOWN

One who is on speaking terms with the headwaiter. *Gideon Wurdz*

MAN (BAD)

In earlier days, a man who went around with niches in his gun. Today, a man who goes around with dents in his automobile fenders.

MAN (FORGOTTEN)

He is the clean, quiet, virtuous, domestic citizen, who pays his debts and his taxes and is never heard of out of his little circle. *William Graham Sumner*

MAN (GREAT)

Meteor designed to burn so that the earth may be lighted. *Napoleon Bonaparte*

MAN (HONEST)

One who is always one step behind opportunity.
The noblest work of God. *Alexander Pope*

MAN (LEARNED)

An idler who kills time by study. *George Bernard Shaw*

MAN (OLD)

A man who is old enough to remember when a job was the first thing you went steady with.

MAN (POLITE)

One who listens with interest to things he knows all about.

when they are told him by a person who knows nothing about them. *Philippe de Morny*

MAN (RICH)
A poor man with money.

MAN (SELF-MADE)
A person who is smart enough to employ college professors to train his children.

One who "worships his creator." *William Cowper*

A man who has a lot of alterations made if he marries.

A person who quit the job too early.

MAN (SUCCESSFUL)
One who can earn more than his wife can spend.

MAN (WHITE COLLAR)
One who carries his lunch in a briefcase instead of a pail.

MAN OF FEW WORDS
One who takes three hours to tell you he is a man of few words. Synonym: Husband.

MAN OF GREAT COMMON SENSE AND GOOD TASTE
A man without originality or moral courage. *George Bernard Shaw*

MANAGEMENT
The marshaling of manpower, resources, and strategy in getting a job done. *Marshall E. Dimock*

MANKIND
A tribe of animals, living by habits and thinking in symbols; and it can never be anything else. *George Santayana*

An incorrigible race. Give them but bugbears and idols—it is all that they ask. *William Hazlitt*

Earthen jugs with spirits in them. *Nathaniel Hawthorne*

MANNERS
The happy ways of doing things . . . if they are superficial, so are the dewdrops, which give such a depth to the morning meadow. *Ralph Waldo Emerson*

The technique of expressing consideration for the feelings of others. *Alice Duer Miller*

The final and perfect flower of noble character. *William Winter*

An expression of the relation of status—a symbolic pantomine of mastery on the one hand and of subservience on the other. *Thorstein Veblen*

MANNERS (GOOD)
The art of making those people easy with whom we converse. Whoever makes the fewest persons uneasy, is the best bred in the company. *Jonathan Swift*

Good manners are made up of petty sacrifices. *Ralph Waldo Emerson*

MANUSCRIPT

Something submitted in haste and returned at leisure. *Oliver Herford*

MARCH

The only windy month, except that in Washington, D. C., it's windy all year long.

> March brings breezes loud and shrill
> Stirs the dancing daffodil.
> *Sara Coleridge*

The month that "comes in like a lion and goes out like a lamb." *English Proverb*

MARKET

A place set apart where men may deceive each other. *Anacharsis*

MARRIAGE

A souvenir of love. *Helen Rowland*

The miracle that transforms a kiss from a pleasure into a duty, and a life from a luxury into a necessity. *Helen Rowland*

Resembles a pair of shears, so joined that they cannot be separated; often moving in opposite directions, yet always punishing anyone who comes between them. *Sydney Smith*

A ceremony in which rings are put on the finger of the lady and through the nose of the gentleman. *Herbert Spencer*

One long conversation, chequered by disputes. *Robert Louis Stevenson*

The only adventure open to the cowardly. *Voltaire*

The one subject on which all women agree and all men disagree. *Oscar Wilde*

A process by which the food market gets the money the clothes shop formerly got.

A condition when there are many pains—in contrast to celibacy which has no pleasures. *Adapted from Samuel Johnson*

A desire on the part of a man to pay a woman's board and room.

A period when you make progress if you break even.

The most dangerous year in married life is the first; then come the second, third, fourth, fifth, etc.

A condition that most women aspire to and most men submit to.

An association of two persons for the purpose of making one the beneficiary.

An institution in which a man constantly faces the music, beginning with, "Here Comes the Bride."

The only life sentence that may be suspended by bad behavior.

An institution. Marriage is love. Love is blind. Therefore marriage is an institution for the blind.

A meal where the soup is better than the dessert. *Austin O'Malley*

A mutual partnership if both parties know when to be mute.

The only known example of the happy meeting of the immovable object and the irresistible force. *Ogden Nash*

A legalized way of suppressing free speech.

Marriage is a very sea of calls and claims, which have but little to do with love. *Henrik Ibsen*

The end of man. *Honoré de Balzac*

The most difficult intelligence test.

A union between two people in which the man pays the dues.

A matter of give and take, but so far I haven't been able to find anybody who'll take what I have to give. *Cass Daley*

That relation between man and woman in which the independence is equal, the dependence mutual, and the obligation reciprocal. *L. K. Anspacher*

A ghastly public confession of a strictly private intention. *Ian Hay*

The way a man finds out what kind of husband his wife would have preferred.

An honorable agreement among men as to their conduct toward women, and it was devised by women. *Don Herold*

The alliance of two people, one of whom never remembers birthdays and the other never forgets them. *Ogden Nash*

A great institution, and no family should be without it. *Channing Pollock*

The greatest educational institution on earth. *Channing Pollock*

A mistake of youth—which we should all make. *Don Herold*

The great puzzle of our day. It is our Sphinx-riddle. Solve it, or be torn to bits, is the decree. *D. H. Lawrence*

That which makes two one, is a lifelong struggle to discover which is that one.

A noose, which, fastened about the neck, runs the closer and fits more uneasy by our struggling to get loose: it is a Gordian knot which none can untie, and, being twisted with our thread of life, nothing but the scythe of death can sever it. *Miguel de Cervantes*

The earliest fruit of civilization and it will be the latest. I think a man and a woman should choose each other for life, for the simple reason that a long life with all its accidents is barely long enough for a man and a woman to understand each other; and in this case to understand is to love. The man who understands one woman is qualified to understand pretty well anything. *William Butler Yeats*

A desperate thing. The frogs in Aesop were extreme wise; they had a great mind to some water, but they would not leap into the well, because they could not get out again. *John Selden*

Has . . . no natural relation to love. Marriage belongs to society; it is a social contract. *Samuel Taylor Coleridge*

To have and to hold from this day forward, for better, for worse, for richer, for poorer, in sickness, and in health, to love and to cherish, till death do us part. *Book of Common Prayer*

A book of which the first chapter is written in poetry and the remaining chapters in prose. *Beverley Nichols*

An end of many short follies—being one long stupidity. *F. W. Nietzsche*

Marriage is the best state for man in general; and every man is a worse man, in proportion as he is unfit for the married state. *Samuel Johnson*

A romance in which the hero dies in the first chapter.

A lottery in which men stake their liberty, and women their happiness. *Mme. de Rieux*

MARRIAGE (HAPPY)
When both parties get better mates than they deserve.
When they are both in love with him.

MARRIAGE (SECOND)
The triumph of hope over experience. *Samuel Johnson*

MARRIAGE (SUCCESSFUL)
When you "treat all disasters as incidents and none of the incidents as disasters." *Harold Nicolson*

One in which two persons learn to get along happily without the things they have no right to expect anyway.

MARRIED LIFE
Just one undarned thing after another.

MARRY
To get a binocular view of life. *Dean William R. Inge*

MARTYR
Any man who is willing to sacrifice others for his "cause." *Elbert Hubbard (The Roycroft Dictionary)*

MARTYRDOM
The only way in which a man can become famous without ability. *George Bernard Shaw*

The blood of the martyrs is the seed of the church. *Adapted from Tertullian*

MARYLAND
Rivers, Heaven and earth never agreed better to frame a place for man's habitation, were it fully manured and inhabited by industrious people. *John Smith (1624)*

MASSES
Those who "do most of the dying for both sides of every conflict." *Joseph Rosenfarb*

MATHEMATICS
A tentative agreement that two and two make four. *Elbert Hubbard (The Roycroft Dictionary)*

The tool specially suited for dealing with abstract concepts of any kind and there is no limit to its power in this field. *P. A. M. Dirac*

The most exact science, and its conclusions are capable of absolute proof. But this is so only because mathematics does not attempt to draw absolute conclusions. All mathematical truths are relative, conditional. *Charles P. Steinmetz*

Mathematics deals exclusively with the relations of concepts to each other without consideration of their relation to experience. *Albert Einstein*

MATHEMATICS (SCIENCE OF PURE)
In its modern developments, may claim to be the most original creation of the human spirit. *Alfred North Whitehead*

MATRIMONY
A bargain, and somebody has to get the worst of the bargain. *Helen Rowland*

The high sea for which no compass has yet been invented. *Heinrich Heine*

MAUSOLEUM
The final and funniest folly of the rich. *Ambrose Bierce*

MAXIMS

The condensed good sense of nations. *Sir James Mackintosh*

Statements of conduct which "are to the intellect what laws are to actions; they do not enlighten, but they guide and direct; and although themselves blind, are protective. They are like the clue in the labyrinth, or the compass in the night. *Joseph Joubert*

Little sermons. *Gelett Burgess*

MAY

The month of gladness. *John Lydgate*

It means youth, love, song, and all that is beautiful in life. *Henry Wadsworth Longfellow*

MAYONNAISE

One of the sauces which serve the French in place of a state religion. *Ambrose Bierce*

ME

The most interesting and important person in the world to each of us.

MEANNESS

To be deaf and not tell your barber.

MECHANICAL TAXPAYER

The dream and hope of every politician.

MEDICINE

The only profession that labors incessantly to destroy the reason for its own existence. *James Bryce*

Consists of amusing the patient while nature cures the disease. *Voltaire*

MEDIEVAL

One college freshman's definition, "Partly evil or bad."

The only place where all the show is stripped off the human drama. You . . . see the human race stark naked—not only physically, but mentally and morally as well. *Martin H. Fischer*

MEDITATION

The nurse of thought, and thought the food of meditation. *C. Simmons*

MEEK

The people who are going to inherit the earth and pay off the mortgage we leave them.

MEEKNESS

Meekness is not a contemplative virtue, it is maintaining peace and patience in the midst of pelting provocation. *Henry Ward Beecher*

MELANCHOLY
> The pleasure of being sad. *Victor Hugo*

MELODY
> The very essence of music. *W. A. Mozart*

MEMOIRS
> Published memoirs indicate the end of a man's activity, and that he acknowledges the end. *George Meredith*

MEMORIES
> What God gave us so that we might have roses in December. *J. M. Barrie*

MEMORY
> A nursery where children grown old play with broken toys.
> The warder of the brain. *Shakespeare*
> The receptacle and sheath of all knowledge. *Cicero*
> The thing one forgets with.
> The diary that we all carry about with us. *Oscar Wilde*
> Memory is the art of attention. *Samuel Johnson*
> The treasury and guardian of all things. *Cicero*
> The library of the mind. *Francis Fauvel-Gourand*

MEN (CLEVER)
> The tools with which bad men work. *William Hazlitt*

MEN (OLD)
> Walking hospitals. *Horace*
> Men who give good advice, to console themselves for being no longer in a position to give bad examples. *La Rochefoucauld*

MERCY
> Nobility's true badge. *Shakespeare*
> Mercy imitates God, and disappoints Satan. *St. John Chrysostom*

MERRY
> Merry is only a mask of sad. *Ralph Waldo Emerson*

METAPHYSICIAN
> A man who goes into a dark cellar at midnight without a light looking for a black cat that is not there. *Ascribed to Baron Bowen*
> Men with no taste for exact facts, but only a desire to transcend and forget them as quickly as possible. *H. L. Mencken*

METAPHYSICS
> The finding of bad reasons for what we believe upon instinct; but to find these reasons is no less an instinct. *F. H. Bradley*

The art of bewildering oneself methodically. *Jules Michelet*

METHOD
The mother of mercy. *Thomas Fuller*

METEOROLOGY
The science of being up in the air and all at sea. *E. L. Hawke*

MICROPHONE
The most tell-tale instrument in the world. *Cesar Saerchinger*

MIDNIGHT
The dusky hour friendliest to sleep and silence. *John Milton*

MILITARISM
A fever for conquest, with peace for a shield, using music and brass buttons to dazzle and divert the populace. *Elbert Hubbard (The Roycroft Dictionary)*

MILTON, JOHN
> That mighty orb of song,
> The divine Milton.
> *William Wordsworth*

The stair or high tableland to let down the English genius from the summits of Shakespeare. *Ralph Waldo Emerson*

MIND
> My mind to me a kingdom is;
> Such present joys therein I find,
> That it excels all other bliss
> That earth affords or grows by kind.
> *Edward Dyer*

MINORITY
Minorities are the stars of the firmament; majorities, the darkness in which they float. *Martin H. Fischer*

Those who are always wrong—at the beginning.

MINORITY (RULE)
A baby in the house. *Milwaukee Journal*

MINUTE
A space of time in which we dream of something that will never come true, or form a resolution that another minute effaces. *Elbert Hubbard (The Roycroft Dictionary)*

MIRACLE
A woman who won't talk. *Gideon Wurdz*

Every cubic inch of space is a miracle. *Walt Whitman*

MIRACLE (CHRISTIAN)
A Christian minister living on a small salary fixed ten years ago, and keeping out of debt.

MIRROR

The thing in a hat store that makes you look foolish.

MIRTH

God's medicine. *Henry Ward Beecher*

Mirthfulness is in the mind and you cannot get it out. It is just as good in its place as conscience or veneration. *Henry Ward Beecher*

Mirth is like a flash of lightning, that breaks through a gloom of clouds, and glitters for a moment; cheerfulness keeps up a kind of daylight in the mind, and fills it with a steady and perpetual serenity. *Joseph Addison*

MISER

A person who has a spendthrift son.

One who "grows rich by seeming poor; an extravagant man grows poor by seeming rich." *Shakespeare*

Misers are very good people; they amass wealth for those who wish their death. *Stanislaus Leszczynski (King of Poland)*

MISFORTUNE

"Something which is not displeasing to us" when our best friends experience it. *La Rochefoucauld*

An experience that is funny when it happens to someone else.

MISFORTUNES

Things "one can endure, they come from the outside; but to suffer for one's faults—ah! there is the sting of life." *Oscar Wilde*

Experiences, like twins, that never come singly. *Josh Billings*

MISTAKE

Evidence that somebody has tried to accomplish something. *John E. Babcock*

MIXED GREENS

An assortment of fives, tens, and twenties.

MOB

A society of bodies, voluntarily bereaving themselves of reason, and traversing its work. The mob is man, voluntarily descending to the nature of this beast. Its fit hour of activity is night; its actions are insane, like its whole constitution. *Ralph Waldo Emerson*

A group of persons with heads but no brains. *Thomas Fuller*

Man voluntarily descending to the nature of the beast. *Ralph Waldo Emerson*

The mob is the mother of tyrants. *Dionysius of Halicarnassus*

MOCKERY

The weapon of those who have no other. *Hubert Pierlot*

Mere poverty of wit. *Jean de La Bruyère*

MODERATION

A fatal thing; nothing succeeds like excess. *Oscar Wilde*

A virtue wherewith to curb the ambition of the great, and to console men of moderate means for their small fortunes and insignificant merits. *La Rochefoucauld*

The inseparable companion of wisdom, but with it genius has not even a nodding acquaintance. *Charles Caleb Colton*

The keynote of lasting enjoyment. *Hosea Ballou*

MODERN ART

A form of painting which convinces you that things can't be as bad as they are painted. *Adapted from M. Walthall Jackson*

MODERN GIRL

A woman who loves a man for all he is worth.

MODERN KITCHEN

Where the pot calls the kettle chartreuse.

MODERN POET

A person who doesn't look like a poet and doesn't write like one either.

MODESTY

The gentle art of enhancing your charm by pretending not to be aware of it. *Oliver Herford*

A quality which is admired in a man "if people ever hear of him." *Edgar W. Howe*

A shining light; it prepares the mind to receive knowledge, and the heart for truth. *François Guizot*

The conscience of the body. *Honoré de Balzac*

To stand in awe of one's self.

The only sure bait when you angle for praise. *Lord Chesterfield*

A kind of fear of falling into disrepute. *Aristotle*

MONARCHY

A merchantman which sails well, but will sometime strike on a rock and go to the bottom; a republic is a raft which will never sink, but then your feet are always in water. *Fisher Ames*

MONDAY

The holiday of preachers. *Thomas Fuller*

MONEY

> A guarantee that we may have what we want in the future. Though we need nothing at the moment, it insures the possibility of satisfying a new desire when it arises. *Aristotle*
>
> What you'd get on beautifully without if only other people weren't so crazy about it. *Margaret Case Harriman*
>
> The thing that made the mare go in contrast to credit that makes automobiles go.
>
> The root of many of the most important family trees.

> > Money. Honey, my little sonny,
> > And a rich man's joke is always funny.
> > > *T. E. Brown*

> The only substance which can keep a cold world from nicknaming a citizen "Hey, you!" *Wilson Mizner*
>
> A good servant but a bad master.
>
> A commodity that won't buy everything, but it keeps you from being more than moderately sullen and depressed.
>
> The fruit of evil as often as the root of it. *Henry Fielding*
>
> The price of life. *Ralph Waldo Emerson*
>
> Money enables a man to get along without education, and education enables him to get along without money. *Marcelene Cox*
>
> Money is the most indispensable tool we have, and while it is a duty to remember that money can be a power for evil, we must not fail to lay equal emphasis on money's power for good. *Presbyterian Life*
>
> A new form of slavery, and distinguishable from the old simply by the fact that it is impersonal—that there is no human relation between master and slave. *Leo Tolstoy*
>
> Money is life to us wretched mortals. *Hesiod* (700 B.C.)

> > Like Heav'n, it bears the orphans' cries,
> > And wipes the tears from widows' eyes.
> > > *John Gay*

MONEY-GETTER

> One who never gets tired.

MONEYGRABBER

> One who grabs more money than you can grab.

MONEYLENDER

> A person who "serves you in the present tense; he lends you in the conditional mood; keeps you in the subjunctive; and ruins you in the future." *Joseph Addison*

MONKEY

An organized sarcasm upon the human race. *Henry Ward Beecher*

Animals "who very sensibly refrain from speech, lest they should be set to earn their livings." *Kenneth Grahame*

MONOLOGUE

A conversation between a woman who spent the summer in Europe and one who didn't.

A conversation between a man and his wife.

Some persons' idea of brilliant conversation.

MONOPOLIST

A person who manages to get an elbow on each arm of his theatre chair.

MONOTONY

The awful reward of the careful. *A. G. Buckham*

MONROE, JAMES

A man whose soul might be turned wrong side outwards, without discovering a blemish to the world. *Thomas Jefferson*

MORAL

What is moral is what you feel good after and what is immoral is what you feel bad after. *Ernest Hemingway*

MORAL INDIGNATION

Jealousy with a halo. *H. G. Wells*

MORALITY

The theory that every human act must be either right or wrong, and that 99 per cent of them are wrong. *H. L. Mencken*

Simply the attitude we adopt towards people whom we personally dislike. *Oscar Wilde*

The custom of one's country and the current feeling of one's peers. Cannibalism is moral in a cannibal country. *Samuel Butler*

A private and costly luxury. *Henry Adams*

An exaltation of personal taste, and taste is something usually sacrificed by leaders of mankind in the mass. *Thomas Beer*

The vestibule of religion. *E. H. Chapin*

The best of all devices for leading mankind by the nose. *F. W. Nietzsche*

MORGUE

Death's shop-window. *Elbert Hubbard* (*The Roycroft Dictionary*)

MORON

> A thing that grieves not and that never hopes,
> Stolid and stunned, a brother to the ox.
>
> > *Edwin Markham*

MORTGAGE (HOUSE WITH MORTGAGE)

A house with a guilty conscience.

MOSES

> A pillar of light on the threshold of history. *Asher Ginzberg*

MOSQUITO

One of the few indestructible objects in the world.

MOTH

An economical insect that eats nothing but holes.

MOTHER

> The holiest thing alive. *Samuel Coleridge*
>
> Motherhood is the keystone of the arch of matrimonial happiness. *Thomas Jefferson (Letter to Martha Jefferson Randolph, 1791).*
>
> The name for God in the lips and hearts of little children. *William Makepeace Thackeray*

MOTHERHOOD

> Neither a duty nor a privilege, but simply the way that humanity can satisfy its desire for physical immortality and triumph over its fear of death. *Rebecca West*
>
> The keystone of the arch of matrimonial happiness. *Thomas Jefferson*

MOTTO (SUCCESSFUL WIFE'S)

If at first you don't succeed, cry, cry again.

MOUNTAINS

> The beginning and the end of all natural scenery. *John Ruskin*
>
> Mountains interposed make enemies of nations. *William Cowper*

MOURNING

> An experience that "teaches charity and wisdom." *St. John Chrysostom*

MOUSE

> An animal that "never trusts his life to one hole only." *Plautus*

MOUTH

> A snare of death. *The Didache*
>
> In man, the gateway to the soul; in women the outlet of the heart. *Ambrose Bierce*

MOVIE

The only art which cannot, or will not, use intelligence. *Frank Craven*

MOZART, W. A.

I tell you before God and on my word as an honest man that your son is the greatest composer I have ever heard of. *Joseph Haydn to Leopold Mozart*

MUCKRAKER

One who sits on the fence and defames American enterprise as it marches by. *Elbert Hubbard (The Roycroft Dictionary)*

MUGWUMP

A person educated beyond his intellect. *Horace Porter*

A fellow with his mug on one side of the fence and his wump on the other. *Harold W. Dodds*

MULTITUDE

A group which "is always in the wrong." *Wentworth Dillon*

MURDER

Always a mistake; one should never do anything that one cannot talk about after dinner. *Oscar Wilde*

MURDERER

Whosoever hateth his brother is a murderer. *I John 3:15*

One who is presumed to be innocent until he is proved insane.

MUSEUM

A sort of mournful place where you conclude "that nothing could ever have been young." *Walter Pater*

MUSIC

The only language in which you cannot say a mean or sarcastic thing. *John Erskine*

Something that is essentially useless, as life is. *George Santayana*

Another lady that talks charmingly and says nothing. *Austin O'Malley*

The only cheap and unpunished rapture on earth. *Adapted from Sydney Smith*

The art of the prophets, the only art that can calm the agitations of the soul; it is one of the most magnificent and delightful presents God has given us. *Martin Luther*

The speech of angels. *Thomas Carlyle*

Music expresses that which cannot be said and on which it it impossible to be silent. *Victor Hugo*

The universal language of mankind. *Henry Wadsworth Longfellow*

Music is a higher revelation than philosophy. *Ludwig von Beethoven*

MUSIC (CLASSICAL)
The kind that we keep hoping will turn into a tune. *Frank M. Hubbard*

MUSICIAN
A person who makes a living by just playing around.
The dullest of the artists, the actor alone excepted. *Paul Rosenfeld*

MYSELF
That favorite subject. *James Boswell*

MYSTERY
How the Joneses do it on that salary.
Another name for our ignorance; if we were omniscient, all would be perfectly plain. *Tryon Edwards*

MYSTICISM
The very pinnacle of individualism. *Bernard Smith*
Sentimentality taken seriously. *Leo Stein*

• N •

NAGGING
The constant repetition of an unpleasant truth.

NAIVE
A word describing anyone who thinks you are interested when you ask how he is.

NAPLES
Naples sitteth by the sea, the keystone of an arch of azure. *M. F. Tupper*

NARROW-MINDED
A common trait of those who disagree with us.

NATIONALISM
A silly cock crowing on its own dunghill. *Richard Arlington*
An infantile disease. It is the measles of mankind. *Albert Einstein*

NATIONALITY
The miracle of political independence.

NATURALNESS
Being natural is simply a pose. *Oscar Wilde*

NATURE
All Nature is but Art, unknown to thee;
All Chance, Direction, which thou canst not see.
Alexander Pope
Nature is a revelation of God; Art a revelation of man. *Henry Wadsworth Longfellow*

The art of God. *Sir Thomas Browne*

What I call God. *Robert Browning*

NECESSITY

The argument of those who have no good reasons.

The plea for every infringement of human freedom. It is the argument of tyrants; it is the creed of slaves. *William Pitt*

The mother of invention. *Jonathan Swift*

The spur of genius. *Honoré de Balzac*

NECKLACE (PEARL)

What "a woman never gets until her neck looks like a pickled peach." *Adapted from Hector Bolitho*

NET

The biggest word in the language of business. *Herbert Casson*

NEUTRALITY

An evidence of weakness. *Louis Kossuth*

NEUTRALS

Scoundrels in the eyes of the combatants. *Ernest Boyd*

NEVER

Never is a long day. *English Proverb*

Hardly ever.

NEVER AGAIN

A phrase meaning until the next time.

NEW ENGLAND

A geographical area where there is a "swaggering underemphasis." *Heywood Broun*

The New Englanders are a people of God, settled in those areas which were once the Devil's territories. *Cotton Mather*

New England is a finished place. Its destiny is that of Florence or Venice, not Milan, while the American empire careens onward toward its unpredicted end. . . . It is the first American section to be finished, to achieve stability in the conditions of its life. It is the first old civilization, the first permanent civilization in America. *Bernard De Voto*

NEW JERSEY

A state that lies behind the billboards. *Irvin S. Cobb*

NEWS

If a man bites a dog, that is news. *Ascribed to John Bogart*

Anything that concerns people, and interests them. *George Washburn*

NEWSPAPER

The ark of God for the safety of the people. *Pennsylvania Gazette* (1768)

Light for all. *Baltimore Sun motto*

An object used by tired men so they can't see a woman standing up in a bus.

A circulating library with high blood pressure. *Arthur Baer*

A manufacturing concern producing goods to sell at a profit, it is also a department store, and has some characteristics that suggest the variety show. *John Macy*

NEWSPAPER (COUNTRY)

Rests entirely upon the theory of the dignity of the human spirit. It is democracy embodied. It emphasizes the individual. *William Allen White*

NEWSPAPERS

The world's mirrors. *James Ellis*

NEW TESTAMENT

The very best book that ever was or ever will be known in the world. *Charles Dickens*

NEWTON, ISAAC

Nature and nature's laws lay hid in night:

God said, Let Newton be! and all was light.

Alexander Pope: Epitaph for Newton

NEW YORK

The nation's thyroid gland. *Christopher Morley*

Hideously ugly for the most part, one yet remembers it as a place of proud and passionate beauty; the place of everlasting hunger, it is also the place where men feel their lives will be gloriously fulfilled and their hunger fed. *Thomas Wolfe*

NEW YORK TIMES

The official leak of the State Department. *Attributed by Mort Sahl to a Friend*

NICKEL

What this country needs—a good five cent one.

A coin that is only one-twentieth of a dollar but which goes to church more often.

NICKNAME

The hardest stone that the Devil can throw at a man. *William Hazlitt*

NIGHT

Night is the time to weep,

To wet with unseen tears

> Those graves of memory where sleep
> The joys of other years.
> > *James Montgomery*
> Night is the time for rest;
> How sweet, when labors close,
> To gather round an aching breast
> The curtain of repose,
> Stretch the tired limbs, and lay the head
> Down on our own delightful bed.
> > *James Montgomery*
> Night is a stealthy, evil Raven,
> Wrapt to the eyes in his black wings.
> > *Thomas B. Aldrich*

Night is the mother of thoughts. *John Florio*
Night is the half of life, and the better half. *J. W. von Goethe*

NOBLE

Noble blood is an accident of fortune; noble actions are the chief marks of greatness. *Carlo Goldoni*

Nobility is nothing but ancient riches. *Proverb*

NOBLE (DEED)

A step towards heaven. *J. G. Holland*

NOISE

One of the essential parts of civilization.

NOON

Dinner time for some folks, but just twelve o'clock for me. *American Negro Saying*

NOSE

A feature which never changes; unless, of course, it's poked once too often into other people's business.

That part of the body which shines, snubs, snoops, and sneezes.

NOSE (SHARP)

A nose that indicates curiosity in contrast to a flat nose which indicates too much curiosity.

NOSTALGIA

To have a deep longing for a place you wouldn't move back to.

NOTHING

Something that has density without weight, like a barber's breath. *Elbert Hubbard (The Roycroft Dictionary)*

NOVEL

Novels are to love as fairy tales to dreams. *Samuel Taylor Coleridge*

A species of composition bearing the same relation to literature that the panorama bears to art. *Ambrose Bierce*

NOVELISTS

Novelists are generally great liars. *St. John Baptist de La Salle*

The business of the novelist is not to relate great events, but to make small ones interesting. *Arthur Schopenhauer*

NOVEMBER

The gloomy month of November, when the people of England hang and drown themselves. *Joseph Addison*

No warmth, no cheerfulness, no healthful ease—
No comfortable feel in any member—
No shade, no shine, no butterflies, no bees,
No fruits, no flowers, no leaves, no birds,
No-vember!

Thomas Hood

NOVOCAIN

A drug that enables the dentist to get you out of his office before you know what's happened.

• O •

OAK (TREE)

An acorn that held its ground!

The perfect image of the manly character. *William Shenstone*

OATH

Oaths are but words, and words but wind. *Samuel Butler*

OATS

A grain, which in England is generally given to horses, but in Scotland supports the people. *Samuel Johnson*

OBEDIENCE

Not to ask the reason why. *Shakespeare*

In a way the mother of all virtues. *St. Augustine*

Obedience . . . makes slaves of men, and, of the human frame, a mechanized automaton. *Percy Bysshe Shelley*

Obedience is not servitude of man to man, but submission to the will of God, who governs through the medium of men. *Pope Leo XIII* (1885)

OBESITY

A condition where you crease a little in the middle to signify you are bowing. *Adapted from Negley Farson*

Obesity is a mental state, a disease brought on by boredom and disappointment. *Cyril Connolly*

OBLIVION

The flower that grows best on graves. *George Sand*

Fame is a vapor; popularity an accident; riches take wings; the only certainty is oblivion. *Horace Greeley*

OBOE

An ill wood-wind that nobody blows good.

OBSOLESCENCE

A factor which says that the new thing I bring you is worth more than the unused value of the old thing. *Charles F. Kettering*

OBSTINACY

The result of the will forcing itself into the place of the intellect. *Arthur Schopenhauer*

OBVIOUS

That which is never seen until someone expresses it simply. *Kahlil Gibran*

OCEAN

A body of water occupying about two-thirds of a world made for man—who has no gills. *Ambrose Bierce*

A body of water which "with its white teeth bites the edges of the continents into new shapes, as a child bites the edges of a biscuit." *Oliver Herford*

OCTOBER

Fresh October brings the pheasant
Then to gather nuts is pleasant.
Sara Coleridge

October is nature's funeral month. Nature glories in death more than in life. The month of departure is more beautiful than the month of coming—October than May. Every green thing loves to die in bright colors. *Henry Ward Beecher*

OFFICE (PUBLIC)

A public trust. *Democratic National Program* (1892)

The last refuge of the incompetent. *Boies Penrose*

OIL

A lubricant except in international affairs.

OKLAHOMA

Where the wind comes sweeping down the plain. *Oscar Hammerstein II*

OLD

You are old when you can pass an apple orchard and not remember the stomach-aches of your youth.

OLD-TIMER

Someone who remembers when people who wore jeans worked.

A person who can remember when a babysitter was called mother.

ONCE

Enough. *Ambrose Bierce*

Once is never. *German Proverb*

ONION

A food that builds you up physically and drags you down socially.

ON THE ROCKS

A phrase meaning a person is either bankrupt or working in jail. The difference is inconsequential.

OOMPH

The noise a fat man makes when he bends over to tie his shoelaces in a telephone booth. *Ann Sheridan*

OPEN MIND

The mind of a man who has the will power to get rid of his present prejudices and take on a new set of prejudices. Sometimes, a case of merely rearranging one's prejudices.

OPENING NIGHT

The night before the play is ready to open. *George Jean Nathan*

OPERA

A magic scene contrived to please the eyes and the ears at the expense of the understanding. *Lord Chesterfield*

OPERATION (MINOR)

One that was performed on the other fellow. *Russell Pettis Askue*

OPINION

A minimum of facts combined with prejudice and emotion.

OPINION (POPULAR)

The greatest lie in the world. *Thomas Carlyle*

When ignorance rules wisdom.

OPINION (PUBLIC)

The greatest force for good, when it happens to be on that side.

What people think other people are thinking.

OPINION SURVEYS

People who don't matter reporting on opinions that do matter. *John A. Lincoln*

OPPONENT
A person to whom you ascribe "motives meaner than your own." *Adapted from J. M. Barrie*

OPPORTUNITY
A favorable occasion for grasping a disappointment. *Ambrose Bierce*
Opportunity merely knocks—temptation kicks the door in!
Something which "has hair in front but is bald behind." *Phaedrus*
A tide in the affairs of men, which, taken at the flood, leads on to fortune. *Shakespeare*

OPTIMISM
The noble temptation to see too much in everything. *G. K. Chesterton*
A kind of heart stimulant—the digitalis of failure. *Elbert Hubbard*
The madness of maintaining that everything is right when it is wrong. *Voltaire*
The instinct to lie. *Elbert Hubbard (The Roycroft Dictionary)*
Fatty degeneration of intelligence. *Elbert Hubbard (The Roycroft Dictionary)*
The content of small men in high places. *F. Scott Fitzgerald*
The determination to see more in something than is there.

OPTIMIST
One who earns $100 a week and buys $200 suits on credit. A pessimist is the one he buys from. *Detroit Free Press*
A person who can always see the bright side of the other fellow's misfortune. *Richmond News-Leader*
A person who looks forward to enjoying the scenery on a detour.
A person who believes that after he pays his taxes he can live on top of the world and put away a nice nest egg of savings.
A husband who double parks while his wife runs into a store for just a minute.
A boy who whistles on his way to school.
A man who looks for lodgings with a trombone under one arm and a saxophone under the other.
A person who, instead of feeling sorry he cannot pay his bills, is glad he is not one of his creditors.
A statistician who says one American in five knows how to drive a car.

A man who thinks the time will come when there will be no more definitions of an optimist.

A person who drops a quarter in the church collection plate and expects a five-dollar sermon.

A person who thinks that when his shoes wear out he will be back on his feet.

A man who does not care what happens, so long as it doesn't happen to him. *Elbert Hubbard* (*The Roycroft Dictionary*)

A lady who starts putting on her shoes when the after dinner speaker says, "Now, in conclusion."

A man who believes the thinning out of his hair is only a temporary matter.

One who proclaims that we live in the best of all possible worlds, and the pessimist fears this is true. *James Branch Cabell*

The sort of man who marries his sister's best friend. *H. L. Mencken*

A fellow who believes a housefly is looking for a way to get out. *George Jean Nathan*

A man who marries his secretary—thinking he'll continue to dictate to her.

A fellow who believes that whatever happens, no matter how bad, is for the best. The pessimist is the fellow to whom it happens.

One who sees an opportunity in every calamity; a pessimist sees a calamity in every opportunity.

One who thinks he knows what the world would be like if it went the way he wants. A pessimist knows what it will be like if it stays the way it is. *John A. Lincoln*

The golfer who said he made fifteen on the first hole, fourteen on the second, thirteen on the third, and then blew up.

One who looks in a cuckoo clock for eggs—or who takes a frying pan on a fishing trip.

One who says his glass is still half full; a pessimist declares that his glass is already half empty.

One who is satisfied with little here below and generally gets below that little.

A guy that has never had much experience. *Don Marquis*

A fellow who looks at the down payment. A pessimist looks at the last installment and the upkeep.

A person who doesn't know anything follows the down payment.

One who makes the best of it when he gets the worst of
it.

> It is not raining rain to me,
> It's raining daffodils;
> In every dimpled drop I see
> Wild flowers on distant hills.
> *Robert Loveman*

One who may be wrong, but who bears mistakes with fortitude.
One who tells you to cheer up when things are going his
way.
A man who thinks he can find some big strawberries in
the bottom of the box.

ORATOR
One who can make men see with their ears. *Arab Proverb*
A person with a flood of words and a drop of reason.
Adapted from Benjamin Franklin

ORATORY
The art of making deep noises from the chest sound like
important messages from the brain. *H. I. Phillips*
The art of making pleasant sounds, which cause the hearers to say "Yes, Yes" in sympathy with the performer,
without inquiring too closely exactly what he means.
Sam Tucker
The power to talk people out of their sober and natural
opinions. *Paul Chatfield*

ORDER
Order is Heaven's first law. *Alexander Pope*

ORIGINALITY
Undetected plagiarism. *Dean William R. Inge*
Nothing but judicious imitation. *Voltaire*
A pair of fresh eyes. *Thomas W. Higginson*
Imitation which is undetected.
Does not consist in saying what no one has ever said before,
but in saying exactly what you think yourself. *James
Fitzjames Stephen*

ORTHODOXY
My doxy; heterodoxy is another man's doxy. *Ascribed to
William Warburton*

OSTENTATION
The signal flag of hypocrisy. *E. H. Chapin*

OSTEOPATH
One who argues that all human ills are caused by the pres-

sure of hard bone upon soft tissue. The proof of his theory is to be found in the heads of those who believe it. *H. L. Mencken*

OVERDRESSED

A condition of being all wrapped up in yourself.

OVERWORKED

To be busy continually. Example: A can opener in a modern home.

OWL

The gravest bird. *Proverb*

OX

The slave of the poor. *Aristotle*

OXFORD UNIVERSITY

A sanctuary in which exploded systems and obsolete prejudices find shelter and protection after they have been hunted out of very corner of the world. *Adam Smith*

A university "so beautiful one expects the people to sing instead of speaking." *William Butler Yeats*

OYSTER

The gravest fish. *Proverb*

A fish built like a nut.

● P ●

PAIN

The thing some people give us.

Pain is in itself an evil, and, indeed without exception, the only evil. *Jeremy Bentham*

Pain is life—the sharper, the more evidence of life. *Charles Lamb*

PANIC

The stampede of our self-possession. *Rivarol*

A manifestation of terror and it would seem that it makes its appearance when a pseudo-social environment is created which removes the customary inhibition to cowardice. *Everett Dean Martin*

Mass hysteria. And hysteria, contrary to the popular impression, is most often seen in persons superficially both cool and collected. *Philip Wylie*

PARADOX

Climbing to the top and remaining on the level.

An efficiency expert out of a job.

PARAGRAPHING

One of the lower forms of cunning, like a way with women. *Harry V. Wade*

PARENT

A person whose only chance to sleep is when the baby isn't looking.

One who strikes a child only for the purpose of discipline or in self-defense.

One who lives "the life of a gambler." *Sydney Smith*

PARENTS

Persons who were invented to make children happy by giving them something to ignore. *Ogden Nash*

PARIS

A city of gaieties and pleasures where four-fifths of the inhabitants die of grief. *Nicholas Chamfort*

A city where great ideas perish, done to death by a witticism. *Honoré de Balzac*

Here nobody ever sleeps; it is not the way. *Thomas Gray*

Paris is nothing but an immense hospitality. *Victor Hugo*

A city where "life passes like a dream." *French Proverb*

PARKING SPACE

The space in which another car is parked.

Where you leave the car to have those little dents made in the fenders.

An unoccupied space about seven feet wide and fifteen feet long next to the curb—on the other side of the street.

Where you leave your car to have the wheel base shortened and the rear end caved in.

An unfillable opening in an unending line of automobiles near an unapproachable fire plug.

The area that disappears while you are making a U-turn.

PARKS

The lungs of a city. *Adapted from William Pitt*

PARLIAMENT

Nothing less than a big meeting of more or less idle people. *Walter Bagehot*

PARSLEY

The food you push aside to see what is under it. *Paul H. Gilbert*

PARTISANSHIP

A partisanship is what someone else does. When I do it, it is taking a stand. *Roger L. Shinn*

PARTY

All parties without exception, when they seek for power, are varieties of absolutism. *P. J. Proudhon*

The historical organ by means of which a class becomes class conscious. *Leon Trotsky*

PASSION

Like a mountain stream; it admits of no impediment; it cannot go backward; it must go forward. *C. N. Bovee*

Universal humanity. Without it religion, history, romance, and art would be useless. *Honoré de Balzac*

The mob of the man, that commits a riot upon his reason. *William Penn*

PASSIONS

The only orators that always persuade; they are, as it were, a natural art, the rules of which are infallible; and the simplest man with passion is more persuasive than the most eloquent without it. *La Rochefoucauld*

Good servants but bad masters. *Sir Roger L'Estrange*

PAST

The best prophet of the future. *John Sherman*

The sepulcher of our dead emotions. *C. N. Bovee*

The dark backward and abysm of time. *Shakespeare*

The misty black and bottomless pit of time. *Thomas Duffett*

The wrecks of days departed. *Percy Bysshe Shelley*

PASTOR

One employed by the wicked to prove to them by his example that virtue doesn't pay. *H. L. Mencken*

PATIENCE

A most necessary qualification for business; many a man would rather you heard his story than granted his request. *Earl of Chesterfield*

A necessary ingredient of genius. *Benjamin Disraeli*

A minor form of despair, disguised as a virtue. *Ambrose Bierce*

A case of not knowing what to do.

The inability to make a decision.

The art of hoping. *Marquis de Vanvenargues*

The best remedy for every trouble. *Plautus*

The key of content. *Mohammed*

An infinite capacity for being bored.

Patience is passion tamed. *Lyman Abbott*

Faith waiting for a nibble. *Josh Billings*

A gift that God gives only to those He loves. *Moroccan Proverb*

PATIENT

One who "must combat the disease along with the physician." *Hippocrates*

PATRIOTISM

The finest flower of western civilization as well as the refuge of the scoundrel. *Leonard Woolf*

It means looking out for yourself by looking out for your country. *Calvin Coolidge*

A variety of hallucination which, if it seized a bacteriologist in his laboratory, would cause him to report the streptococcus pyrogenes to be as large as a Newfoundland dog, as intelligent as Socrates, as beautiful as Mont Blanc, and as respectable as a Yale professor. *H. L. Mencken*

The last refuge of a scoundrel. *Samuel Johnson*

Your conviction that this country is superior to all other countries because you were born in it. *George Bernard Shaw*

The willingness to kill and be killed for trivial reasons. *Bertrand Russell*

Often an arbitrary veneration of real estate above principles. *George Jean Nathan*

A sense of partisan solidarity in respect of prestige. *Thorstein Veblen*

Patriotism is not, as sentimentalists like to assert, one of the profoundest of man's noblest instincts. *I. A. R. Wylie*

A kind of religion; it is the egg from which wars are hatched. *Guy de Maupassant*

PATRON

A wretch who supports with insolence, and is paid with flattery. *Samuel Johnson*

PAWNBROKER

A mercenary man to whom money is the one redeeming quality. *Gideon Wurdz*

PEACE

In international affairs, a period of cheating between two periods of fighting. *Ambrose Bierce*

The short interval when nations toil to pay the costs of past and future wars.

A monotonous interval between fights. *Elbert Hubbard (The Roycroft Dictionary)*

A moribund condition, caused by a surplus of civilians, which war seeks to remedy. *Cyril Connolly*

Order based on law. There is no other imaginable definition. Any other conception of peace is sheer Utopia. *Emery Reves*

When the wolf "shall dwell with the lamb." *Isaiah 11:6*

A beautiful concept of the human mind. It is as unique as it is beautiful. *John Hodgdon Bradley, Jr.*

Not a passive, but an active virtue. *Monsignor Fulton J. Sheen*

A mere skeleton in armor.

Peace is the soft and holy shadow that virtue casts. *Josh Billings*

Peace is our final good. *St. Augustine*

Peace, dear nurse of arts, plenties and joyful births. *Shakespeare*

PEACEMAKER

The children of God. *Matt.* 5:9

How beautiful upon the mountains are the feet of him that bringeth good tidings, that publisheth peace. *Isaiah* 52:7

PEDAGOGUE

One who casts false pearls before real swine.

PEDANTRY

Stupidity that read a book.

The unseasonable ostentation of learning. *Samuel Johnson*

PEDESTRIAN

A person who crosses the street and hopes to get the brakes. *Harvard Lampoon*

One who has bought a used car.

An individual who has found that it doesn't pay to go straight, especially across a street.

A car owner with a wife and a grown-up son or daughter.

A person who needs automobile insurance. *Judge*

One who is safe only when he is riding. *Helena Independent*

PEDESTRIANS

Consist of two groups—the quick and the dead.

PEERAGE

The best thing in fiction the English have ever done. *Oscar Wilde*

PEN

Pen and ink is wit's plow. *John Clarke*

The tongue of the mind. *Miguel de Cervantes*

A formidable weapon, but a man can kill himself with it a great deal more easily than he can other people. *George Denison Prentice*

That mighty instrument of little men. *Lord Byron*

PEN (FOUNTAIN)

An instrument that writes, and having writ, blots.

PENGUIN

A bird that flies backwards because he doesn't care to see where he's going, but wants to see where he's been. *Fred Allen*

PENNSYLVANIA

The cradle of toleration and freedom of religion. *Thomas Jefferson*

A state that "has produced but two great men: Benjamin Franklin of Massachusetts, and Albert Gallatin of Switzerland." *J. J. Ingalls* (1885)

PENNY

A coin that "will hide the biggest star in the universe if you hold it close enough to your eye." *Samuel Grafton*

PEOPLE

The greatest undeveloped resources of any nation.

That part of the state which does not know what it wants. *G. W. F. Hegel*

The people are a many-headed beast. *Alexander Pope*

The people are the only sure reliance for the preservation of our liberty. *Thomas Jefferson*

PERFECT PERSONS

Bachelors' wives and old maids' children. *Nicholas Chamfort*

PERFECTION

What American women expect to find in their husbands . . . but English women only hope to find in their butlers. *W. Somerset Maugham*

An alarm clock that doesn't ring.

PERFECTIONIST

One who takes infinite pains and gives them to others.

PERFUME

Any smell that is used to drown a worse one. *Elbert Hubbard*

PERPETUAL HOLIDAY

A good working definition of hell. *George Bernard Shaw*

PERSIA

The country that gave us the dismal system of mathematics.

PERSISTENCY

A fool's best asset.

PERSON (IGNORANT)

One who doesn't know anything about what you know, and knows things you don't know anything about.

PERSONALITY
> Personality is to a man what perfume is to a flower. *C. M. Schwab*

PESSIMISM
> Only the name that men of weak nerves give to wisdom. *Bernard De Voto*

PESSIMIST
> One who, when he has the choice of two evils, chooses both.
> A man who thinks everybody as nasty as himself, and hates them for it. *George Bernard Shaw*
> One who forgets to laugh whereas an optimist laughs to forget.
> One who makes difficulties of his opportunities; an optimist is one who makes opportunities of his difficulties. *Vice Admiral Mansell, R. N.*
> A fellow who lives with an optimist.
> One who sizes himself up and gets angry.
> A person who expects nothing on a silver platter except tarnish.
> An optimist who endeavored to practice what he preached.
> A person who never develops eyestrain looking on the bright side of things.
> An individual who is happy when he is wrong.
> A person who suffers seasickness during the entire journey of life.
> One who feels sad when he feels good for fear he will feel worse when he feels better.
> A person who blows out the candle to see how dark it is.

PETS (DOMESTIC)
> Animals that grow dull because "they miss the stimulus of fleas." *Sir Francis Galton*

PHILANTHROPIST
> A rich (and usually bald) old gentleman who has trained himself to grin while his conscience is picking his pocket. *Ambrose Bierce*

PHILANTHROPY
> The refuge of people who wish to annoy their fellow-creatures. *Oscar Wilde*
> The process of giving it back to the people from whom you got it.

PHILISTINE
> A term of contempt applied by prigs to the rest of their species. *Sir Leslie Stephen*

What we call bores, dullards, children of darkness. *Thomas Carlyle*

A low practical man, who pays his debts, I hate him. *C. F. Brown (Artemus Ward)*

PHILOLOGY

The art of reading with profit—the capacity for absorbing facts without interpreting them falsely and without losing caution, patience, and subtlety in the effort to understand them. *F. W. Nietzsche*

PHILOSOPHER

A man who, instead of crying over spilt milk, consoles himself with the thought that it was four-fifths water anyway.

One who thinks in order to believe; one who formulates his prejudices and systematizes his ignorance. *Elbert Hubbard (The Roycroft Dictionary)*

A person who will not believe what he sees because he is too busy speculating about what he does not see. *La Bovier de Fontenello*

All are lunatics, but he who can analyze his delusion is called a philosopher. *Ambrose Bierce*

One who doubts. *Michel de Montaigne*

The pioneers of revolution. *Robert V. Harper*

The servants of posterity. *Francis Bacon*

One who desires to discern the truth. *Plato*

A fool who torments himself while he is alive, to be talked about after he is dead. *Jean Le Rond D'Alembert*

PHILOSOPHY

Common sense. If it isn't common sense, it isn't philosophy. *Edgar W. Howe*

When he who hears doesn't know what he who speaks means, and when he who speaks doesn't know what he himself means. *Voltaire*

A route of many roads leading from nowhere to nothing. *Ambrose Bierce*

The art of living. *Plutarch*

Something that enables the rich to say there is no disgrace in being poor. *Gideon Wurdz*

Any system of thought which enables one to be unhappy intelligently.

The attempt to make manifest the fundamental evidence as to the nature of things. *Alfred North Whitehead*

Unintelligible answers to insoluble problems. *Henry Adams*

The art of lying about the art of living. *D. G. Kin*

Can never be defined because it is the search for the indefinable. *Dagobert D. Runes*

Philosophy may teach us to bear with equanimity the misfortunes of our neighbors. *Oscar Wilde*

Nonsense. *Samuel Butler*

A filter turned upside down, where what goes in clear comes out muddy.

PHILOSOPHY (COMMUNIST)

The belief that if you keep the people in poverty, poverty will keep them in communism.

PHILOSOPHY (DOCTOR OF)

The kind of doctor who doesn't do you any good.

PHOTOGRAPHY

The latest form of art—instantaneous art for busy people, simplified art for people without artistic training, mechanical skill and genius for mass production turned to art. *M. F. Agha*

PHYSICIAN

Only a consoler of the mind. *Petronius Arbiter*

Only nature's assistant. *Galen*

> One who grants the husband's pray'rs
> Or gives relief to long-expecting heirs.
> > *Jonathan Swift*

A person who gets no pleasure out of the health of his friends. *Michel de Montaigne*

PIANO

A bourgeois instrument. (*London*) *Left Review*

PICCOLO

The smallest instrument a musician may play in public and still maintain his self-respect. *Emile Gauvreau*

PICKPOCKET

The optimist in a crowd.

A person who believes every crowd has a silver lining.

PICTURE

An intermediate something between a thought and a thing. *Samuel Taylor Coleridge*

A poem without words. *Horace*

Pictures are the books of the ignorant. *English Proverb*

A picture is a mute poem. *Latin Proverb*

PIONEER

Shall I tell you who he is, this key figure in the arch of our enterprise? That slender, dauntless, plodding, modest figure is the American pioneer. *Franklin K. Lane*

The first settler in the woods is generally a man who has outlived his credit or fortune in the cultivated parts. *Benjamin Rush*

PIONEER (WOMAN)

An old-fashioned woman who crossed the Western plains and the Rocky Mountains in a skirt, but has a granddaughter who puts on slacks to shop at the supermarket.

PIQUE

The spur the devil rides the noblest tempers with. *Sir George Savile*

PITY

Imagination or fiction of future calamity to ourselves, proceeding from the sense of another man's calamity. But when it lighteth on such as we think have not deserved the same, the compassion is greater because there then appeareth more probability that the same may happen to us; for the evil that happeneth to an innocent man may happen to every man. *Thomas Hobbes*

Often a perception of our own troubles through the woes of others; it is a clever anticipation of the misfortunes which may befall us. We help our neighbor to make sure of his assistance under similar circumstances; hence the kindness we do others is in truth an anticipated kindness we do ourselves. *La Rochefoucauld*

A scent sachet that serves to stop your nose. *Jules Romains*

More than any other feeling, is a "learned" emotion; a child will have it least of all. *Thomas Wolfe*

The feeling which rests the mind in the presence of whatsoever is grave and constant in human sufferings and unites it with the human sufferer. *James Joyce*

Pity makes the world soft to the weak and noble for the strong. *Edwin Arnold*

PLAGIARISM

Taking something from one man and making it worse. *George Moore*

The only 'ism' Hollywood believes in. *Dorothy Parker*

PLAGIARIST

One who helps to preserve what is best.

A gatherer and disposer of other men's stuff. *Henry Wotton*

Those who are "suspicious of being stolen from—as pickpockets are observed commonly to walk with their hands in their breeches' pockets." *Samuel Taylor Coleridge*

PLATITUDE

A truth we are tired of hearing. *Godfrey Nicholson*

PLATITUDES
> The Sundays of stupidity.

PLATO
> One who raised "all fundamental questions without answering them." *Alfred North Whitehead*

PLAYING BY NOTE
> To learn to play the piano by note instead of by ear. Twelve payments on the note and the piano is yours to learn to play.

PLEASURE
> Pleasure is the first good . . . It is the absence of pain in the body and of trouble in the soul. *Epicurus*
>
> Nature's test, her sign of approval. When we are happy we are always good, but when we are good we are not always happy. *Oscar Wilde*
>
> Pain past is pleasure. *Thomas Fuller*

PLEASURES (SIMPLE)
> The last refuge of the complex. *Oscar Wilde*

PLYMOUTH ROCK
> A doorstep into a world unknown, the cornerstone of a nation. *Henry Wadsworth Longfellow*
>
> The rock underlies all America: it only crops out here. *Wendell Phillips*

POE, EDGAR ALAN
> Poe is a kind of Hawthorne and delirium tremens. *Leslie Stephen*
>
> > There comes Poe with his raven
> > like Barnaby Rudge,
> > Three-fifths of him genius, and
> > two-fifths sheer fudge.
> >   *James Russell Lowell*

POET
> A person born with the instinct of poverty. *Elbert Hubbard* (*The Roycroft Dictionary*)
>
> > Poets are all who love, who feel great truths,
> > And tell them.
> >
> >   *Philip James Bailey*
>
> The most precious jewel of a nation. *Ludwig von Beethoven*
>
> Poets are prophets whose prophesying never comes true. *E. W. Howe*
>
> Those who "utter great and wise things which they do not themselves understand." *Plato*

Terribly sensitive people and one of the things they are most sensitive about is cash. *Robert Penn Warren*

POETRY

The language in which man explores his own amazement. *Christopher Fry*

A form of writing that "can never be concocted by any purely intellectual process. It has nothing to do with the intellect; it is, in fact, a violent and irreconcilable enemy to the intellect. Its purpose is not to establish facts, but to evade and deny them." *H. L. Mencken*

The rhythmical creation of beauty. Its sole arbiter is taste. *Edgar Allan Poe*

An art in which the artist by means of rhythm and great sincerity can convey to others the sentiment which he feels about life. *John Masefield*

Poetry is vocal painting, as painting is silent poetry. *Simonides*

That thirst, or aspiration . . . for something purer and lovelier, something more powerful, lofty and thrilling, than ordinary or real life affords. *William Ellery Channing*

The utterance of deep and heart-felt truth. The true poet is very near the oracle. *E. H. Chapin*

Something to make us better and wiser by continually revealing those types of beauty and truth which God has set in all men's souls. *James Russell Lowell*

"Poetry," said Emilia, "seems like talking on tiptoe." *George Meredith*

Truth dwelling in beauty. *Robert Gilfillan*

POISE

What the Dutchman said girls go out with.

The art of raising the eyebrows instead of the roof.

POLICE

Employees of the city who could arrange for us to have less crime news in the newspapers.

POLICE DEPARTMENT

A bureau in each city that has the most magnificent collection of clues in existence.

POLICEMAN (TRAFFIC)

A man who stays mad all the time.

POLICY

Leaving a few things unsaid. *Elbert Hubbard (The Roycroft Dictionary)*

POLITENESS

Fictitious benevolence. *Samuel Johnson*

One of those advantages which we never estimate rightly but by the inconvenience of its loss. *Samuel Johnson*

The flower of humanity. He who is not polite enough, is not human enough. *Joseph Joubert*

A desire to so contrive it, by word and manner, that others will be pleased with us and with themselves. *C. L. de Montesquieu*

A tacit agreement that people's miserable defects, whether moral or intellectual, shall on either side be ignored and not be made the subject of reproach. *Arthur Schopenhauer*

The most acceptable hypocrisy. *Ambrose Bierce*

One half good nature and the other half good lying. *Mary Wilson Little*

To cover your mouth when you yawn.

Politeness is an easy virtue, and has great purchasing power. *A. B. Alcott*

The chief sign of culture. *Baltasar Gracian*

POLITICAL DEBATE

An enthusiastic presentation of organized emotions.

POLITICAL ECONOMY

The dismal science. *Thomas Carlyle*

A field of knowledge that "has nothing to do with either politics or economy." *Stephen Leacock*

POLITICAL PARTY

A kind of conspiracy against the rest of the nation. *Lord Halifax*

The madness of many, for the gain of a few. *Alexander Pope*

POLITICAL PLUM

One result of careful grafting.

POLITICIAN

An animal who can sit on a fence and yet keep both ears to the ground. *Oscar Wilde*

A person with whose politics you won't agree; if you agree with him he is a statesman. *David Lloyd George*

Like quicksilver; if you try to put your fingers on him, you will find nothing under it. *Austin O'Malley*

A person without capacity who has the ability to turn out resounding phrases.

A person who realizes you can't fool all the people all of the time, but is satisfied with a majority.

One who "thinks of the next election; a statesman, of the next generation." *James Freeman Clarke*

A person who doesn't stand on his record, but jumps on the other fellow's.

A person who keeps the people loyal to him by keeping them angry at some one else.

A person who keeps his ear to the ground and his hand in the taxpayer's pocket.

A person who is never as bad as he is painted by his enemies or as good as he is whitewashed by his friends.

The only person who asks you to help him and then sends you the bill for it.

A person who keeps his ear to the ground and limits his vision.

A person who has prejudices enough to suit the needs of all his constituents.

One who hopes to swap his bunk for a berth.

One who talks himself "red, white, and blue in the face." *Clare Booth Luce*

One that would circumvent God. *Shakespeare*

A person who shakes your hand before election and your confidence afterwards.

A person who can take a popular economic fallacy and make a major plank for his party.

An individual who makes life a bed of ruses.

Any citizen with influence enough to get his old mother a job as charwoman in the City Hall. *H. L. Mencken*

Persons who "neither love nor hate. Interest, not sentiment, directs them." *Earl of Chesterfield*

POLITICIAN (CHEAP)
There isn't any such thing.

POLITICIAN (CONSERVATIVE)
One in office. *Columbia Record*

POLITICIAN (HONEST)
One who when he is bought will stay bought. *Simon Cameron*

POLITICS
An activity in which the choice is constantly between two evils. *John Morley*

Perhaps the only profession for which no preparation is thought necessary. *Robert Louis Stevenson*

The art of being wise for others—policy of being wise for self. *Edward Bulwer-Lytton*

An occupation where the blind lead the blind.

Consists in serving God in such a manner as not to offend the devil. *Thomas Fuller*

The science of how who gets what, when and why. *Sidney Hillman*

A strife of interests masquerading as a contest of principles. The conduct of public affairs for private advantage. *Ambrose Bierce*

The art of looking for trouble, finding it everywhere, diagnosing it wrongly, and applying unsuitable remedies. *Sir Ernest Benn*

A perpetual emergency. *Ralph Roeder*

At its worst is a device for keeping people—and peoples—apart. At its best it is a means of bringing them together. *Cesar Saerchinger*

Nothing but good manners in public. *Lincoln Steffens*

The science of exigencies. *Theodore Parker*

Practical politics consists in ignoring facts. *Henry Adams*

Politics is but the common pulsebeat, of which revolution is the fever-spasm. *Wendell Phillips*

I believe that politics is a science. It's a scientific approach to handling human beings. *James A. Farley*

Nothing but corruptions. *Jonathan Swift*

POLITICS (POWER)
The diplomatic name for the law of the jungle. *Ely Culbertson*

POLITICS (PRACTICAL)
Consists in ignoring facts. *Henry Brooks Adams*

POLLING PLACE
A place where you stand in line for a chance to decide who will spend your money.

PONTIUS PILATE
The first great censor and Jesus Christ the first great victim of censorship. *Ben Lindsay*

POOL (CAR)
Four men and a sucker.

POOR
The one class in the community that thinks more about money than the rich. *Oscar Wilde*

A condition that "necessitates the cultivation of the virtues." *Jerome K. Jerome*

Those who expect "no change for the worse." *Demetrius*

POOR PEOPLE
The only consistent altruists; they sell all that they have and give to the rich. *Holbrook Jackson*

POOR RELATION
The most irrelevant thing in nature. *Charles Lamb*

POPULAR SONG
A song which fortunately is not popular very long.

POPULAR SONG WRITING
Generally an occupation for illiterates.

POPULARITY
A crime from the moment it is sought; it is only a virtue where men have it whether they will or no. *Lord Halifax*

The capacity for listening sympathetically when men boast of their wives and women complain of their husbands. *H. L. Mencken*

It is glory's small change. *Victor Hugo*

The triumph of the commonplace. *Elbert Hubbard (The Roycroft Dictionary)*

POSITIVE
Being mistaken at the top of one's voice. *Ambrose Bierce*

POSTERITY
What an author writes for after publishers reject him.

POSTPONEMENT
The father of failure. *Elbert Hubbard (The Roycroft Dictionary)*

POVERTY
An anomaly to rich people. It is very difficult to make out why people who want dinner do not ring the bell. *Walter Bagehot*

A great enemy to human happiness; it certainly destroys liberty, and it makes some virtues impracticable, and others extremely difficult. *Samuel Johnson*

No disgrace to a man, but it is confoundedly inconvenient. *Sydney Smith*

A condition caused by trying to keep up with the Joneses.

The wicked man's temper, the good man's perdition, the proud man's curse, the melancholy man's halter. *Edward Bulwer-Lytton*

The parent of revolution and crime. *Aristotle*

The lack of ability, in any given set of circumstances, to get whatever is necessary for comfortable living. *Edward H. Faulkner*

The step-mother of genius. *Josh Billings*

Poverty is not merely deprivation; it means shame, degradation. *Henry George*

It is life near the bone, where it is sweetest. *Henry David Thoreau*

Poverty is a teacher of all the arts. *Plautus*

Poverty is a pain, but no disgrace. *James Kelly*

POWER

Power is always right, weakness always wrong. Power is always insolent and despotic. *Noah Webster*

Power is an emotionally charged word. When we possess it we call it *influence,* but when it is held by someone else we are content to use the ugly word. Yet there is nothing wrong with power; it takes power to get things done. Power is the application of intelligence to force. A river may be a terrific force, but it develops power only when directed through a turbine. *Arthur F. Corey*

Power is a relative thing, and no nation, or group of nations, can become relatively stronger without making other nations relatively weaker. If each nation had sought to excel in the arts, in learning or well-being, its success would not have meant failure for the others. But with each nation . . . aiming at an increase in power, we have entered an era of perpetual warfare . . . burdensome and fruitless. *Glenn E. Hoover*

Power is poison. Its effect on Presidents has been always tragic, chiefly as an almost insane excitement at first, and a worse reaction afterwards; but also because no mind is so well balanced as to bear the strain of seizing unlimited force without habit or knowledge of it; and finding it disputed with him by hungry packs of wolves and hounds whose lives depend on snatching the carrion. *Henry Brooks Adams*

Political power is merely the organized power of one class to oppress another. *Karl Marx and Friedrich Engels*

A great nation which bans fireworks and produces H-bombs.

PRAGUE

A city in which every stone has in it a bit of history.

PRAISE

Like ambergris: a little whiff of it, and by snatches, is very agreeable; but when a man holds a whole lump of it to your nose, it is a stink, and strikes you down. *Alexander Pope*

Only a debt, but flattery is present. *Samuel Johnson*

A debt we owe unto the virtue of others. *Sir Thomas Browne*

Incense to the wisest of us. *Benjamin Disraeli*

PRAISE (UNDESERVED)

Satire in disguise.

PRAYER

A wish turned God-ward. *Phillips Brooks.*

The very highest energy of which the mind is capable. *Samuel Taylor Coleridge*

Our deepest source of power and perfection. *Adapted from Alexis Carrel*

A power that "moves the Hand which moves the world." *John Aikman Wallace*

Prayer is releasing the energies of God. For prayer is asking God to do what we cannot do. *Charles Trumbull*

To ask not what we wish of God, but what God wishes of us.

Prayer is not only worship; it is also an invisible emanation of man's worshipping spirit—the most powerful form of energy that one can generate. *Alexis Carrel*

Prayer is a force as real as terrestrial gravity. *Alexis Carrel*

Prayer is a binding necessity in the lives of men and nations. *Alexis Carrel*

Prayer is not using God; it is more often to get us in a position where God can use us. I watched the deck hands on the great liner *United States,* as they docked that ship in New York Harbor. First, they threw out a rope to the men on the dock. Then inside the boat the great motors went to work and pulled on the great cable. But oddly enough, the pier wasn't pulled out to the ship; but the ship was pulled snugly up to the pier. Prayer is the rope that pulls God and man together. But it doesn't pull God down to us: it pulls us to Him. We must learn to say with Christ, the master of the art of praying, "Not my will; but thine be done." *Billy Graham*

Personal prayer, it seems to me, is one of the simple necessities of life, as basic to the individual as sunshine, food and water—and at times, of course, more so. By prayer I believe we mean an effort to get in touch with the Infinite. We know that our prayers are imperfect. Of course they are. We are imperfect human beings. A thousand experiences have convinced me beyond room of doubt that prayer multiplies the strength of the individual and brings within the scope of his capabilities almost any conceivable objective. *Dwight D. Eisenhower*

The voice of faith. *Richard H. Horne*

Conversation with God. *Clement of Alexandria*

Prayer is a cry of hope. *French Proverb*

PRAYER (LORD'S)

The sum total of religion and morals. *Duke of Wellington*

PREACHING

Preaching has been compared with the discharge of a pipette of eye medicine from a third story window into a crowded street in the hope that it will hit someone in the right place. *Harry Emerson Fosdick*

Constantly to remind mankind of what mankind are constantly forgetting . . . to fortify the feebleness of human resolutions. *Sydney Smith*

PREJUDICE

A vagrant opinion without visible means of support. *Ambrose Bierce*

The reason of fools. *Voltaire*

The child of ignorance. *William Hazlitt*

The twin of illiberality. *G. D. Prentice*

The dislike for all that is unlike. *I. Zangwill*

PREJUDICE (RACE)

A convenient device for the exploitation of one group by another. *Buel G. Gallagher*

PRESS

The foe of rhetoric, but the friend of reason. *Charles Caleb Colton*

Broadly speaking, is a servile instrument of wealthy men. Owned by them, in a degree ever more concentrated, dependent for its profits on wealthy advertisers whom it dare not offend, it pours forth a stream of tendentious news the main purpose of which is to maintain an atmosphere favorable to the maintenance of inequality. *Harold J. Laski*

A great industry and therein lies the logic of its behavior. *J. B. S. Hardman*

The press is the best instrument for enlightening the mind of man, and improving him as a rational, moral and social being. *Thomas Jefferson*

PRESS (FREEDOM)

Freedom of the press is the staff of life for any vital democracy. *Wendell L. Willkie*

PRIDE

Pride is a kind of pleasure produced by a man thinking too well of himself. *Baruch Spinoza*

Pride eradicates so many vices, letting none subsist but itself, that it seems as if it were a great gain to exchange vanity for pride. Pride can go without domestics, without fine clothes, can live in a house with two rooms, can eat potato, purslain, beans, lyed corn, can work on the soil, can travel afoot, can talk with poor men, or sit silent well contented in fine saloons. But vanity costs money, labor, horses, men, women, health and peace, and is still nothing at last, a long way leading nowhere. Only one drawback: proud people are intolerably selfish, and the vain are gentle and giving. *Ralph Waldo Emerson*

A human characteristic that "plays a greater part than kindness in our censure of a neighbor's faults. We criticize faults less to correct them than to prove we do not possess them." *La Rochefoucauld*

A sign of self-centered view, of a lack of objectivity. *Fritz Kunkel*

The basis of all true courage. There never was a hero without pride, never a coward who could boast of having it.

The master sin of the devil. *E. H. Chapin*

PRINTING PRESS
Either the greatest blessing or the greatest curse of modern times, one sometimes forgets which. *J. M. Barrie*

PRISON WARDEN
A person who makes his living by his pen.

PRIVATE ENTERPRISE
Really consists of harnessing men, money and ideas, and the genius of investors and technologists with the savings of the thousands. *Malcolm Muir*

PROBLEM
An opportunity in work clothes. *Henry J. Kaiser, Jr.*

PROCRASTINATION
The thief of time. *Edward Young*
A relief.
The art of keeping up with yesterday. *Don Marquis*

PRODUCTION
The goose that lays the golden egg. Payrolls make consumers. *George Humphrey*
The only answer to inflation. *Chester Bowles*

PRODUCTIVITY
That capacity of any organism, of an individual or even a group, to solve a problem in a new way so that new means appear and new forms arise, never existent before. *Fritz Kunkel*

PROFANITY
A way of escape for the man who runs out of ideas.
The effort of a feeble mind to express itself forcibly.

PROFESSOR
> One who talks in someone else's sleep. *W. H. Auden*
> A scholar who is paid to study the sleeping habits of students.
> A man whose job it is to tell students how to solve the problems of life which he himself has tried to avoid by becoming a professor.
> One who knows very little of a single subject and nothing about any others.
> A person who is too smart to be a university dean.

PROFESSIONAL ATHLETE
> An athlete who is paid by check in contrast to an amateur athlete who receives cash.

PROFESSIONAL CHARITY
> The milk of human blindness. *Tom Mason*

PROGRESS
> The victory of laughter over dogma. *Benjamin De Casseres*
> The result of a universal innate desire on the part of every organism to live beyond its income. *Samuel Butler*
> The onward stride of God. *Victor Hugo*
> Men have learned to travel farther and faster, though on errands not conspicuously improved. This, I believe, is called progress. *Willis Fisher*
> The activity of today and the assurance of tomorrow. *Ralph Waldo Emerson*
> The art of progress is to preserve order amid change, and to preserve change amid order. *Alfred North Whitehead*
> The fact of progress is written plain and large on the page of history; but progress is not a law of nature. The ground gained by one generation may be lost by the next. *H. A. L. Fisher*

PROGRESSIVE SCHOOL
> One where "none of the teachers ever raised his voice. None of the children ever lowered his, except through hoarseness." *Emily Hahn*

PROMISE
> The pitfalls of fools. *Baltasar Gracian*
> A promise is a kind of debt. *Moroccan Proverb*

PRONOUN
> A pronoun is used instead of a noun,
> as "James was tired and he sat down."
> *English Rhyme*

PROPAGANDA
> Expression of opinion or action by individuals or groups

deliberately designed to influence opinions or actions of other individuals or groups with reference to predetermined ends. *Institute for Propaganda Analysis*

PROPAGANDIST

A specialist in selling attitudes and opinions. *Hans Speier*

PROPERTY

Property is the fruit of labor; property is desirable; is a positive good in the world. *Abraham Lincoln*

The consequence and the basis of the state. *Mikhail Bakunin*

Theft. *Pierre J. Proudhon*

Property exists by grace of the law. It is not a fact, but a legal fiction. *Max Stirner*

A natural right. It is the safeguard of family life, the stimulus and the reward of work. *Letter of the French Roman Catholic Hierarchy* (1919)

PROPHET

The best guesser.

Those who were twice stoned—first in anger, then, after their death, with a handsome slab in the graveyard. *Christopher Morley*

PROSE

Prose is where all the lines but the last go on to the margin —poetry is where some of them fall short of it. *Jeremy Bentham*

PROSPERITY

A period when there are a lot of after-dinner speakers after dinners to speak after.

When it is easy to borrow money to buy things which you should be able to pay for out of your own income.

Tom Bright, once a candidate for governor of Maryland, defined prosperity as follows: "I want chicken legs raining down on this state like a snowstorm in Chicago; I want turkey gravy dripping out of your mouths like Niagara Falls; I want you to have porterhouse steaks for breakfast!"

The one thing that cannot be endured continually. *Adapted from J. W. von Goethe*

An instrument to be used; not a deity to be worshiped. *Calvin Coolidge*

A time when "our friends know us; in adversity we know our friends." *Churton Collins*

A period when we pay a little more for things we shouldn't buy anyway.

An economic condition the businessman creates and the politician takes credit for.

A period when all of us have more installment payments due than we can pay.

The surest breeder of insolence. *Mark Twain*

PROSPERITY (COOLIDGE)

The triumph of the perfected beltline—a device which stamped, pressed, cut, drilled, abraded, sawed, spun, polished, and lacquered a profusion of commodities, conveniences, luxuries, and variegated gadgets in ever increasing quantities at every decreasing cost. *Henry Morton Robinson*

PROVERB

A short sentence based on long experience. *Cervantes*

Much matter decocted into few words. *Thomas Fuller*

The philosophy of the common people. *James Howell*

The sanctuary of the intuitions. *James Russell Lowell*

One man's wit and all men's wisdom. *Ascribed to Lord John Russell*

PRUDENCE

An attitude that "keeps life safe, but does not often make it happy." *Samuel Johnson*

To know the useful art of acting dumb. *G. Crabbe*

PSYCHIATRIST

A mind sweeper.

A person who convinces you that your parents were failures because you turned out to be such a louse.

A person who asks you a lot of expensive questions that your wife asks for nothing.

PSYCHOLOGIST

A person who watches everyone else when a good looking girl comes into the room.

Has been slanderously defined as a man who tells you what everybody knows in language nobody can understand. *Joseph Jastrow*

PSYCHOTIC

One who believes that two and two make five whereas a neurotic knows that two and two are four, but it makes him nervous.

PUBLIC

The public is a fool. *Alexander Pope*

A ferocious beast: one must either chain it up or flee from it. *Voltaire*

Just a great baby. *John Ruskin*

PUBLIC INTEREST
Term used by every politician to support his ideas. *W. M. Kiplinger*

PUBLIC LIBRARY BUILDING
The tallest building in town—it has more stories than any other.

PUBLIC SPEAKER
A person whose mind sits down when he stands up.

PUBLISHERS
Publishers are demons, there's no doubt about it. *William James*

PUN
The lowest form of humor—when you don't think of it first. *Oscar Levant*

Among the smaller excellencies of lively conversation. *James Boswell*

A noble thing *per se* . . . it is as perfect as a sonnet; better. *Charles Lamb*

PUNCTUALITY
The thief of time. *Oscar Wilde*

A practice that makes the person who does it very lonely.

A cheap virtue. *Benjamin Franklin*

The art of guessing how late the other fellow is going to be.

PUNISHMENT
The justice that the guilty deal out to those who are caught. *Elbert Hubbard (The Roycroft Dictionary)*

Punishment brings wisdom; it is the healing art of wickedness. *Plato*

All punishment in itself is evil. *Jeremy Bentham*

PUNNING
A talent which no man affects to despise but he that is without it. *Jonathan Swift*

Like poetry, is something every person belittles and everyone attempts. *Louis Untermeyer*

PUPPETS
Little men without ego. *Gordon Craig*

Puppets are people, and the way they play depends on how they are made and the way their strings are pulled. Through them we may see ourselves in miniature. *Catherine Reighard*

PUPPY LOVE
Friendship with chocolate sodas.

Love that is dangerous because it may lead to a dog's life.

PURITAN
> A person who pours righteous indignation into the wrong things. *G. K. Chesterton*
>
> One who "prostrated himself in the dust before his Maker; but he set his foot on the neck of his king." *Thomas B. Macaulay*

PURPOSELESSNESS
> The fruitful mother of crime. *C. H. Parkhurst*

• Q •

QUARREL
> The interruption of an argument. *Adapted from G. K. Chesterton*
>
> The weapon of the weak. *Hebrew Proverb*

QUID PRO QUO
> No checkee; no shirtee. *Saying Credited to Chinese Laundrymen*

QUIET
> What home would be without children.

QUOTATION
> The act of repeating erroneously the words of another. *Ambrose Bierce*

• R •

RABBIT
> A little animal that grows the fur other animals get credit for when it's made into a lady's coat. *Cincinnati Enquirer*

RACE TRACK
> A place where the windows clean the people.

RADICAL
> A man with both feet firmly planted in the air. *Franklin D. Roosevelt*

RADICALISM
> The conservatism of tomorrow injected into the affairs of today. *Ambrose Bierce*

RADICALS
> Those who advance and consolidate a position for conservatives to occupy a little later.

RADIO
> A means of communication which is used to demonstrate that the country is full of people who can't sing.
>
> An advertisement with knobs.

An instrument of communication from which you learn that the whole country is full of bad sopranos.

The rape of the elements. *Jimmy Cannon*

The triumph of illiteracy. *John Dos Passos*

An instrument "of unique usefulness for bringing peoples together." *Albert Einstein*

RAGE

Mental imbecility. *Hosea Ballou*

Vulgar passion with vulgar ends. *Ernst von Feuchtersleben*

RAIN

Something that when you take your umbrella it doesn't.

RAINBOW

God's illumined promise. *Henry Wadsworth Longfellow*

RAISE

The increase in pay you get just before going into debt a little further.

RARE

The way a restaurant serves roast beef when you order it well done.

RARE (BOOK)

A book that comes back when you loan it to a friend.

RASHNESS

The characteristic of ardent youth, and prudence that of mellowed age. *Cicero*

RATIONALIZING

The self-exculpation which occurs when we feel ourselves, or our group, accused of misapprehension or error. *James Harvey Robinson*

REACTION

The consequence of a nation waking from its illusions. *Benjamin Disraeli*

REACTIONARY

A somnambulist walking backward. *Franklin D. Roosevelt*

READING

Thinking with someone else's head instead of one's own. *Arthur Schopenhauer*

An ingenious device for avoiding thought. *Sir Arthur Helps*

Reading is the work of the alert mind, is demanding, and under ideal conditions produces finally a sort of ecstasy. This gives the experience of reading a sublimity and power unequaled by any other form of communication. *E. B. White*

REAL ESTATE AGENT

The man who puts you on his wailing list.

REAL ESTATE BOOM

When no one buys property with the expectation of keeping it.

REALIST

A man who insists on making the same mistakes his grandfather made. *Benjamin Disraeli*

The man, who having weighed all the visible factors in a given situation and having found that the odds are against him, decides that fighting is useless. *Raoul de Sales*

REASON

The arithmetic of the emotions. *Elbert Hubbard (The Roycroft Dictionary)*

Seldom or never the ruler: it is the servant of instinct. *Clarence Day*

The mistress and queen of all things. *Cicero*

The wise man's guide; example, the fool's. *Welsh Proverb*

RECEIVER

A person appointed by the court to take what's left. *Robert Frost*

RECESSION

A period in which you tighten up your belt. In a depression you have no belt to tighten up—and when you have no pants to hold up, it's a panic.

The period when the right to strike seems less important than the right to work.

A time when it is more difficult to borrow money to buy things you don't need.

RECITAL (ORGAN)

Two persons discussing their operations.

RECKLESS DRIVING

A woman with a hammer and some nails working on a freshly painted, living room wall.

REDUCING MACHINE

A machine that costs so much you have to starve yourself to keep up the payments.

REFLECTION

This is to colors what echo is to sounds. *Joseph Joubert*

REFORM

A correction of abuses; a revolution is a transfer of power. *Edward Bulwer-Lytton*

REFORMER

A man who rides through a sewer in a glass-bottomed boat. *James J. Walker*

One who insists on his conscience being your guide.

One who makes his associates feel miserable about their pleasures.

REGRET
An appalling waste of energy; you can't build on it; it's only good for wallowing in. *Katherine Mansfield*

A woman's natural food—she thrives upon it. *Arthur Wing Pinero*

REJECTED PLAY MANUSCRIPT
A case of all work and no play.

RELATIVES
Simply a tedious pack of people who haven't got the remotest knowledge of how to live nor the smallest instinct about when to die. *Oscar Wilde*

The worst friends.

Persons we do not like because "we can't stand other people having the same fault as ourselves." *Oscar Wilde*

RELIGION
Religion should be the motor of life; the central heating plant of personality; the faith that gives joy to activity, hope to struggle, dignity to humility, zest to living. *William Lyon Phelps*

The opium of the people. *Karl Marx*

Nothing else but love to God and man. *William Penn*

Pure religion, and undefiled before God and the Father, is this. To visit the fatherless and widows in their affliction, and to keep himself unspotted from the world. *James 1:27*

The best armor in the world, but the worst cloak. *John Newton*

Religions are opposed to one another in their form, in the material details of the cult, and in the human interpretations of symbols. They all agree on the existence of God, on the virtues, and on moral rules. Purity, goodness, beauty, faith are venerated everywhere, and it is they which should rule. *Lecomte du Nouy*

A monumental chapter in the history of human egotism. *William James*

A sum of scruples which impede the free exercise of our faculties. *Salomon Reinach*

The indispensable basis of democracy. *John A. Ryan*

Religion may be defined, as objectively, "the sum of the ties or relations which bind men to God"; subjectively, as the recognition of these ties or relations and the acceptance of the obligations therein implied. *John A. Ryan*

A process of turning your skull into a tabernacle, not of going up to Jerusalem once a year. *Austin O'Malley*

The root, without which morality would die. *C. A. Bartol*

When religion is banished, human authority totters to its fall. *Pope Benedict XV*

RELIGIOUS

To be thoroughly religious, one must, I believe, be sorely disappointed. One's faith in God increases as one's faith in the world decreases. The happier the man, the farther he is from God. *George Jean Nathan*

RELIGIOUSNESS

The most beautiful and most profound emotion we can experience is the sensation of the mystical. It is the power of all true science. . . . To know that what is impenetrable to us really exists, manifesting itself as the highest wisdom and the most radiant beauty which our dull faculties can comprehend only in their most primitive forms—this knowledge, this feeling, is at the center of true religiousness. *Albert Einstein*

REMEMBRANCE

A form of meeting. *Kahlil Gibran*

REMORSE

Regret that one waited so long to do it. *H. L. Mencken*

The echo of a lost virtue. *Edward Bulwer-Lytton*

Beholding heaven and feeling hell. *George Moore*

The pain of sin. *Theodore Parker*

The anticipation of the pain to which our offense has exposed us. *C. A. Helvetius*

A sign that it wasn't quite as pleasant as one expected it to be.

REPARTEE

What you wish you'd said. *Heywood Broun*

Something we think of twenty-four hours too late. *Mark Twain*

An insult with its dress suit on.

A duel fought with the points of jokes. *Max Eastman*

The highest order of wit, as it bespeaks the coolest yet quickest exercise of genius at a moment when the passions are aroused. *Charles Caleb Colton*

What a person thinks on his way home.

A clever reply you think of after you could have used it.

The clever reply some one else gave and which you wish you had said.

REPENTANCE
Not so much regret for the ill we have done as fear of the
ill that may happen to us in consequence. *La Roche-
foucauld*
Repentence is being so sorry for sin you quit sinning.
Repentence is a change of heart, not an opinion.
Another name for aspiration. *Henry Ward Beecher*
Something more than mere remorse for sins; it compre-
hends a change of nature befitting heaven. *Lew Wallace*
When you are angry with yourself.

REPETITION
A good means of making or keeping impressions vivid, and
almost the only means of keeping them unchanged.
George Santayana

REPUBLIC
Governments which "are brought to their ends by luxury;
monarchies by poverty." *C. L. de Montesquieu*
Where "all are masters and each tyrannizes over the others."
Max Stirner

REPUTATION
What others are not thinking about you. *Tom Masson*
A mixture of what your friends, enemies and relatives say
behind your back.
Reputation is in itself only a farthing candle, of a wavering
and uncertain flame, and easily blown out, but it is the
light by which the world looks for and finds merit. *James
Russell Lowell*
What men and women think of us; character is what God
and the angels know of us. *Thomas Paine*
A bubble which man bursts when he tries to blow it for
himself. *Will Carleton*
What people say behind your back is your standing in the
community. *Edgar Watson Howe*

RESEARCH
An organized method for keeping you reasonably dissatisfied
with what you have. *Charles F. Kettering*
An organized method of finding out what you are going to
do when you can't keep on doing what you are doing now.
Charles F. Kettering

RESISTANCE (SALES)
The triumph of mind over patter.

RESORT
A place where the natives live on your vacation money until
next summer.

A place that overlooks a lake, and also overlooks comfortable beds, good food, and the conveniences of home.

RESPONSIBILITY

The price of greatness. *Winston Churchill*

REST

The sweet sauce of labor. *Plutarch*

RETRIBUTION

Retribution is one of the grand principles in the divine administration of human affairs. There is everywhere the working of the everlasting law of requital: man always gets as he gives. *John Foster*

REVENGE

Often like biting a dog because the dog bit you. *Austin O'Malley*

A kind of wild justice, which the more man's nature runs to, the more ought law to weed it out. *Francis Bacon*

A morsel reserved for God. *Italian Proverb*

REVIEWERS

Usually people who would have been poets, historians, biographers, if they could: they have tried their talents at one or the other, and have failed; therefore they turn critics. *Samuel Taylor Coleridge*

REVOLUTION

A successful effort to get rid of a bad government and set up a worse. *Oscar Wilde*

In politics, an abrupt change in the form of misgovernment. *Ambrose Bierce*

The larva of civilization. *Victor Hugo*

RHETORIC

Reason well dressed, and argument put in order. *Jeremy Collier*

RHETORICIAN

One who is "inebriated with the exuberance of his own verbosity." *Benjamin Disraeli*

RHEUMATISM

Nature's first primitive effort to establish a weather bureau.

RICH MAN

A man who has so much money he doesn't even know his son is in college.

One who doesn't know who his friends are.

RICHES

Riches are like muck, which stink in a heap, but spread abroad, make the earth fruitful.

RIDICULE
The first and last argument of fools. *C. Simmons*
The language of the devil. *Thomas Carlyle*

RIGHT
Right is the eternal sun; the world cannot delay its coming. *Wendell Phillips*

RIGHTEOUS INDIGNATION
Your own wrath as opposed to the shocking bad temper of others. *Elbert Hubbard*

RING (ENGAGEMENT)
The only sign of toil on the hand of a modern girl.

RIO DE JANEIRO
The city whose first view "persuades the son of Adam to forgive the Creator for having consented to Jersey City." *Hubert Herring*
A sun-browned woman adorned with flowers and stretched out in the sun on the sands of the Atlantic. *Erico Verissimo*

RIVER
Roads that move. *Blaise Pascal*

ROAD HOG
Some other motorist.

ROMANCE
The only sport in which the animal that gets caught has to buy the license.

ROME
Rome? The city of all time, and of all the world. *Nathaniel Hawthorne*
The capital of the world. *Pope Innocent II* (1139)
Rome, the mother of men. *Latin Phrase*

ROSE
A rose is a rose is a rose. *Gertrude Stein*

ROUGHING IT
To do without radio or television on a camping trip.

RUMMAGE
What you buy at a charity sale to store in your attic.

RUMOR
A favorite weapon of the assassins of character. *Ambrose Bierce*
Half a lie. *Thomas Fuller*

RUSSIA
A riddle wrapped in a mystery inside an enigma. *Winston Churchill*
A country where you can talk your head off.

• S •

SABBATH

Day of the Lord, as all our days should be. *Henry Wadsworth Longfellow*

When a man labors not for a livelihood, but to accumulate wealth, then he is a slave. Therefore it is that God granted the Sabbath. For it is by the Sabbath that we know that we are not working animals, born to eat and to labor. We are men. It is the Sabbath which is man's goal; not labor, but the rest which he earns from his labor. It was because the Jews made the Sabbath holy to God that they were redeemed from slavery in Egypt. It was by the Sabbath that they proclaimed that they were not slaves but free men. *Sholem Asch*

SABOTAGE

A management consultant reorganizing a business.

SACRED

To have friends whose lives we can elevate or depress by our influence is sacred. To be entrusted with little children is sacred. To have powers by which we can make this earth a more decent place is sacred. To be a child of God is sacred. And honor, honesty, truthfulness, fidelity, and love are sacred. *Harry Emerson Fosdick*

SACRIFICE

The sacrifices of God are a broken spirit: a broken and a contrite heart. *Ps. 51:17*

SALAD

Herbaceous treat. *Sydney Smith*

Four persons are wanted to make a good salad: a spendthrift for oil, a miser for vinegar, a counselor for salt, and a madman to stir all up. *Abraham Hayward*

SALT

Salt is what makes things taste bad when it isn't in them.

SALVATION

"Salvation" is one of religion's greatest words. It is well to see what is its true and full meaning. To some it means a drunkard saved from the ditch, to others escape from hell or reaching heaven . . . this is true, but not enough. Salvation means three things: (1) deliverance from evil, evil of every kind, within and without, now and to come; (2) the gaining of good, good of every kind but especially the highest good, the life with God and all that this brings; (3) the help of God. In a word, salvation is deliverance and life by the help of God. . . . "You did he make alive," Paul writes. "That is salvation, being alive to God and to every good which God's world can bring us." *H. F. Rall*

All that is necessary to salvation is contained in two virtues: faith in Christ, and obedience to laws. *Thomas Hobbes*

Salvation comes from God alone. *Old Latin Proverb*

SANITY

A madness put to good uses; waking life is a dream controlled. *George Santayana*

SARCASM

The language of the devil; for which reason I have long since as good as renounced it. *Thomas Carlyle*

Intellect on the offensive.

SATIETY

The most famous reformer.

SATIRE

The boldest way, if not the best,
To tell men freely of their foulest faults,
To laugh at their vain deeds and vainer thoughts.
John Sheffield

A lonely and introspective occupation, for nobody can describe a fool to the life without much patient self-inspection. *Frank Moore Colby*

Consists of "lies about literary men while they live, and eulogy lies about them when they die." *Voltaire*

A sort of glass wherein beholders do generally discover everybody's face but their own. *Jonathan Swift*

The last flicker of originality in a passing epoch as it faces the onroad of staleness and boredom. Freshness has gone: bitterness remains. *Alfred North Whitehead*

To "leave a sting within a brother's heart." *Edward Young*

SAVAGE

A person whose manners differ from ours. *Benjamin Franklin*

SAVING

It is a game that can be played by day, by night, at home and abroad, and at which you must win in the long run. . . . What an interest it imparts to life! *William Makepeace Thackeray*

SAVINGS

Delayed expenditures.

SAXOPHONE

The heart, soul, mind, body and spirit of the jazz orchestra. *Henry S. Osgood*

SCANDAL

Scandal is but amusing ourselves with the faults, foibles, follies and reputations of our friends. *Royall Tyler*

Gossip made tedious by morality. *Oscar Wilde*

The sweetener of a female feast. *Edward Young*

The thing that makes the whole world chin.

SCHOLAR

One who "possessing nothing of this world's goods, is like unto God." *Pope Xystus I*

A medieval owl that roosts in universities, especially those that are endowed. *Elbert Hubbard (The Roycroft Dictionary)*

A man, long on advice but short on action, who thinks he thinks. *Elbert Hubbard (The Roycroft Dictionary)*

The favorite of Heaven and earth, the excellency of his country, the happiest of men. *Ralph Waldo Emerson*

One who sells his "birthright for a mess of learning." *Henry David Thoreau*

One who "is surrounded by wiser men than he." *Ralph Waldo Emerson*

SCHOOL

School is not preparation for life, but school is life. *John Dewey*

SCHOOL (ART)

A place for young girls to pass the time between high school and marriage. *Thomas Hart Benton*

SCHOOLBOY

A boy with a "shining morning face, creeping like snail unwillingly to school." *Shakespeare*

SCHOOLHOUSES

The republican line of fortifications. *Horace Mann*

SCHOOLMASTER

A person who spends his life telling the same people the same things about the same things. *Greek Proverb*

SCOTSMAN

The only golfer who wouldn't knock a golf ball out of sight.

A person of whom "much may be made . . . if he be caught young." *Samuel Johnson*

SCOUNDREL

Every man over forty. *George Bernard Shaw*

SCULPTOR

A person who cuts away marble that isn't needed.

SEA

The sea drowns out humanity and time: it has no sympathy

with either, for it belongs to eternity, and of that it sings
its monotonous song for ever and ever. *Oliver Wendell
Holmes*
The great devourer of men. *Pio Baroja*
The waste basket of the world. *Rodger L. Simons*

SEASONS
Spring is a virgin, Summer a mother, Autumn a widow, and
Winter a step-mother. *Polish Proverb*

SECRET
Something that's not worth keeping or too good to keep.
Something you tell to only one person at a time.
What you ask someone not to tell because you can't keep
it.

SECRETS
Things we give to others to keep for us. *Elbert Hubbard*

SECRETARY (CLUB)
The person who keeps the minutes and wastes the hours.

SEEING
Believing.

SELF
The only prison that can ever bind the soul. *Henry Van
Dyke*

SELF-ABNEGATION
The rare virtue that good men preach and good women
practice. *Oliver Wendell Holmes*

SELF-COMPLACENCY
The death of the artist. *W. Somerset Maugham*
The great menace to the life of an industry. *David Sarnoff*

SELF-CONFIDENCE
The first requisite to great undertakings. *Samuel Johnson*
Faith in fools. *Edgar Allan Poe*
To be firmly convinced of what you think.

SELF-CONQUEST
The greatest of victories. *Plato*

SELF-DECEPTION
The thing all of us like most to do.

SELF-DEFENSE
The clearest of all laws, and for this reason: the lawyers
didn't make it. *Douglas Jerrold*
Nature's eldest law. *John Dryden*

SELF-DENIAL
Self-denial is not a virtue; it is only the effect of prudence
on rascality. *George Bernard Shaw*

SELF-DISTRUST
The cause of most of our failures. *C. N. Bovee*

SELF-ESTEEM
The most voluble of the emotions. *Frank Moore Colby*

SELF-HELP
To act with the knowledge that "God is a hard worker, but he likes to be helped." *Basque Proverb*

SELF-INTEREST
The dynamo of our economic system is self-interest which may range from mere petty greed to admirable types of self-expression. *Felix Frankfurter*

The thing to which wisdom yields.

SELFISHNESS
The greatest curse of the human race. *William E. Gladstone*

That detestable vice which no one will forgive in others and no one is without in himself. *Henry Ward Beecher*

Selfishness is not living as one wishes to live; it is asking others to live as one wishes to live. And unselfishness is letting other people's lives alone, not interfering with them. Selfishness always aims at creating around it an absolute uniformity of type. Unselfishness recognizes infinite variety of type as a delightful thing, accepts it, acquiesces in it, enjoys it. *Oscar Wilde*

The only real atheism; aspiration, unselfishness, the only real religion. *Israel Zangwill*

SELF-KNOWLEDGE
To know thyself, and "the first step to self-knowledge is self-distrust." *J. C. and A. W. Hare*

SELF-LOVE
An attitude "often rather arrogant than blind; it does not hide our faults from ourselves, but persuades us that they escape the notice of others." *Samuel Johnson*

Self-love is a cup without any bottom; you might pour all the great lakes into it, and never fill it up. *Oliver Wendell Holmes*

The greatest of all flatterers. *La Rochefoucauld*

Self-love . . . attends us first, and leaves us last. *Jonathan Swift*

To love one's self is the beginning of a life-long romance. *Oscar Wilde*

SELF-MADE
One who has made himself. John Bright said of Benjamin Disraeli, "He is a self-made man and worships his Creator."

SELF-PITY
> One of the last things that any woman surrenders. *Irvin S. Cobb*

SELF-PRESERVATION
> The first law of nature. *English Proverb*

SELF-RELIANCE
> The name we give to the egotism of the man who succeeds. *Elbert Hubbard*

SELF-REPROACH
> To blame one's self. "When we blame ourselves we feel no one else has a right to blame us." *Oscar Wilde*

SELF-RESPECT
> The secure feeling that no one, as yet, is suspicious. *H. L. Mencken*
>
> The cornerstone of all virtue. *John Herschel*

SELF-RESTRAINT
> Feeling your oats without sowing them. *Shannon Fife*

SELF-SACRIFICE
> Enables us to sacrifice other people without blushing. *George Bernard Shaw*
>
> An action which is "demoralizing to the people for whom one sacrifices oneself." *Oscar Wilde*

SELF-SATISFACTION
> To excuse one's ignorance, stupidity, and mistakes.

SELF-TAUGHT
> To have an ignoramus for one's teacher.

SENATE
> A body of elderly gentlemen charged with high duties and misdemeanors. *Ambrose Bierce*
>
> The greatest deliberative body in the world, but a group of bricklayers will run it a close second.

SENATOR
> One whose job it is to satisfy the farmers, consumers, labor unions, and businessmen.

SENIOR
> A student who feels that the university is going to the little children. *Adapted from Tom Masson*

SENSE (COMMON)
> The knack of seeing things as they are, and doing things as they ought to be done. *C. E. Stowe*
>
> Common sense is instinct, and enough of it is genius. *Josh Billings*
>
> Common sense is the measure of the possible. *H. F. Amiel*
>
> Common sense "is of the soul." *Walt Whitman*

SENSE (HORSE)
What keeps horses from betting on what people will do.

SENSE OF HUMOR
What makes you laugh at something which would make you mad if it happened to you.

SENSUALITY
The grave of the soul. *William E. Channing*

SENTIMENT
The poetry of the imagination. *Alphonse de Lamartine*
An emotion that masters reason.

SENTIMENTALIST
The barrenest of all mortals is the sentimentalist. *Thomas Carlyle*

SEPTEMBER
Warm September brings the fruit,
Sportsmen then begin to shoot.
Sara Coleridge

SERMON
The sermon is an effort to help and encourage and to feed the hunger of the hearts of those who have come seeking and expecting help. *Charles L. Allen*

SERVANT
One who "must always come when he's called, do what he's bid, and shut the door after him." *Jonathan Swift*
One who "hears, but doesn't hear. He is nothing but eyes and feet." *J. C. F. Schiller*

SERVANT (PUBLIC)
Persons chosen by the people to distribute the graft. *Mark Twain*

SEVENTY
To be seventy years old is like climbing the Alps. You reach a snow-crowned summit, and see behind you the deep valley stretching miles and miles away, and before you other summits higher and whiter, which you may have strength to climb, or may not. Then you sit down and meditate and wonder which it will be. *Henry Wadsworth Longfellow*

SEVENTY-FIVE
An age at which few grow stronger. *Adapted from Horace Walpole*

SEWING BASKET
A basket with needles, thread and other sewing equipment which can generally be found where father left it the last time he sewed on a button.

SEWING CIRCLE

The Protestant confessional, where each one confesses, not her own sins, but the sins of her neighbors. *Charles B. Fairbanks*

SHAKE

A greeting used by a citizen of Florida when he meets a citizen of California who has felt some earthquakes.

SHAKESPEARE, WILLIAM

A dramatist of note who lived by writing things to quote. *Henry Cuyler Bunner*

A savage with sparks of genius. *Voltaire*

SHARP TONGUE

The only edged tool that grows keener with constant use. *Washington Irving*

SHAW, GEORGE BERNARD

An author who "discovered himself and gave ungrudgingly of his discovery to the world." *Saki*

An excellent man; he has not an enemy in the world, and none of his friends like him. *Oscar Wilde*

SHEEPSKIN

A helpful tool in earning a living which ranks next to shoe leather in importance.

SHOEHORN

An instrument that only plays foot notes.

SHOT (BIG)

A potential big bore.

SHOWER (WEDDING)

The beginning of the end of a man's reign.

SHYNESS

The protective fluid within which our personalities are able to develop into natural shapes. *Harold Nicolson*

SICKNESS

A belief, which must be annihilated by the divine mind. *Mary Baker Eddy*

SILENCE

The unbearable repartee. *G. K. Chesterton*

The greatest persecution. *Blaise Pascal*

The fool's wisdom. *Spanish Proverb*

Silence is the perfectest herald of joy: I were but little happy, if I could say how much. *Shakespeare*

One great art of conversation. *William Hazlitt*

A conversation with an Englishman. *Heinrich Heine*

Silence is God, and it will be the only thing to last longer than eternity. *Ramon de la Serna*

Sometimes the severest criticism. *Charles Buxton*
Wisdom in dead storage.
Silence is a figure of speech, unanswerable, short, cold, but
    terribly severe. *Theodore Parker*
One of the hardest arguments to refute. *Josh Billings*
What would follow if the average politician spoke his
    mind.

SILK
The thing that makes the difference in Adam's children.
    Adapted from Thomas Fuller

SIMILE
To compare one thing with another, often with *as* or *like*.
    Example: R is silent as in Harvard.

SIMPLICITY
An exact medium between too little and too much. *Sir
    Joshua Reynolds*
In character, in manner, in style, in all things, the supreme
    excellency is simplicity. *Henry Wadsworth Longfellow*
The peak of civilization. *Jessie Sampter*
The glory of expression. *Walt Whitman*
The characteristic of all high bred deportment, in every
    country. *James Fenimore Cooper*
To be simple is to be great. *Ralph Waldo Emerson*

SIN
A departure from God. *Martin Luther*
Anything that separates us from God. If we are so good that
    we don't feel any need for God's mercy, then our goodness
    is sin. *Alexander Purdy*
Sin is twisting and distorting out of its proper shape a
    human personality which God designed to be a thing of
    beauty and a joy forever. *Walter L. Carson*

SIN (WAGES OF)
The price a confession magazine pays for a story.

SINCERITY
A mental attitude acquired after long practice by man, in
    order to conceal his ulterior motives. *Elbert Hubbard
    (The Roycroft Dictionary)*
A sincere person is one who bluffs only a part of the time.
    Elbert Hubbard (The Roycroft Dictionary)

SKEPTIC
A dogmatist. He enjoys the delusion of complete futility.
    Alfred North Whitehead

SKEPTICISM
The first attribute of a good critic. *James Russell Lowell*

The mark and even the pose of the educated mind. *John Dewey*

The first step on the road to philosophy. *Denis Diderot*

Means, not intellectual doubt alone, but moral doubt. *Thomas Carlyle*

SKIING

A winter sport that people learn in several sittings.

SLANDER

A vice that strikes a double blow, wounding both him that commits, and him against whom it is committed. *Saurin*

The revenge of a coward, and dissimulation his defense. *Samuel Johnson*

Slander . . . makes an evil man . . . executioner of the innocent. *Jeremy Taylor*

SLANG

The speech of him who robs the literary garbage carts on their way to the dumps. *Ambrose Bierce*

Language that takes off its coat, spits on its hands, and goes to work. *Carl Sandburg*

SLEEP

An excellent way of listening to an opera. *James Stephens*

So like death, I dare not trust it without my prayers. *Sir Thomas Browne*

The death of each day's life, sore labor's bath, balm of hurt minds, great nature's second course, chief nourisher in life's feast. *Shakespeare*

Sleep, Silence's child, sweet father of soft rest,
Prince whose approach peace to all mortals brings,
Indifferent host to shepherds and to kings,
Sole comforter of minds with grief opprest.
                    William Drummond

The twin of death. *Homer*

Sleep, rest of nature, O sleep, most gentle of the divinities, peace of the soul, thou at whose presence care disappears, who soothest hearts wearied with daily employments, and makest them strong again for labor. *Publius Ovidius Naso*

The image of cold death. *Ovid*

Sleep is a death. *Sir Thomas Browne*

SLOGANS

Slogans are both exciting and comforting, but they are also powerful opiates for the conscience. *James Bryant Conant*

SMALLPOX

Smallpox in its ordinary form, is simply an effort of the

blood to rid itself of impurities. It is invariably followed
by more vigorous health. *Voltaire* (1723)

SMILE
A pleasant wrinkle.

SMILE (PERPETUAL)
A pathetic mask. *P. K. Thomajan*

SNAIL
An ingenious animal. "When it encounters a bad neighbor it takes up its house and moves away." *Philemon*

SNEER
The weapon of the weak. *James Russell Lowell*

SNOBBERY
The pride of those who are not sure of their position. *Ber-
ton Braley*

SNORER
A sound sleeper.

SNORING
Sheet music.

SOAP
A measure of the prosperity and culture of a nation. *Jus-
tus von Liebig*

SOCIAL ADVANTAGE
To have the license number of one's automobiles as low
as possible in America. *André Maurois*

SOCIALISM
A sincere, sentimental, beneficient theory, which has but
one objection, and that is, it will not work. *Elbert Hubbard (The Roycroft Dictionary)*

Participation in profits without responsibility as to deficits.
Elbert Hubbard (The Roycroft Dictionary)

That contemplated system of industrial society which pro-
poses the abolition of private property in the great material instruments of production, and the substitution
therefor of collective property; and advocates the collective management of production, together with the distribution of social income by society, and private property in the larger proportion of this social income. *Richard T. Ely*

Venomous teachings. *Pope Leo XIII*

Socialism is a stage in social development from a society
guided by the dictatorship of the proletariat to a society
wherein the state will have ceased to exist. *Joseph Stalin*
(1925)

Socialism is not at all the enemy of civilization. It only

wants to extend civilization to all humanity; under capitalism, civilization is the monopoly of a privileged minority. *William Liebknecht*

What is characteristic of socialism is the joint ownership by all members of the community of the instruments and means of production, which carries with it the consequence that the division of all the produce among the body of owners must be a public act performed according to the rules laid down by the community. *John Stuart Mill*

SOCIETY

Two great classes: those who have more dinners than appetite, and those who have more appetite than dinners. *Nicholas Chamfort*

A lot of nobodies talking about nothing. *Oscar Wilde*

A producer of "rogues, and education makes one rogue cleverer than another." *Oscar Wilde*

"A hospital of incurables." *Ralph Waldo Emerson*

One polish'd horde, form'd of two mighty tribes, the bores and bored. *Lord Byron*

A masked ball, where every one hides his real character, and reveals it by hiding. *Ralph Waldo Emerson*

Other people are quite dreadful. The only possible society is oneself. *Oscar Wilde*

SOLAR SYSTEM

A system that "has no anxiety about its reputation." *Ralph Waldo Emerson*

SOLDIERS

Theirs not to make reply,
Theirs not to reason why,
Theirs but to do and die.
Alfred Tennyson

Citizens of death's gray land. *Siegfried Sassoon*

SOLEMNITY

A trick of the body to hide the faults of the mind. *La Rochefoucauld*

SOLITUDE

Where we are least alone. *Lord Byron*

The best nurse of wisdom.

I am never less alone than when alone.

A good place to visit but a poor place to stay. *Josh Billings*

SONG

The licensed medium for bawling in public things too silly or sacred to be uttered in ordinary speech. *Oliver Herford*

SONS

The anchors of a mother's life. *Sophocles*

SOPHISTICATION

The art of admitting that the unexpected is just what you anticipated.

The trusted weapon of defense against ridicule. *L. Wardlaw Miles*

Means one sort of an experience—a wide experience of the wrong and evil of the world, combined with a modish tolerance and an amused interest. *L. Wardlaw Miles*

SORROW

Sorrow . . . makes the night morning, and the noon-tide night. *Shakespeare*

A kind of rust of the soul, which every new idea contributes in its passage to scour away. *Samuel Johnson*

SORROWS

Like thunderclouds—in the distance they look black, over our heads scarcely gray. *Jean Paul Richter*

SO-SO

Good, very good, very excellent maximum; and yet it is not; it is but so-so. *Shakespeare*

SOUND-EFFECTS MAN

The fellow in the radio station who can wreck a train, shoot a policeman and burn a house all in an evening's work.

SOUTH

A section of the United States where the people raise cotton but wear silk and nylon.

SPACE

This is to place what eternity is to time. *Joseph Joubert*

There is beauty in space, and it is orderly. There is no weather, and there is regularity. It is predictable . . . Everything in space obeys the laws of physics. If you know these laws and obey them, space will treat you kindly. And don't tell me man doesn't belong out there. Man belongs wherever he wants to go. *Wernher von Braun*

SPEAKEASY

During the prohibition era, a business place where every knock was a customer.

SPEAKER (AFTER DINNER)

Someone who knows how to dilute a two-minute idea into a two-hour speech.

One who says nothing and takes 30 minutes to say it.

SPEAKING (PUBLIC)
>The art of making an audience believe that deep noises from the chest are important messages from the brains.

SPECIALIST
>One who limits himself to his chosen mode of ignorance. *Elbert Hubbard (The Roycroft Dictionary)*

SPEECH
>A faculty given to man to conceal his thoughts. *Charles Talleyrand*
>Human nature itself, with none of the artificiality of written language. *Alfred North Whitehead*
>The supreme art of man. *Mathurin Dondo*
>Speech is power: speech is to persuade, to convert, to compel. *Ralph Waldo Emerson*
>Speech is the mirror of the soul; as a man speaks, so he is. *Publius Syrus*

SPEECHLESS
>What some people would be if they said what they thought.

SPINACH
>Spinach is the broom of the stomach. *French Proverb*

SPINE
>What your head sits on and you sit on.

SPINNING A ROPE
>A lot of fun—providing your neck ain't in it. *Will Rogers*

SPONTANIETY
>What he who laughs last hasn't.

SPORTS
>Activities which make the people of a nation hardy, such as sitting on a cold slab of concrete in the rain in a stadium.

SPRING
>Makes everything young again except man. *Jean Paul Richter*
>When a young man's fancy lightly turns—and turns—and turns. *Helen Rowland*
>Spring is a call to action, hence to disillusion, therefore April is called "the cruelest month." *Cyril Connolly*
>Ethereal mildness. *James Thomson*
>When daffodils begin to peer. *Shakespeare*

STABILITY
>Nothing else than a more sluggish motion. *Michel de Montaigne*

STAGECRAFT
>Nothing more than the tail to the poet's kite. Designer

and mechanic held the string so that the kite can soar. *Lee Simonson*

STARS

Candles in Heaven.

The forget-me-nots of the angels. *Henry Wadsworth Long-fellow*

STARVATION

A cure for indigestion. *Elbert Hubbard (The Roycroft Dictionary)*

STATE

An organized society of individual human beings who determine its structure, the equality of its social relations, its laws, and the objects pursued by its government. *Leonard Woolf*

States are great engines moving slowly. *Francis Bacon*

No more than a machine for the oppression of one class by another; this is true of a democracy as well as of a monarchy. *Friedrich Engels*

A perfect body of free men, united together to enjoy common rights and advantages. *Hugo Grotius*

STATESMAN

One who "shears the sheep, the politician skins them." *Austin O'Malley*

One who thinks he belongs to the state, whereas a politician thinks the state belongs to him.

A person who takes his ears from the ground and listens to the still small voice.

A politician who is held upright by equal pressure from all directions. *Eric A. Johnston*

A successful politician who is dead. *Thomas Buchanan Reed*

One who has beliefs, but doesn't believe them too hard. *Adapted from James Russell Lowell*

Persons who "face facts; politicians distort them." *John A. Lincoln*

STATESMAN (ELDER)

Somebody old enough to know his own mind and keep quiet about it. *Bernard Baruch*

STATESMANSHIP

The art of understanding and leading the masses, or the majority. Its glory is to lead them, not where they want to go, but where they ought to go. *Joseph Joubert*

When you get the formalities right; never mind about the moralities. *Mark Twain*

The act of changing a nation from what it is to what it ought to be. *W. R. Alger*

STATESMANSHIP (HONEST)
The wise employment of individual meanness for the public good. *Abraham Lincoln*

STATISTICIAN
A person who diligently collects facts and figures and from them draws any number of confusions.

STATISTICS
Figures used "as a drunken man uses lamp posts—for support rather than for illumination." *Andrew Lang*
Mendacious truths. *Lionel Strachey*

STAY
A charming word in a friend's vocabulary. *Bronson Alcott*

STEAM
Water which is crazy with the heat.

STINGY
To be poor always.

STOMACH
An organ that serves "instead of a clock." *Jonathan Swift*
A slave that must accept everything that is given to it, but which avenges wrongs as slyly as does the slave. *Emile Souvestre*

STONE AGE
A prehistoric period when man stopped at the red traffic light to let a dinosaur go by.

STORK
A bird with a big bill.
The only bird that discriminates against the common people.

STORY (DETECTIVE)
The normal recreation of noble minds. *Philip Guedalla*

STORYTELLER
A person who has a good memory and hopes other people haven't. *Irvin S. Cobb*

STRATEGY
Strategy is a system of makeshifts. *Helmuth von Moltke*

STUDY
The noblest exercise of the mind within doors, and most befitting a person of quality, is study. *William Ramesy*
Study serves for delight, for ornament, and for ability. *Francis Bacon*

STUPIDITY
Unconscious ignorance. *Josh Billings*

STYLE

The ultimate morality of the mind. *Alfred North White-head*

Doing things not in any way but in the best way. *Gelett Burgess*

A wonderful pickle that is able to preserve mediocrity of thought under favorable conditions for many centuries. *F. S. Oliver*

The dress of thoughts. *Lord Chesterfield*

SUBSIDY

A formula for handing you back your own money with a flourish that makes you think it's a gift. *Jo Bingham*

SUBURBANITE

A man who hires someone to mow his lawn so he will have time to play golf for exercise.

SUBWAY

A form of transportation which is generally so crowded even the men can't all get seats.

SUCCESS

The necessary misfortune of life, but it is only to the very unfortunate that it comes early. *Anthony Trollope*

Something that "covers a multitude of blunders." *George Bernard Shaw*

Self-expression at a profit. *Marcelene Cox*

The ability to hitch your wagon to a star while keeping your feet on the ground. *Marcelene Cox*

Getting what you want. In contrast, happiness is wanting what you get.

To work faithfully eight hours a day so you may eventually get to be a boss and work twelve hours a day. *Adapted from Robert Frost*

Making more money to meet obligations you wouldn't have if you didn't have so much money. *Marcelene Cox*

Little more than a chemical compound of man with moment. *Philip Guedalla*

When you live miserably in order to die rich.

The end of hope.

Getting up just one more time than you fell down.

SUCCESS (LITERARY)

Success that "liberates the tensions of a hostile environment by removing the environment and so prepares the way for literary failure." *Cyril Connolly*

SUICIDE

Cheating the doctors out of a job. *Josh Billings*

SUMMER
>When a Scotsman throws his Christmas tree away.
>Summer is the mother of the poor. *Italian Proverb*

SUN
>My almighty physician. *Thomas Jefferson*

>Center and sire of light,
>The keystone of the world-built arch of heaven.
>*Philip J. Bailey*

SUNDAY
>The golden clasp that binds together the volume of the week. *Henry Wadsworth Longfellow*
>The day that "clears away the rust of the whole week. *Joseph Addison*
>The core of our civilization, dedicated to thought and reverence. *Ralph Waldo Emerson*

SUNDAY AFTERNOON
>The period during the week when all the automobiles in the United States are laid end to end.

SUNDAY SCHOOL
>A prison in which children do penance for the evil conscience of their parents. *H. L. Mencken*

SUN DIAL
>An old-timer.

SUNRISE
>When "o'er night's brim, day boils at last." *Robert Browning*

SUPERFLUOUS
>A very necessary thing. *Voltaire*

SUPERIORITY
>There are three marks of a superior man: being virtuous, he is free from anxiety; being wise, he is free from perplexity; being brave, he is free from fear. *Confucius* (500 B.C.)

SUPERSTITION
>The religion of feeble minds. *Edmund Burke*

SURGERY
>It separates the patient from his disease. It puts the patient back to bed and the disease in a bottle. *Logan Clendening*
>By far the worst snob among the handicrafts. *Austin O'Malley*

SUSPENSE
>The life of a spider. *Jonathan Swift*

SYMPATHY

A virtue unknown in nature. *Paul Eipper*

What one woman gives another in exchange for all the details.

Two hearts tugging at one load. *C. H. Parkhurst*

SYNONYM

A word to use when you can't spell the other word.

• T •

TABLOID

A newspaper with a permanent crime wave.

A newspaper which covers a multitude of sins.

TACT

Knowing how far we may go too far. *Jean Cocteau*

Be kind and considerate to others, depending somewhat upon who they are. *Don Herold*

The ability to describe others as they see themselves. *Abraham Lincoln*

The ability to make advice agreeable.

A human quality which should be cultivated as a help to avoid telling the truth in embarrassing situations.

A quality that "comes as much from goodness of heart as from fineness of taste." *Endymion*

Looking around to be sure no one is related to the person about whom you are going to gossip.

The ability to close your mouth before somebody else wants to.

Tact is one of the first mental virtues, the absence of which is often fatal to the best of talents; it supplies the place of many talents. *W. G. Simms*

TALENT

The ability to do things tolerably well; genius does them intolerably better.

Talent is that which is in a man's power; genius is that in whose power a man is. *James Russell Lowell*

A human quality "nurtured in solitude; but character is best formed in the stormy billows of the world." *J. W. von Goethe*

TALKING

The way women "cure all their sorrows." *Jean Paul Richter*

The disease of age. *Ben Jonson*

TARIFF

A scale of taxes on imports, designed to protect the domestic producer against the greed of his consumer. *Ambrose Bierce*

TASTE

The feminine of genius. *Edward FitzGerald*

A quality possessed by persons without originality or moral courage. *Adapted from George Bernard Shaw*

Fine taste is an aspect of genius itself, and is the faculty of delicate appreciation, which makes the best effects of art our own. *N. P. Willis*

Nothing but a delicate good sense. *M. J. de Chénier*

TAVERN (HOTEL)

A house kept for those who are not housekeepers. *Paul Chatfield*

TAVERNS

Places where madness is sold by the bottle. *Jonathan Swift*

TAXATION

Plucking the goose as to obtain the largest amount of feathers with the least possible amount of hissing. *Jean Baptiste Colbert*

TAXES

The sinews of the state. *Cicero*

Without a doubt the simplest leverage known to society for directing social impulses. *Morris L. Ernst*

The thing generally raised on city land is taxes. *C. D. Warner*

TAXPAYER

One who has the government on his payroll.

TEACHER

A person who "should have an atmosphere of awe, and walk wonderingly, as if he was amazed at being himself." *Walter Bagehot*

One who, in his youth, admired teachers. *H. L. Mencken*

Like the candle which lights others in consuming itself. *Ruffini*

A person, either male or female, who instils into the head of another person, either voluntarily or for pay, the sum and substance of his or her ignorance. *Elbert Hubbard* (*The Roycroft Dictionary*)

A person who "should be sparing of his smile." *William Cowper*

TEACHER (BALLET)

A teacher who criticizes her students in order to keep them on their toes.

TEACHER (MUSIC)

A teacher who is hired to bridge the awful gap between his students and Chopin. *Adapted from George Ade*

TEARS

The noble language of the eye. *Robert Herrick*

The telescope by which men see far into heaven. *Henry Ward Beecher*

The most efficient water power in the world—woman's tears. *Wilson Mizner*

Tears are not the mark of weakness but of power. They speak more eloquently than ten thousand tongues. *Washington Irving*

Tears are the tribute of humanity to its destiny. *W. R. Alger*

Summer showers to the soul. *Alfred Austin*

The silent language of grief. *Voltaire*

Holy water. *Shakespeare*

TEASING

A sure sign of love.

TELEPHONE

An instrument used for long periods when youth calls to youth.

A wonderful instrument because it connects you with so many strangers.

TELEVISION

Radio with eyestrain.

TELEVISION (PORTABLE)

An instrument of communication which enables a person in the end seats to see the football game and hear the band.

TEMPERAMENT

Temper that is too old to spank. *Charlotte Greenwood*

TEMPERAMENT (ARTISTIC)

A disease that afflicts amateurs. *G. K. Chesterton*

TEMPERANCE

The noblest gift of the Gods. *Euripides*

The moderating of one's desires in obedience to reason. *Cicero*

The greatest of all virtues. *Plutarch*

A disposition of the mind which sets bounds to the passions. *Thomas Aquinas*

TEMPTATION

An irresistible force at work on a moveable body. *H. L. Mencken*

Temptation is a part of life. No one is immune—at any age. For temptation is present wherever there is a choice to be made, not only between good and evil, but also between a higher and lower good. For some, it may be a temptation to sensual gratification; for others a temptation to misuse their gifts, to seek personal success at the cost of the general welfare, to seek a worthy aim by unworthy means, to lower their ideal to win favor with the electorate, or with their companions and associates. *Ernest Trice Thompson*

TESTIMONIAL

An endorsement you believe and act on to your great regret.

TEXAN

A wealthy man who has ranch to ranch carpeting.

TEXAS

The place where there are the most cows and the least milk and the most rivers and the least water in them, and where you can look the furthest and see the least.

THEATER

A place for entertainment where people go who have colds. *Adapted from James Agate*

A form of entertainment which does not hold a mirror up to life, but to a keyhole.

THEFT

It is rascally to steal a purse, daring to steal a million, and a proof of greatness to steal a crown. The blame diminishes as the guilt increases. *J. C. F. Schiller*

THEOLOGY

The most noble of studies. *Pope Leo XIII*

A science of mind applied to God. *Henry Ward Beecher*

THIEF

One who thinks everybody steals. *Danish Proverb*

One who considers he is honest if he has no chance to steal. *Hebrew Proverb*

THIEF (AUTO)

A person who steals automobiles and is known in Texas as a Cadillac rustler.

THINKING

The hardest work there is, which is the probable reason why so few engage in it. *Henry Ford*

The talking of the soul with itself. *Plato*

To think is to live. *Cicero*

The magic of the mind. *Lord Byron*

THIRTY-FIVE YEARS
>One backward look—the last—the last!
>One silent tear—for youth is past.
>>*N. P. Willis*

THIRTY YEARS
>The age of a woman who is forty.

THOUGHT
>The universal consoler. *Chamfort*
>The seed of action. *Emerson*
>An idea in transit. *Pythagoras*

THOUGHTLESS
>Describes a person who is seldom quiet.

THRONE
>A glorious sepulcher. *Empress Theodora*

THUNDER
>That great artillery of God Almighty. *William Temple*

TIBET
>The roof of the world. *T. E. Gordon*
>The forbidden land. *Walter Savage Landor*

TIGHTWAD
>A despicable person, but the one from whom the good fellows borrow money.

TIME
>A babbler, and speaks even when not asked. *Euripides*
>A sort of river of passing events, and strong is its current; no sooner is a thing brought to sight than it is swept by and another takes its place, and this too will be swept away. *Marcus Aurelius Antoninus*
>A system of folds which only death can unfold. *Jean Cocteau*
>Time is what we want most, but what alas! we use worst. *William Penn*
>Time is an herb that cures all diseases. *Benjamin Franklin*
>Time is like money; the less we have of it to spare the further we make it go. *Josh Billings*
>The most valuable thing a man can spend. *Theophrastus*
>A great legalizer, even in the field of morals. *H. L. Mencken*
>A very shadow that passeth away. *Wisdom of Solomon 2:5*
>The wisest of all counsellors. *Plutarch*
>The father of truth. *John Florio*
>The avenger. *Lord Byron*

TIPS
>Wages we pay other people's employees. *Gideon Wurdz*

TO BE MISERABLE
To have no troubles to talk about.

TOASTMASTER
A person whose job it is to bore you so that you will think the speaker is good.

Living proof that all oil cans aren't in the toolbox.

TOBACCO
A product found in certain Southern States and in some cigars.

A lone man's companion, a bachelor's friend, a hungry man's food, a sad man's cordial, a wakeful man's sleep, and a chilly man's fire. *Charles Kingsley*

> Tobacco is an evil weed
> It was the Devil sowed the seed;
> It stains your fingers, burns your clothes
> And makes a chimney of your nose.

TOBACCO (HAVANA)
A product you find in Cuba and in a few cigars.

TODAY
The obscurest epoch. *Robert Louis Stevenson*
Yesterday's pupil. *Benjamin Franklin*

TOIL
The sire of fame. *Euripides*
The law of life and its best fruit. *Lewis Morris*

TOLERANCE
Another word for indifference. *W. Somerset Maugham*
An agreement to tolerate intolerance. *Elbert Hubbard (The Roycroft Dictionary)*
Tolerance does not lie in denying the possibility of truth or its claim on man, as some would have it. To deprive a man of the right to live according to the truth as he understands it is to rob him of all that makes life human. Tolerance does lie . . . in truly grasping what the other person understands by truth and judging him as a person not by one's own standards but by his own, however misguided they might be. This does not mean indifferentism. Each man has to serve the truth as we may well believe that some men who think they are serving the truth are in fact bound to superstition or ignorance. False ideas have no claim on tolerance. The central figure in tolerance is the person, infinitely worthy of respect. *John Cogley*
The only real test of civilization. *Arthur Helps*

TOLERATION

The best religion. *Victor Hugo*

To gently scan your brother man. *Robert Burns*

TOMB

The clothes of the dead. A grave is but a plain suit, and a rich monument is one embroidered. *Thomas Fuller*

TOMBSTONE

About the only thing that can stand upright and lie on its face at the same time. *Mary Wilson Little*

TOMORROW

The day when idlers work, and fools reform, and mortal men lay hold on heaven. *Edward Young*

The mother of regret. *Elbert Hubbard* (*The Roycroft Dictionary*)

TONGUE

It is an unruly evil, full of deadly poison. *James 3:8*

A woman's sword and she never lets it rust.

The pen of a ready writer. *Ps. 14:1*

TOOL

The extension of a man's hand, and a machine is but a complex tool. And he that invents a machine augments the power of a man and the well-being of mankind. *Henry Ward Beecher*

TOOTHACHE

A pain that drives you to extraction.

TOOT ENSEMBLE

Two hundred cars lined up at a traffic intersection.

TOTALITARIANISM

A system in which no disagreement on ends is allowed, whereas the means are not restricted by any previous agreement. The end justifies the means, which therefore range from persuasion to coercion, from compromise to terror. *Hans Simons*

TOURIST

A person who changes the car oil every four days and his shirt once a week.

A person who travels hundreds of miles in order to get a snapshot of himself standing by his automobile.

TOWN (HICK)

One where there is no place to go where you shouldn't be. *Alexander Woollcott*

TOWN (HOME)

Where they think you are in some kind of trouble if you return for a visit.

TOWN (SMALL)
A place where everybody knows whose check is good.

TRADE-MARKS
The lines and wrinkles in a person's face.

TRADITION
A method of holding the many back while some man does the thing which they declare is impossible. *Elbert Hubbard (The Roycroft Dictionary)*

An extension of the franchise. Tradition means giving votes to the most obscure of all classes, our ancestors. It is the democracy of the dead. *G. K. Chesterton*

One of the most cherished and most dangerous possessions of the human race. *C. C. and S. M. Furnas*

TRAFFIC COP
A large forceful person of few words, but often.

TRAFFIC LIGHT
A device that helps you get halfway across the street safely.

TRAGEDY
A bride without a can opener.
A California citizen dying in Florida.

TRANQUILITY
The summum bonum of old age. *Thomas Jefferson*

TRAVEL
An experience that broadens one—sometimes just going across the street.

Activity that broadens the mind, flattens the traveler, and lengthens conversation.

One way of lengthening life, at least in appearance. *Benjamin Franklin*

TREAT (DUTCH)
When two businessmen have dinner and each uses his own expense account.

TREATY
A system under which the faithful are always bound and the faithless always free. *Lord Vansittart*

TREE
An object that will stand in one place for years, then jump in front of a lady driver. *Ruth Lemezis*

A shaft of beauty towering high. *Henry C. Bunner*

TROUBLE
Trouble is the next best thing to enjoyment; there is no fate in the world so horrible as to have no share in either its joys or sorrows. *Henry Wadsworth Longfellow*

TROUBLES
   The tools by which God fashions us for better things. *Henry Ward Beecher*

TRUTH
   The object of philosophy, but not always of philosophers. *John Churton Collins*

   The one thing that nobody will believe. *George Bernard Shaw*

   What men kill each other for. *Herbert Read*

   The opinion that still survives. *Elbert Hubbard* (*The Roycroft Dictionary*)

   The strongest argument. *Sophocles*

   The foundation of all knowledge and the cement of all societies. *John Dryden*

   A universal error. *Elbert Hubbard* (*The Roycroft Dictionary*)

   What God says about a thing.

   The rarest quality in an epitaph. *Henry David Thoreau*

   Truth is the secret of eloquence and of virtue, the basis of moral authority; it is the highest summit of art and of life. *H. F. Amiel*

   > Truth ever lovely—since the world began,
   > The foe of tyrants, and the friend of man.
   > *Thomas Campbell*

TUNAFISH
   A fish in a can that comes out when unexpected company calls.

TURKEY
   An old bird that strutted and got caught.

TWENTY-ONE
   The age of complete confidence.

TWINS
   Two things in this life for which we are never fully prepared. *Josh Billings*

● U ●

UGLINESS
   A point of view: an ulcer is wonderful to a pathologist. *Austin O'Malley*

UKULELE
   A so-called musical instrument which, when listened to, you cannot tell whether one is playing on it, or just monkeying with it. *Will Rogers*

UMBRELLA
Common property. One man's loss is another man's umbrella.

UMPIRE
A retired baseball player whose eyesight began to fail him.

UNBELIEF
A confession of ignorance where honest inquiry might easily find the truth. "Agnostic," is but the Greek for "ignoramus." *Tryon Edwards*

UNDERGRADUATE
One who devotes to the adornment of his person such time as he can spare from the neglect of his duties. *Samuel Butler*

UNDERWORLD
The world that is on top.

UNHAPPINESS
Not knowing what we want and killing ourselves to get it. *Don Herold*

UNION (LABOR)
An elemental response to the human instinct for group action in dealing with group problems. *William Green*

UNITED STATES
I believe in the United States of America as a government of the people, by the people, for the people; whose just powers are derived from the consent of the governed; a democracy in a republic, a sovereign nation of many sovereign states; a perfect union, one and inseparable; established upon those principles of freedom, equality, justice and humanity for which American patriots sacrificed their lives and fortunes. I therefore believe it is my duty to my country to love it, to support its constitution, to obey its laws, to respect its flag, and to defend it against all enemies. *William Tyler Page*
The greatest poem. *Walt Whitman*

UNIVERSITY
An educational institution in which young men and women work their parents through college.
A collection of books. *Thomas Carlyle*
A place where 2,000 can sit in the classrooms and 50,000 in the stadium.
The university is a place where inquiry is pushed forward, and discoveries verified and perfected, and rashness rendered innocuous, and error exposed, by the collision of

mind with mind and knowledge with knowledge. It is the place where the professor becomes eloquent, and is a missionary and a preacher displaying his science in its most complete and most winning form, pouring it forth with the zeal of enthusiasm, and lighting up his own love of it in the breasts of his hearers. It is the place where the catechist makes good his ground as he goes treading in the truth day by day into the ready memory, and wedging and tightening it into the expanding reason. It is a place which wins the admiration of the young by its celebrity, kindles the affections of the middle-aged by its beauty, and rivets the fidelity of the old by its associations. It is a seat of wisdom, a light of the world, a minister of the faith, an Alma Mater of the rising generation. *Cardinal Newman*

A place of light, of liberty, and of learning. *Benjamin Disraeli*

UNIVERSITY (AMERICAN)
Defined by a Chinese student as an athletic institution in which a few classes are held for the feeble-minded.

UNNECESSARY THINGS
Our only necessities. *Oscar Wilde*
Today's luxuries but tomorrow's necessities.

U. S.
Stands for Unlimited Spending. *Tampa Tribune*

UTOPIA
All the road-hogs laid end to end.

● V ●

VACATION
What you need just after you have had it.
A period of travel and relaxation when you take twice the clothes and half the money you need.

VACILLATION
The prominent feature of genius. Alternately inspired and depressed, its inequalities of mood are stamped upon its labors. *Edgar Allan Poe*

VAGABOND
A tramp who is called a tourist when rich. *Adapted from Paul Richard*

VALET
The difference between a man and his valet: they both smoke the same cigars, but only one pays for them. *Robert Frost*

VALOR
> To do without witnesses what one would do before all the world. *La Rochefoucauld*

VAN WINKLE, RIP
> A man who was able to sleep for twenty years because there were no alarm clocks and the neighbors didn't have radios.

VANITY
> The greatest of all flatterers. *La Rochefoucauld*
>
> Keeps persons in favor with themselves who are out of favor with all others. *Shakespeare*
>
> The highest form of vanity is love of fame. *George Santayana*
>
> One of the most positive human traits, probably having its roots in nothing more noxious than the normal desire to win the approval of others. *Hamilton Basso*
>
> The quicksand of reason. *George Sand*
>
> A strange passion: rather than be out of a job it will brag of its vices. *Josh Billings*

VARIETY
> Variety's the very spice of life,
> That gives it all its flavor.
> *William Cowper*

VEGETARIANISM
> A diet that "is harmless enough, although it is apt to fill a man with wind and self-righteousness." *Robert Hutchinson*

VELOCITY
> What a person puts a hot plate down with.

VENICE
> A fine city if it were only drained. *Ascribed to U. S. Grant*

VERSE (FREE)
> The triumph of mind over meter.

VICE
> Vice is a monster of so frightful mien
> As to be hated needs but to be seen;
> Yet seen too oft, familiar with her face,
> We first endure, then pity, then embrace.
> *Alexander Pope*
>
> A creature of such hideous mien that the more you see it, the better you like it. *F. P. Dunne*

VICE-PRESIDENT
> A title given to a bank officer in place of a raise in salary.
> An unknown person ranking next to the President.

A spare tire on the automobile of government. *John N. Garner*

VICTORY

A matter of staying-power. *Elbert Hubbard (The Roycroft Dictionary)*

What is victory? Victory is that which must be bought with the lives of young men to retrieve the errors of the old. Victory is a battered thing courage must salvage out of the wreckage which stupidity has wrought. Victory is redemption purchased for men's hope at a cost so terrible that only defeat could be more bitter. *Gordon R. Munnoch*

When the conquered mourn.

VIGILANCE (ETERNAL)

The price of liberty. *John Philpot Curran*

VILLAGE

A community where no one knows a rich policeman.

A place where everyone knows whose check is good.

Where the folks know all the news before the paper comes out, but merely take it to see whether the editor got the stories the way they heard them.

A village is a hive of glass,
Where nothing unobserved can pass.
C. H. Spurgeon

VIOLET

The blue eyes of Springtime. *Heinrich Heine*

VIRTUE

A quality that "has never been as respectable as money." *Mark Twain*

The first title of nobility. *Jean B. P. Molière*

Virtue consists, not in abstaining from vice, but in not desiring it. *George Bernard Shaw*

Virtue does not consist in the absence of the passions, but in the control of them. *Josh Billings*

An angel, but she is a blind one, and must ask of knowledge to show her the pathway that leads to her goal. *Horace Mann*

VIRTUES

Most frequently but vices disguised. *La Rochefoucauld*

VISION

The art of seeing things invisible. *Jonathan Swift*

VOCABULARY

What a man acquires when he marries.

VOICE (OF THE PEOPLE)
The voice of God. *Alcuin*

VOTE
The instrument and symbol of a freeman's power to make a fool of himself and a wreck of his country. *Ambrose Bierce*

VOW
A snare for sin. *Samuel Johnson*

VULGARITY
An inadequate conception of the art of living. *Mandell Creighton*

The conduct of other people, just as falsehoods are the truths of other people. *Oscar Wilde*

The rich man's modest contribution to democracy.

• W •

WAGNER, RICHARD
A musician who wrote music which "is better than it sounds." *Mark Twain*

WAITRESS
A girl who thinks money grows on trays.

WALKING
The means by which one gets to the garage.

WALL (WHITE)
Fool's writing paper. *Dutch Proverb*

WANT
The mistress of invention. *Susanna Centlivre*

WAR
A perpetual violation of every principle of religion and humanity. *Edward Gibbon*

What distinguishes war is, not that man is slain, but that he is slain, spoiled, crushed by the cruelty, the injustice, the treachery, the murderous hand of man. *William Ellery Channing*

Death's feast. *George Herbert*

Much too important a matter to be left to the generals. *Georges Clemenceau*

Mainly a catalog of blunders. *Winston Churchill*

That mad game the world so loves to play. *Jonathan Swift*

The business of barbarians. *Napoleon Bonaparte*

The greatest plague that can afflict humanity; it destroys religion, it destroys states, it destroys families. Any scourge is preferable to it. *Martin Luther*

An activicy that makes rattling good history: but peace is poor reading. *Thomas Hardy*

An ugly mob-madness, crucifying the truthtellers, choking the artists, side-tracking reforms, revolutions, and the working of social forces. *John Reed*

A disaster to the soldier; to the general a spectacle. *Isaac Goldberg*

The great failure of man, out of fear, lust for power, injustice, or misery left unrectified. *Cordell Hull*

Not a moral picnic. *Lancelot Hogben*

A national calamity whether victorious or not. *General Von Moltke*

The greatest destroyer of democracy in the world. *H. E. Fosdick*

The science of destruction. *J. S. C. Abbott*

> Ez for war, I call it murder,—
>> There you hev it plain and flat;
> I don't want to go no furder
>> Than my Testyment for that.
>>> *James Russell Lowell*

War means fightin' and fightin' means killin'. *Nathan Bedford Forrest*

War is the concentration of all human crimes. It turns man into a beast of prey. *Walter Ellery Channing*

Wars are not "acts of God". They are caused by man, by man-made institutions, by the way in which man has organized his society. What man has made, man can change. *Fred Vinson*

WAR (POLITICAL)

One in which everyone shoots from the lip. *Raymond Moley*

WARDEN

The most anxious man in a prison. *George Bernard Shaw*

WASHINGTON, D. C.

A city full of big guns that are smooth bores.

A place where they take the taxpayer's shirt and have a bureau in which to put it.

The only city where a few people are paid to keep the rest of us worried.

WATER

The only drink for a wise man. *Henry David Thoreau*

A liquid which "the people of England drink . . . at certain times for penance." *John Fortescue*

WATERLOO

A battle of the first rank won by a captain of the second. *Victor Hugo*

WATERMELON

A good fruit—you eat, you drink, and you wash your face. *Enrico Caruso*

WEALTH

Consists not in having great possessions but in having few wants. *Epicurus*

A cunning device of fate whereby men are made captive and burdened with responsibilities from which only death can file their fetters. *Elbert Hubbard* (*The Roycroft Dictionary*)

The savings of many in the hands of one. *Eugene V. Debs*

To be content with a little.

Wealth may be an excellent thing, for it means power, it means leisure, it means liberty. *James Russell Lowell*

The product of labor. *John Locke*

Wealth is power. *Edmund Burke*

Evidence of greatness. *Thomas B. Reed*

WEALTH (SURPLUS)

A sacred trust which its possessor is bound to administer in his lifetime for the good of the community. *Andrew Carnegie*

WEBSTER, DANIEL

A steam engine in trousers. *Sydney Smith*

WEBSTER, NOAH

The author who had the biggest vocabulary.

WEDDING

The point at which a man stops toasting a woman and begins roasting her. *Helen Rowland*

A significant event; before it the woman cries, and afterward the man.

WEDLOCK

Padlock. *John Ray*

WEED

A plant which never dies.

A plant whose virtues have not been discovered. *Ralph Waldo Emerson*

WELFARE

A liberal defines it as share-the-wealth; a conservative defines it as soak-the-rich.

WELL-BRED

What everyone considers himself to be.

WEST

The West begins where the average annual rainfall drops below twenty inches. When you reach the line which marks that drop—for convenience, the one-hundredth meridian—you have reached the West. *Bernard De Voto*
The land of the heart. *G. P. Morris*

Out where the handclasp's a little stronger,
Out where the smile dwells a little longer,
That's where the West begins.
Arthur Chapman

WESTERN (ADULT)

One in which the plot is more than twenty years old.

WHEELBARROW

The greatest of human inventions is the wheelbarrow. It taught some people to walk upon their hind legs.

WHISKY

Trouble put up in liquid form. *Gideon Wurdz*

WHISTLER, JAMES A. MCN.

A painter who "always spelt art with a capital I." *Oscar Wilde*

WHO'S WHO

A directory of persons who know What's What.

WICKEDNESS

A myth invented by good people to account for the curious attraction of others. *Gideon Wurdz*
Weakness. *John Milton*

WIFE

One who is sorry she did it, but would undoubtedly do it again. *H. L. Mencken*
A person who sits up with you when you are sick and puts up with you when you are not.
A man's booin' companion.
A woman who keeps breaking things, like five, ten, and twenty dollar bills.
A person who can look in a bureau drawer and find her husband's cuff links that aren't there.
A woman who remembers when and where she got married but not why.

Teacher, tender comrade, wife,
A fellow-farer true through life.
Robert Louis Stevenson
The weaker vessel. *I Peter 3:7*

Man's best possession. *Robert Burton*
Heaven's last best gift. *John Milton*
The rainbow in the storms of life. *Lord Byron*

WIFE (GOOD)
A married woman who is blind whereas a good husband is a married man who is deaf.

WIFE (MODERN)
A woman who knows what her husband's favorite dishes are and the restaurants that serve them.

WILL
Character in action. *William McDougall*
The master of the world. *Ferdinand Brunetière*

WINDMILL
An object well known in the Netherlands and which resembles college cheer leaders in action.

WINE

> John Barleycorn was a hero bold,
> Of noble enterprise,
> For if you do but taste his blood,
> 'Twill make a man forget his woe;
> 'Twill heighten all his joy.
> *Robert Burns*

The blood of grapes. *Gen. 49:11*
Claret is the liquor for boys; port for men; but he who aspires to be a hero must drink brandy. *Samuel Johnson*
The most healthful and most hygienic of beverages. *Louis Pasteur*
A turncoat; first a friend, and then an enemy. *Thomas Fuller*

WINTER (ENGLISH)
A period of time—"ending in July, to recommence in August." *Lord Byron*

WISDOM
There are more fools than wise men and even in the wise man himself there is more folly than wisdom. *Nicholas Chamfort*
The perfect good of the human mind; philosophy is the love of wisdom and the endeavor to attain it. *Seneca*
Wisdom is knowing what to do next; virtue is doing it. *David Starr Jordan*
It is wisdom to believe the heart. *George Santayana*

WISE
They only are wise who know that they know nothing. *Thomas Carlyle*

WIT

A clever idea that "sometimes enables us to act rudely with impunity." *La Rochefoucauld*

A form of lightning calculation; humor, the exploitation of disproportion. *Russell Green*

The salt of conversation, not the food. *W. Hazlitt*

Wit consists in knowing the resemblance of things which differ, and the difference of things which are alike. *Mme. De Stael*

Intellect on a spree.

True wit is nature to advantage dress'd,
What oft was thought, but ne'er so well expressed.
                                        Alexander Pope

The unexpected explosion of thought. *E. P. Whipple*

Educated insolence. *Aristotle*

The thing that helps us play the fool with more confidence. *Thomas Fuller*

WITNESS

A liar who swears to another liar's testimony.

WIVES

Young men's mistresses; companions for middle age; and old men's nurses. *Francis Bacon*

Women nobody knows how to manage well but bachelors. *Adapted from George Colman*

WIZARD

A person who can save money. Synonym: miser.

A husband who can keep up with the neighbors and the instalment payments.

WOMAN

One who "inspires us to great things—and prevents us accomplishing them." *Alexander Dumas*

A woman is only a woman, but a good cigar is a smoke. *Rudyard Kipling*

The last thing civilized by man. *George Meredith*

The peg on which the wit hangs his jest, the preacher his text, the cynic his grouch, and the sinner his justification. *Helen Rowland*

A man's solace, but if it wasn't for her he wouldn't need any solace.

A tyrant until she's reduced to bondage, and a rebel until she's well beaten. *George Meredith*

An evil, and he is a lucky man who catches her in the mildest form. *Menander*

A person who "will buy anything she thinks the store is losing money on." *Kin Hubbard*

Like your shadow follow her, she flies; fly from her, she follows. *S. R. N. Chamfort*

Only one of nature's agreeable blunders. *Abraham Cowley*

The weaker vessel. *I Peter* 3:7

In the beginning, said a Persian poet—Allah took a rose, a lily, a dove, a serpent, a little honey, a Dead Sea apple, and a handful of clay. When he looked at the amalgam —it was a woman. *William Sharp*

A ministering angel. *Walter Scott*

WOMAN (FASHIONABLE)
One who is always in love—with herself. *La Rochefoucauld*

WOMAN'S AMBITION
To be weighed and found wanting.

WOMAN'S INTUITION
Often nothing more than man's transparency. *George Jean Nathan*

WOMAN'S VOCABULARY
Only about five hundred words, but with a heavy turnover.

WOMEN AND ELEPHANTS
Two groups that "never forget an injury." *Saki*

WOMEN'S TEARS
The most effective water power in the world. *Wilson Mizner*

WONDER
Involuntary praise. *Young*

Men love to wonder and that is the seed of our science. *Ralph Waldo Emerson*

The basis of worship. *Thomas Carlyle*

Implies the desire to learn. *Aristotle*

WOODEN-HEADED DRIVER
A type of golf club; also a type of motorist.

WOODS
A place where "it rains twice." *German Proverb*

God's first temples. *William Cullen Bryant*

WORD
The only things that last forever. *William Hazlitt*

The airy, fairy humming-birds of the imagination. *Elbert Hubbard (The Roycroft Dictionary)*

Tools which automatically carve concepts out of experience. *Julian S. Huxley*

Words are the clothes that thoughts wear—only the clothes. *Samuel Butler*

The most powerful drug used by mankind. *Rudyard Kipling*

We should have a great many fewer disputes in the world if words were taken for what they are, the signs of our ideas only, and not for things themselves. *John Locke*

The shadows of deeds. *Baltasar Gracian*

WORK

The greatest thing in the world, so we should always save some of it for tomorrow. *Don Herold*

The hardest way to make a living.

The inevitable condition of human life, the true source of human welfare. *Leo Tolstoy*

A form of nervousness. *Don Herold*

A necessity for man. Man invented the alarm clock. *Pablo Picasso*

What one does to please oneself, leisure the time one has to serve the community. *Eric Gill*

What consists of whatever a body is obliged to do, and play consists of whatever a body is not obliged to do. *Mark Twain*

Work is something you want to get done; play is something you just like to be doing. *Harry Leon Wilson*

God gave man work, not to burden him, but to bless him, and useful work, willingly, cheerfully, effectively done, has always been the finest expression of the human spirit. *Walter R. Courtenay*

Work is love made visible. And if you cannot work with love but only with distaste, it is better that you should leave your work and sit at the gate of the temple and take alms of those who work with joy. *Kahlil Gibran*

WORKERS

The saviors of society, the redeemers of the race. *Eugene V. Debs*

Soldiers with different weapons but the same courage. *Winston Churchill*

WORLD

Nothing but vanity cut out into several shapes. *Lord Halifax*

Nothing more than a larger assembly of beings, combining to counterfeit happiness which they do not feel. *Samuel Johnson*

A gambling table so arranged that all who enter the casino must play, and all must lose more or less heavily in the long run, though they win occasionally by the way. *Samuel Butler*

A comedy to those who think, a tragedy to those who feel. *Horace Walpole*

A globe "to be inhabited by beasts, but studied and contemplated by man." *Sir Thomas Browne*

I count it not an inn, but a hospital, and a place, not to live, but to die in. *Sir Thomas Browne*

A stage, but the play is badly cast. *Oscar Wilde*

God's workshop for making men. *Henry Ward Beecher*

> This world is all a fleeting show,
> For man's illusion given
> The smiles of joy, the tears of woe,
> Deceitful shine, deceitful flow,—
> There's nothing true but Heaven.
>
> *Thomas Moore*

WORLD SERIES
An example of typical American modesty.

WORRY
Interest paid on trouble before it is due. *Dean William R. Inge*

A morbid anticipation of events which never happen. *Russell Green*

A thin stream of fear trickling through the mind. If encouraged, it cuts a channel into which all other thoughts are drained. *Arthur Somers Roche*

WORSHIP
Fellowship with God.

WRESTLERS
A mass of mute meat. *Joel Sayre*

WRESTLING
The one hazardous occupation in the sports department of journalism because the wrestlers are vindictive in a dumb way and one can never tell when one of them will pick up another and throw him at a correspondent sitting at the ringside. *Westbrook Pegler*

WRIGLEY, PHILIP K.
The first man to discover that American jaws must wag; so why not give them something to wag against? *Will Rogers*

WRINKLES
The deathbed wherein women bury their illusions.

WRITER (HOLLYWOOD)
A writer who puts "on a sport jacket and takes off his brain." *Adapted from Ben Hecht*

WRITING

The art of applying the seat of the pants to the seat of the chair. *Mary Heaton Vorse*

One of the cruelest of professions. *James T. Farrell*

A different name for conversation. *Laurence Sterne*

• Y •

YAWN

A silent shout. *G. K. Chesterton*

Bad manners, but an honest expression of opinion.

The short period a married man gets to open his mouth.

YES

The answer to any question the boss asks.

A married man's last word.

YESTERDAY

One evil less and one memory more. *Elbert Hubbard (The Roycroft Dictionary)*

YOURS

"Anything which up to the present time" others have "not been able to get away from you." *Elbert Hubbard (The Roycroft Dictionary)*

YOUTH

A period when "we believe many things that are not true; in old age we doubt many truths." *German Proverb*

A wonderful thing; what a crime to waste it on children. *George Bernard Shaw*

A young person "must be strong, unafraid, and a better tax-payer than its father." *Harry V. Wade*

Someone who is young enough to know everything. *J. M. Barrie*

The age of striving and selfishness; old age the period of dreaming dreams for the young and for the future that age is not to see. *Arthur Brisbane*

Youth is the only season for enjoyment, and the first twenty-five years of one's life are worth all the rest of the longest life of man, even though those five-and-twenty be spent in penury and contempt, and the rest in the possession of wealth, honors, respectability. *George Borrow*

A blunder; manhood a struggle; old age a regret. *Benjamin Disraeli*

• Z •

ZEAL

Fanaticism with tolerance.

The enthusiasm with which we look after someone else's affairs.

True zeal is a strong, steady, uniform, benevolent affection; but false zeal is a strong, desultory, boisterous, selfish passion. *Nathaniel Emmons*

ZOO

A place devised for animals to study the habits of human beings. *Oliver Herford*